PIOUS FASHION

PIOUS FASHION

How Muslim Women Dress

ELIZABETH BUCAR

HARVARD UNIVERSITY PRESS

Cambridge, Massachusetts ◆ London, England ◆ 2017

Library of Congress Cataloging-in-Publication Data
Names: Bucar, Elizabeth M., author.
Title: Pious fashion : how Muslim women dress / Elizabeth Bucar.
Description: Cambridge, Massachusetts : Harvard University Press, 2017. |
Includes bibliographical references and index.
Identifiers: LCCN 2017010500 | ISBN 9780674976160 (alk. paper)
Subjects: LCSH: Muslim women—Clothing—Iran—Tehran. | Muslim
women—Clothing—Turkey—Istanbul. | Muslim
women—Clothing—Indonesia—Yogyakarta. | Muslim
women—Iran—Tehran—Conduct of life. | Muslim
women—Turkey—Istanbul—Conduct of life. | Muslim
women—Indonesia—Yogyakarta—Conduct of life. | Clothing and
dress—Social aspects—Asia.
Classification: LCC BP190.5.C6 B84 2017 | DDC 297.5/76—dc23
LC record available at https://lccn.loc.gov/2017010500

CONTENTS

PREFACE

I reached into my carry-on to feel for two items I had brought with me, wanting to reassure myself that they were still there: a black head-scarf and a long black overcoat. The flight attendant passed by, collecting plastic cups and wrappers of overly sweet breakfast pastry. I looked around the cabin and saw only two women wearing head-scarves. When was the right time to change? I had not wanted to show up at the airport in full fieldwork garb. That somehow seemed inappropriate, as though I were trying too hard to blend in. But now that we were getting close to landing, I wondered when I was going to put on my *hijab*, and who was going to make sure I was covered properly.

Six months before, I had been informed by the Islamic Republic of Iran that my visa was contingent on my abiding by local laws, including wearing "proper *hijab* according to the sharia." But no description was offered as to what that entailed. I had trouble deciding what to wear to enter the country and had finally settled on borrowing an outfit from an Iranian friend, presuming that she had a better grasp of the unwritten dress norms in Iran than I did. But what if she had neglected something? Would I have trouble getting through passport control if my outfit was judged inadequate? Would my clothing be considered appropriately modest? Professional? Stylish? Feminine?

My worrying was interrupted by the pilot's voice over the audio system, asking the flight attendants to prepare the cabin for our initial descent into Tehran Imam Khomeini International Airport. I heard a slight rustling and looked over at the woman across the aisle from me. Thirty-something, dressed in skinny jeans and a Diane von Furstenberg patterned silk blouse. She caught me staring, smiled, and then winked. Out of her Louis Vuitton bag came an overcoat and a Gucci scarf. I followed her lead. The mass wardrobe change had begun.

◆ ◆ ◆

FOR THE REST OF THE SUMMER, I lived in Tehran, studying Persian, perusing the Khomeini archives, and interviewing leaders of local women's groups. At the time I was researching a different project having to do with women's advocacy programs, so Islamic dress was not my focus. That is not to say that veiling did not occupy a lot of my time and energy. I still had to figure out how to follow the ambiguous dress code and decide what the culturally appropriate form of dress was for different activities, including meeting with government officials, interviewing activists, visiting official archives, and socializing. Despite my lack of confidence, it turned out I was adequately covered for my entry into Iran, wearing what I came to identify as a very formal style of *hijab*. As I stood in line at passport control—in my long black crepe overcoat and plain black scarf, surrounded by women in stylishly cut and colorful coats and tunics—I realized I had probably overcompensated and worn something too demure. Contrary to the assumptions of outsiders, women's dress in Iran continued to be enormously varied even after the legalization of mandatory *hijab*. This is even more the case in the bustling cosmopolitan capital, Tehran, where on a single block one can see women wearing styles that range from full-body black *chador* to grungy punk.

In the first weeks, I felt awkward and a little embarrassed in *hijab*. It was a form of dress I was unaccustomed to wearing, so it seemed to me as though it drew more, not less, attention. And because I am not Muslim, it felt inappropriate, almost deceptive, even though it was legally required. Early on, I had a few fashion failures. But I soon began to understand what was appropriate in various contexts. I noticed the subtle differences in women's headscarves and admired the splendid diversity of their modest outfits. I started shopping for Islamic clothing when I needed a break from my research: a culturally appropriate form of retail therapy.

When I left Iran, I spent a few weeks in Istanbul before returning to the United States. Veiling is optional in Turkey. In 2004, it was heavily regulated and was even banned in some locations. It would have seemed odd for a non-Muslim woman to cover her hair in a city like Istanbul, so I did not. But bareheaded and without an overcoat, I immediately noticed some differences. Without my modest dress I was more aware of being a woman traveling alone than I had been in Tehran. I also noticed that Muslim women's modest dress was quite different in Turkey. In contrast to the loosely draped shawls that had been popular in Tehran that summer, women's headscarves in Istanbul were tightly pinned and were shaped to make the head appear very large and round. In Tehran, women pushed the limits of acceptable exposure of skin, but Muslim women in Turkey were carefully covered from the neck down. They were no less stylish but differently so. This contrast intrigued me, and I decided to begin a comparative research project on Muslim women's fashion—what I call "pious fashion"—in Tehran and Istanbul. Later, I added a location in Indonesia for reasons I will explain in the Introduction.

During my summer in Iran, I realized that modest dress had a moral effect on me. It altered how I saw myself and how I interacted with others, and it influenced my expectations for how Islamic public space should be organized in terms of gender segregation. It also had an aesthetic effect on me, shaping what I expected from and admired about Muslim women's clothing. This is all to say that I found surprise, pleasure, and delight in pious fashion, as well as an intellectual challenge to the neat boxes I had once put things in: modest dress as imposed on women, fashion as a symptom of patriarchy, and aesthetics as separate from ethics. This book is an exploration of this delight and challenge.

PIOUS FASHION

Introduction

Many Westerners view modest clothing as the ultimate sign of Muslim women's oppression. They assume that the concept of the veil, whether a headscarf or a full-body covering, is based on the outdated idea that women's bodies are overly sexual and must be hidden. The veil covers women, effaces them, signals that they are less valuable than men. According to this line of thought, the veil is either forced on women by Muslim men or is an expression of an over-zealous form of piety. As a global phenomenon, it is regarded as the sign of a worrisome creep of Islam.

While modest clothing can indeed be used as a form of social control or as a display of religious orthodoxy, in practice, it is both much less and much more. Much less, because for many Muslim women, it is simply what they wear. Much more, because like all clothing, Muslim women's clothing is diverse, both historically and geographically, and is connected with much broader cultural systems. The decision to wear modest clothing is usually motivated by social and political reasons as well as religious ones. Islam may be an important factor in what Muslim women wear, but it is not the only one.

In *Pious Fashion*, I investigate Muslim women's modest clothing in three locations—Iran, Indonesia, and Turkey—in order to describe the wide range of meanings conveyed by what women wear. Colors and textures are combined to express individual tastes and challenge aesthetic conventions. Brand-name overcoats, scarves, and handbags are used to display social distinction. More than just a veil, this is pious fashion head to toe, which both reflects and creates norms and ideas related to self-identity, moral authority, and consumption. It is part of a communication system that is understood locally, but not always by outsiders. This book aims to make that communication explicit—deciphering how Muslim women negotiate a variety of aesthetic and moral pressures. Muslims' lives, it turns out, are not completely dictated by religious dogma or law. In fact, they are not all that different from non-Muslims' lives.

I do not view Muslim women's modest clothing as a "problem" that needs to be solved. But I am also aware of the risks involved in wearing or celebrating pious fashion, such as inadvertently validating the gender norms that are associated with it. Indeed, pious fashion is a style of clothing that provokes controversy both within and outside Muslim communities. At the same time, it has benefits for women, such as creating opportunities to claim a form of religious expertise within Muslim communities and to participate fully in consumer culture. I will be exploring all of these themes in depth.

Before we go any further, let's take a look at the meaning of some of the important concepts in this book: fashion, piety, and modesty. Clothing is a cultural practice that is governed by social forces as well as daily individual choices.[1] I use the term "fashion" to refer to clothing that does more than keep us warm. It can be used to protect and attract, decorate and display, reveal and conceal. Through fashion, people can do a number of things, such as construct identities, communicate status, and challenge aesthetic preferences.[2] And these functions are all possible because fashion is situated within a context that makes it intelligible, as I discuss below.

"Modest" and "pious" are two adjectives often used to describe Muslim women's clothing. "Modest" usually refers to clothing that does not show too much of a person's body. It is generally assumed that the goal of wearing modest clothing is to be decent and demure, and to discourage sexual attention. Through the course of this book we will see that modest dress has a much wider array of functions, many of which go beyond issues of bodily presentation.

"Pious" is used to describe a person who is devout, or something that is expressive of deep religious devotion. Thus, pious clothing for a Muslim woman is clothing that expresses her devotion to Islam. "Piety" has also become a general placeholder for ethics, so that a "good" Muslim woman is described as "pious." Similarly, pious clothing is connected with morality because it is a disciplinary practice that helps form a woman's character and serves to establish public norms of dress. The nature of piety is constantly being redefined through debates about what Muslim women should wear, as well as through their everyday choices about what they actually do wear. We will see that piety is judged not only in terms of personal submission to Islam or sexual docility, but also in terms of public display that is in good taste.

I chose to use the term "pious fashion" in this book for several reasons. For one thing, other commonly used terms do not adequately capture the head-to-toe looks that are part of Muslim women's modest dress. The word "veil" brings to mind a headscarf or full-face covering, whereas I am also concerned with tunics, pants, shoes, and accessories that are all part of the sartorial practices of Muslim women. "Fashion veiling" is too limiting for the same reason.

The terms "Muslim clothing" or even "gendered Muslim clothing" are also not quite right because I focus not on any clothing worn by a Muslim woman, but rather on clothing practices that are intentionally stylish and respond to global fashion trends. "Modest fashion" is also insufficient, not only because it does not indicate the religious aspect of the clothing I study, but also because part of the goal of this book is to redefine what we mean by the concept of modesty. The word "pious" is more appropriate than "modest" because it captures a number of ethical and religious dimensions of this clothing, such as character formation through bodily action, regulating sexual desires between men and women, and creating public space organized around Islamic moral principles.

"Pious fashion" is also meant to be slightly provocative. These two terms do not sit easily together: fashion is often thought of as a way to express materialistic desires, whereas piety is the mechanism through which unruly desires are suppressed. But my goal is to unsettle these assumptions: fashion is not merely superficial, and piety does not efface the body. These terms do not conflict but rather inform each other when used together to help us understand the complexities of Muslim women's actual sartorial practices.

Comparing Style on Location

To study pious fashion, I conducted research in three Muslim-majority countries, focusing on major cities where Islamic dress is common: Tehran, Iran; Yogyakarta, Indonesia; and Istanbul, Turkey.[3] The popularity of pious fashion in these locations does not mean it has gone uncontested. In all three cities, political, social, and religious controversies contribute to debates over how Muslim women should dress.

While there have been studies of Muslim women's clothing in many individual countries, there are few cross-cultural and transnational comparisons of pious fashion. Notable exceptions are Amelie Barras's work on legal regulation of headscarves in France and Turkey, and Reina Lewis's examination of Muslim style in Britain and Turkey.[4] The limited number of comparative studies is unsurprising. It is complicated enough to study pious fashion in a single location, and analysis across multiple locations is a daunting task. Many scholars devote their careers to becoming experts in one geographic location, learning the language, customs, narratives, and norms. The careful work of these scholars informs many parts of this book.

But comparison of several Muslim-majority cultures can bear its own fruit, at both the local and the cross-cultural level. For instance, the discovery that pious fashion comes in many forms prevents us from viewing one particular form of Muslim dress as representative of piety or style. I also intentionally selected locations that are not part of the Arab world. Westerners tend to assume that Muslim dress around the world is based on the styles of Cairo, Mecca, or Abu Dhabi. The three countries treated in this book have fraught political and cultural relationships with Arab nations and societies, which play out in interesting ways in how women dress. Observing pious fashion in non-Arab countries underscores the global diversity of this practice. In addition, it provides a way to challenge both the conception of an unchanging Islamic orthodoxy and the idea that Islamic expertise is greater the closer one is to Mecca.

Comparison also highlights the local specificity of pious fashion. The presence of skull motifs and bright red in styles in Tehran is all the more striking when contrasted with the lace and pastels of Yogyakarta. The large round shape of a popular Turkish headscarf style is even more obvious once we look at it next to the loosely draped scarves of Tehran or the elaborately pinned styles in Yogyakarta. These details show us how local histories, politics, and aesthetics have invested Muslim women's clothing with varied meanings.

Finally, a comparative framing of this topic highlights commonalities of Muslim women's modest dress. While the story of pious fashion is not the same everywhere, we do find similar concerns over virtue, expertise, judgment, consumption, and beauty. In all three locations, women's pious fashion styles are influenced by prevailing standards of beauty that are based on viewing women as objects of desire and subjects of moral judgment. We will also see similar anxieties about overconsumption along with an acknowledgment that some form of consumption is necessary for pious fashion. And in each location, aesthetic failures are harshly judged and presumed to be outward manifestations of moral failures.

When a Muslim woman decides what to wear, she does so within a framework of limits that are specific to her national context. Pious fashion in Tehran, for example, is highly regulated. Since shortly after the Islamic Revolution of 1979, women in Iran, including non-Muslims and foreign visitors, have been legally required to wear *hijab,* or clothing that conforms with sharia. According to Article 638 of the 1991 version of the Iranian Penal Code, women who appear in public without proper *hijab* can be sentenced to a period of up to two months in jail or a fine of 50,000 to 500,000 rials (approximately $5 to $50).[5] Enforcement varies depending on the political climate. To further complicate the issue, there is no clear definition of *hijab* in the penal code. This gives Iranian women some flexibility in deciding what to wear. Furthermore, since women's dress is explicitly defined as a political issue in post-revolutionary Iran, pious fashion is a political opportunity: stylistic choices provide a way for women to contribute to local debates about gender norms in Muslim politics.

It would make sense to include a case study of Indonesia based on its status as the most populous Muslim nation in the world. But my actual reason for choosing this location has more to do with aesthetics than demographics. Muslim women's modest clothing looks very different in Indonesia than in Iran or Turkey, a difference that results in part from the country's history. Indonesian women did not historically wear head coverings, as uncovered hair and shoulders are part of the traditional Javanese aesthetic of beauty.[6] Thus, the increasing popularity of modest dress cannot be understood as a return to tradition. A headscarf, not a bare head, is what reads as new, fresh, and forward-thinking in this location.

If pious fashion is compulsory in Iran, and rather new to Indonesia, it has a long history of being stigmatized and strictly regulated in Turkey. The choice to wear a headscarf has been interpreted for most of the last hundred years as a challenge to the nation's determinedly secular tradition. But this is changing, in part because of the rise of an Islamic middle class. Because Islamic modest dress has been so controversial, women express extraordinary concern about their appearance. It is considered important to select a modest outfit and headscarf that is visually pleasing in public. This allows a Turkish woman to represent Islamic piety in the best way possible, as well as to avoid the harsh critiques of the secular elite that veiled women are ugly and unfashionable.

In all three locations, modest dress has long been politicized, though in very different ways. At the beginning of each chapter, I include brief overviews of the relevant political history of each country. We will see different forms of political Islam, expressed through public norms and embodied in female fashion. Indeed, Iran is the only one of the three countries in which pious fashion was imposed by an authoritarian regime focused on establishing Islamic institutions. As the scholars Olivier Roy and Amel Boubekeur have pointed out, political Islam has become more complex, and recent Islamist movements have often been motivated by concerns for public morality and social justice.[7] Pious fashion is just one example of how Muslim politics permeates the everyday lives of ordinary Muslims.

Different terms are used to refer to Muslim women's modest clothing in Iran, Indonesia, and Turkey. All three terms derive from Arabic but have been adopted into local languages. In Tehran, the Arabic word *hijab* is used to refer to Muslim women's required dress. This term is mentioned in Quran 33:53, sometimes referred to as "the verse of the *hijab*," in which Muslim men are told that if they address the Prophet's wives, there should be a *hijab* between themselves and the women. Although *hijab* is commonly used in Western scholarship and the media to refer to women's Islamic dress, in this verse it is best translated simply as "curtain."

Most Indonesians use a different Arabic word from the Quran, *jilbab*, to refer to Muslim women's modest dress. The plural form of *jilbab* (*jalabib*) is mentioned in Quran 33:59, a verse in which all Muslim women are encouraged to wear this item of clothing so that they will be recognized, and not harassed or molested. There is no way to know for sure what seventh-century *jilbab* looked like, but scholarly consensus is that it was probably some sort of total body covering, and it is often translated as "outer garment" or "cloak." While there are a number of other Indonesian and Arabic words that have come in and out of popular use, *jilbab* has been the most common term used in Indonesia in the past decade to refer to Muslim women's modest fashion.

In Turkey, the word *tesettür* has been used since the 1980s to refer to a modern version of women's modest dress, and women who wear it are referred to as *tesettürlü* women. *Tesettür* is a Turkish word with an Arabic root, s-t-r, which refers to covering or concealing. Scholars have often translated this as "veiling-fashion," but it is used to refer to entire outfits, not just the use of a headscarf.

Since different terms for pious fashion are used in these three locations, whenever possible I use *hijab* when referring to local pious fashion in Iran, *jilbab* in Indonesia, and *tesettür* in Turkey.

Reading Fashion

In the fall of 2016, I had an enthusiastic group of honors freshmen in my seminar "The Politics of the Veil," who allowed me to try out ideas and material for this book. After a heavy theoretical class discussion, a student named Nathan Hostert sent me a link to a YouTube video along with the message, "Today's class discussion reminded me of this." I rewrote this section of my introduction that night and promised Nathan I would credit him for providing me with this outstanding illustration of what it means to "read" fashion.

The video was a clip of a monologue from the 2006 film *The Devil Wears Prada*. Meryl Streep plays Miranda Priestly, a high-powered editor of a fashion magazine loosely based on Anna Wintour, the editor of *Vogue*. Anne Hathaway plays Andy, Priestly's new assistant, who longs for a "real" publishing job at the *New Yorker* and considers fashion quite trivial. In the scene that leads up to the monologue, Andy has been told to "watch and listen" as Priestly and her team of stylists put together an outfit for a shoot. After a dress is selected, one of the stylists pulls out two turquoise belts, almost identical in color. "It's a tough call. They are so different," she remarks. Andy lets out an audible snort. Everyone glares. She realizes her faux pas and tries to cover. "It's just that both those belts look exactly the same to me, you know, I'm still learning about this stuff." "This *stuff*?" Priestly retorts in a cool tone. "Oh, okay, I see, you think this has nothing to do with you. You go to your closet and you select out, oh I don't know, that lumpy blue sweater, for instance, because you're trying to tell the world that you take yourself too seriously to care about what you put on your back. But what you don't know is that that sweater is not just blue, it's not turquoise, it's not lapis, it's actually cerulean." Priestly goes on to provide a stinging "read" of Andy's lumpy blue sweater. The color cerulean blue, Priestly explains, made its way from an Oscar de la Renta collection, to the collections of other designers, to department stores, to a clearance bin in a discount store, to Andy's closet. "That blue," Priestly informs Andy, "represents millions of dollars and countless jobs, and it's sort of comical how you think that you've made a choice that exempts you from the fashion industry when, in fact, you're wearing the sweater that was selected for you by the people in this room from a pile of *stuff*."[8]

The bookish Andy thinks fashion is of interest only to silly, superficial people. She thus represents the long-standing scholarly tendency to devalue the significance of dress as a cultural and economic phenomenon.[9] But the display of Priestly's expertise makes Andy the fool in the room, not the stylists. If Andy knew even part of the story behind her lumpy sweater she might not find it so trivial. Likewise, close readings of pious fashion allow us to understand the nuances of Muslim women's dress. Just as a blue sweater is never just blue, pious fashion is never merely clothing.

Clothing everywhere can be read, and in our own culture we do it all the time. I might note how my student's T-shirt, my colleague's suit, or the height of my friend's boots convey social privilege, gender norms, or power. But when we try to read clothing in other cultures, we often make mistakes because we base our interpretations on our own aesthetic and moral assumptions. So the first step to reading fashion is to acquire some fluency in local styles and ethics.

With this goal in mind, I completed fieldwork in Tehran (2004 and remotely in 2011), Istanbul (2004, 2012, and 2013), and Yogyakarta (2011). On location, I collected information through three ethnographic methods: observing what women were wearing in a variety of public settings, participating in shopping and other activities associated with pious fashion, and asking questions of local informants about values and other meanings connected with pious fashion. For the first task, I embedded myself in public places where pious fashion was the norm—such as cafés, campuses, offices, and popular pedestrian shopping districts. I watched social interactions, noted details and general clothing trends, and took photographs. I also shopped for clothing and headscarves and, when appropriate, dressed modestly in public settings. Stories of my first-hand experiences as a non-Muslim woman who nevertheless engaged in practices required for pious fashion punctuate each chapter. They represent some of the moments in the field when my preexisting assumptions were challenged, and they became opportunities for deeper and more nuanced understanding.

In each location I also conducted informal interviews and focus groups with women who wear pious fashion. Through these interactions I learned about how various styles were interpreted, as well as about tensions and debates over pious fashion that exist within the local Muslim community. My interlocutors were young women from eighteen to thirty years old, whom I refer to using pseudonyms. I chose to focus on younger women in part because that was the age group I had the easiest access to through my local contacts, and it was a group willing to talk at length with me about fashion. Clothing styles also vary by age, so it was helpful to focus on one age group. This difference is most striking in Indonesia, where many of the young women I spoke with had mothers who did not wear pious fashion. In Iran, a woman's age also affects her relationship to clothing. The Iranian women I worked with were all born after 1979, and thus have only known a political context that legally mandates Islamic clothing. In addition, Iran's population is overwhelmingly skewed young—according to the 2011 census, 55 percent of the population at that time was under thirty. Turkey has one of the youngest populations in Europe, with a median age of just over thirty. The young Muslim women I spoke with in Istanbul had come of age after the 2002 electoral success of the AKP (Justice and Development Party), which ushered in a political situation much different from the secularism that had dominated Turkish politics for the preceding eight decades. Young people are also a powerful collective group of tastemakers. Fashion designers often borrow trends from youth culture for high-end collections: Marc Jacobs made Seattle grunge glamorous, and Hedi Slimane drew inspiration from Berlin-based punks for his couture. Today, young people are not only sources for the next cool thing—they are arbiters and promoters of fashion. Muslim youth are no exception; they function as important fashion icons and consumers of stylish clothing.

In each chapter, I divide discussion of my data into two main sections: "style snapshots" and "aesthetic authorities." The style snapshots focus on one or two season's trends. Sometimes I linger on the details of an outfit—its fabric, tailoring, buttons, patterns, structure, color, and so on. At other times I consider broader trends, such as the introduction of a new style of headscarf wrapping or a new cut of an overcoat. These descriptions are not meant to provide an exhaustive overview of pious fashion in each city. Given how quickly clothing trends shift, that task would be impossible. However, by concentrating on a particular season, I can make correlations between clothing trends and the pressures that influence them.

Each chapter includes a set of photographs taken by locally based photographers. While these photographs show versions of the clothing details and trends I identify, they do not illustrate the specific outfits I describe in the text. The photographs function somewhat independently from the text; they provide a set of head-to-toe looks for each location that the reader can practice their own "read" on. No single image encapsulates local pious fashion, but together each set creates a "visual poem," displaying local aesthetic and moral values in lieu of rhyme schemes.

Most of the photographs were taken from December 2016 to January 2017. This allows a real-time comparison of clothing styles and highlights the differences in climate between Yogyakarta, where it is warm and humid all year round, and Tehran and Istanbul, where temperatures fall into the forties in the winter. I invite you to linger over these images and think about how specific outfits convey meanings through coordination and concealment, attraction and disruption, or embellishment and harmony.

Since these sets were curated in a collaborative process between myself and local photographers, they are influenced by the photographers' style of composition, taste, and relationship to pious fashion. The Tehran photographs were taken by Donya Joshani and Anita Sepehry, who are both frequent contributors to the fashion blog *The Tehran Times*. Donya says that the goal of her photographs of *hijab* in Tehran is "to show that we don't live in an abandoned desert and we don't ride camels to work. We know high fashion and we have our own fashion." Shortly after completing this project, Donya moved to Berlin to study photography. Anita is a Tehran-based photographer who says she "likes to portray what goes beyond style." In her artistic street-style shots, she is particularly interested in capturing styles of *hijab* modified to express personal taste. Benita Amalina, who photographed *jilbab* in Yogyakarta, is a graduate of Gadjah Mada University, where she majored in American Studies. She describes herself as having a keen interest in popular culture and gender. Photography is a hobby for her, but she has an active Instagram account. When she first agreed to help with this project she did not wear a headscarf, but during the six months we worked together she began to wear *jilbab,* at which point this project took on a new level of personal significance. Monique Jaques is an Istanbul-based photojournalist who focuses on the Middle East. Her stunning images of Istanbul Modest Fashion Week were published by the *New York Times,* and her photo essay about the Turkish Islamic fashion magazine *Âlâ* appeared in *Newsweek.* Born in the United States and holding an MFA from New York University, she is not Muslim and does not herself wear *tesettür.*

In each chapter, the style snapshots are followed by descriptions of a range of aesthetic authorities—including people, institutions, and ideologies—that provide perspective on the structural factors that regulate proper dress in that location.[10] Although pious fashion is never merely the result of religious coercion, neither is it merely the expression of a woman's autonomy, personal taste, or religious identity. Self-appointed experts of women's dress—political leaders, clerics, designers, and bloggers—attempt to dictate what counts as appropriate attire for Muslim women. These experts create impressions, alter perceptions, elicit emotions, make demands, and assert pressures in their efforts to implement particular forms of Muslim dress.[11] They thereby help form the context within which a Muslim woman decides what to wear each and every day.

The style snapshots combined with the descriptions of aesthetic authorities enable us to see how women negotiate the forces that regulate proper dress through the variety of styles they wear and the way they participate in discussions about them. What does the incorporation of embroidery on a hemline mean? Why that handbag, with those shoes, and that overcoat? Does a particular shape of a headscarf challenge an aesthetic preference? What social status does a certain ensemble communicate?

If Miranda Priestly's read of the cerulean sweater is my model for how to interpret fashion, there is one caveat: my goal is to provide a nuanced read of various styles of pious fashion—not to inflict the kinds of brutal insults that Priestly excels at. Indeed, I admire the personal style of the women I study. And, unlike Priestly, I am neither a fashion icon nor a powerful editor of a fashion magazine. Quite the contrary: I am an academic whose best attempt at fashion involves Camper boots and a Diane von Furstenberg wrap-dress, both designed to emphasize comfort over appearance. Priestly's read is authoritative for two reasons: her understanding of the history of meaning in fashion, and her status as a major contributor to that meaning. I only aspire to the first type of expertise, striving to identify pious fashion's political and social potency, despite its apparent superficiality.

This is not to say that I shy away from critique. Some of the most interesting styles of pious fashion are the ones my local informants identified as failures for aesthetic or moral reasons. These failures are a central analytical category I develop throughout the book. Andy's lumpy sweater is a fashion failure, but nevertheless we learn an extraordinary amount from Priestly's interpretation of it: how colors become mass trends, what the role of designers is, and how items flow into retail outlets. Similarly, for each location I discuss pious fashion that fails to read as pious or fashionable: impious fashion or unfashionable piety. Local judgments about why specific outfits fail to meet the bar of pious fashion help make clear what is at stake in claiming that others succeed.

Because my analysis involves scrutinizing women's public dress, it might be seen as contributing to a broader social practice in which women's public appearance is the object of judgment. This scrutiny is not limited to Muslim-majority cultures. I still bristle at the memory of a conversation I had with a senior professor when I was first on the academic job market about the importance of having more than one suit. "Men can get away with one suit for a two-day campus visit," he declared, "but not women. It is expected you will have a significant wardrobe change for day two. It's just common sense: what women wear matters more." Another professor, this one female, urged me not to wear "aggressive shoes, red lipstick, or skirts above the knee." I was annoyed that my competency, unlike that of my male colleagues, would apparently be assessed based on my footwear, cosmetics, and hemline. I acknowledge that my subject matter and research design participates in a similar practice of gendered scrutiny, and thus reinforces the notion that a woman's appearance is a significant marker of her agency, competency, and identity. But it is only by participating in this process that I am able to describe it accurately. In part this is because how we experience dress depends on how others evaluate it, so scrutiny is a necessary part of my ethnographic method.

What, then, can we actually learn by analyzing fashion? It is helpful here to bring in Erving Goffman's insight that fashion is a nonverbal form of communication. Pious fashion, for example, communicates moral beliefs, such as the meaning and relationship of key values (modesty, modernity, beauty). It communicates a vision of what successful cultivation of character entails for women (disciplined sartorial practices), and what it looks like (a specific public presentation of femininity). It communicates acceptance or challenge of existing sources of moral authority. Pious fashion can also communicate what Goffman calls "a moral demand on others": by wearing modest religious dress, an individual claims to be a pious woman, and that claim in turn demands that she be treated accordingly.[12] In addition, pious fashion, like any sartorial practice, can communicate an individual's social position.[13]

Class, as grounded in material circumstances such as income, occupation, education, and wealth, influences pious fashion. But exactly how is not simple. Certainly, some items are available only to the very rich, and a person with a well-trained eye can place women wearing specific forms of pious fashion within a socioeconomic class. But often class is more difficult to read. A Gucci label on a scarf is just as likely to indicate a cheap fake as an expensive designer item. Although certain types of black fabric used for *chador* are signs of wealth, it can be hard to tell, especially from a distance, if the fabric is an expensive silk crepe or a cheap polyester blend. And the wide availability of inexpensive clothing means that those with limited resources can create personal styles, as well as imitate styles originally marketed to the wealthy. Reading dress as a marker of class is also complicated because dress is a reflection not only of who a woman is but also who she wants to be. The class conveyed by a particular form of pious fashion might merely be aspirational. Thus, instead of focusing on what a woman's outfit can tell us about her material circumstances, I pay attention primarily to showing how clothing conveys boundaries and distinctions between individuals and groups.[14]

Finally, a note about what religious sources have to say about pious fashion. There are scattered references to modest dress in the sacred written sources of Islam, the Quran and the hadith, but these sacred texts were not a touchstone for the women I interviewed.[15] Muslim women wearing pious fashion all accept that they should dress modestly. They accept that revelation tells them this. But debates about what to wear are almost never based on engagement with sacred texts.

The real interpretative work occurs not by textual exegesis but by putting outfits together every day.

Muslim Ethics of Dress: Action, Society, and Aesthetics

We express our values, norms, and virtues in the circumstantial actions of our daily lives. Or as the anthropologist Michael Lambek puts it, "the ordinary is intrinsically ethical and ethics intrinsically ordinary."[16] The study of pious fashion builds on this insight, highlighting the role of physical acts, the importance of a social context, and the relationship of aesthetics to Muslim ethics.

We can start with the general observation that certain physical acts, such as praying and fasting, are pillars of a pious Muslim life. It follows that belief, understanding, and instruction are not enough to transform a person into a moral Muslim: actual actions—repetitive behavior and physical habits—are also part of moral development.[17] These practices transform the person who does them by creating virtues or dispositions to behave a certain way: daily prayer cultivates humility and submission in the person who prays, and fasting during Ramadan cultivates devotion.[18] Similarly, by wearing pious fashion every day, a Muslim woman can change the sort of person she is. This is one way pious fashion is "pious": it embodies and displays norms that cultivate a good character.

When my students question my claim that wearing specific clothing can change who you are, I usually relate the experience I had traveling in Turkey after I had been in Tehran, which I described in the Preface. I had not freely chosen to wear *hijab* in Tehran; it was a legal requirement of appearing in public. I did not believe *hijab* was necessary for me to be a good person. But the practice of dressing modestly did have an effect on me. When I got to Istanbul I was startled by the tourists' strappy tank tops, even though I had a drawer full of them back home in the United States. When a man touched my hand or held my gaze as he gave me change, I was uncomfortable. I found it difficult to navigate crowded buses without the gender segregation of Tehran's mass transport. Despite my lack of intention, wearing *hijab* had made me more modest, or at least more aware of modesty's social role.

Even though we often consider the cultivation of character to be a personal task, pious fashion is acutely social. Dressing in proper pious fashion depends on learning social norms about what to wear and being embedded in a society that serves as an audience for the sartorial practice. Pious fashion is also valuable in part because it contributes to the community's well-being, not just the well-being of the woman who wears it, by helping to create norms for the public face of Islam.

The social nature of pious fashion falls into four categories. First, the modest aspect of pious fashion manifests itself during interactions with strangers in the public sphere. Second, wearing pious fashion properly requires gleaning advice from others. There is no centralized rulebook of proper modest dress. Women learn from peers and various experts what successful pious fashion consists of. Third, community and social institutions help women reflect on their own style of pious fashion. As a woman begins to dress modestly, the sartorial practices of those around her act as a mirror within which she gauges her own success. Fourth, debates about pious fashion are at one level about the appropriate role of Islam in public, particularly in forming an Islamic social sphere through expressions of Islamic norms. Take the case of Iran, where *hijab* is mandatory for all women, including non-Muslim Iranians and non-Iranian visitors. Iranian leaders have decided that it is not enough for most women to wear *hijab* in public; all women must do so. That is why I am required to wear *hijab* when I am in Iran doing research. My clothing is just as important for public modesty as that of the most pious Iranian Muslim.

This social aspect of pious fashion explains how it can function as both a form of control and a form of rebellion. Sartorial practices are part of the politics of appearance, grounded in gender-specific norms that serve to mold and control women. As a result, pious fashion is the realm where changes to these underlying norms can take place. Disproportionate attention to women's public presentation makes women's dress an opportunity: if pious fashion changes how women are seen, it can also influence the evaluation schemes (norms of ideal womanhood, visions of gendered piety) behind that seeing. Religious ethics influence dress codes; but practices of dress can in turn be used to critique these ethics.

Throughout this book, I emphasize both individual actions and the specific social context within which they occur, a theory of agency that I have described elsewhere as "creative conformity." In this understanding, agency is defined as a tactical engagement within a structural context. Like many feminist scholars, I affirm a woman's ability to make choices while acknowledging that these choices are limited by factors, pressures, and expectations outside her control.[19] This means that for a faithful Muslim woman, choices about appropriate dress and behavior are shaped by discussions among multiple stakeholders about what it means to be a good Muslim woman. This situation is not unlike that for the non-Muslim woman, who likewise lives within the constraints of patriarchy and others' expectations concerning her behavior and conduct.

The anthropologists Ann Marie Leshkowich and Carla Jones use a similar idea of agency to develop a theoretical framework for studying clothing that they refer to as "performance practices." The word "performance," which draws on the work of Judith Butler, emphasizes the idea that clothing choices involve a kind of role playing, much like an actor playing a role on stage. The word "practices" builds on the insights of theorists like Michel de Certeau, who have shown that daily practices are not free of structural constraints—whether based on social class, religious authority, or political institutions—but rather take place within those structures and often reinforce them when people try to "play by the rules."[20] This emphasis on clothing as a form of practice helps prevent us from painting an overly rosy picture of what pious fashion can do. As a practice, pious fashion is not entirely empowering for Muslim women, since it relies on traditional gender ideologies and structural injustices. However, pious fashion is a form of meaning-making that can succeed as political critique, rework the ethical meanings of clothing, and shift the visual culture of public religion.

Finally, in terms of everyday ethics, pious fashion demonstrates a strong link between aesthetics and ethics, since much of this clothing is designed to display aesthetic, as well as moral value. This is not surprising, since the Muslim community has long embraced beauty as an important value to pursue, based on a number of hadith reports attributed to the Prophet Muhammad, including "God is beautiful and He loves beauty."[21] Although there is no specific genre of Islamic texts on aesthetics like there is on virtue (*adab*) and law (*fiqh*), a connection between ethics and aesthetics is found in classic Islamic writings. The twelfth-century Islamic thinker al-Ghazali, for example, wrote, "The interior luminescence illuminated the exterior by giving it ornamentation and luster," and "Whose heart is not a niche for divine lights, the beauty of prophetic example will not radiate."[22] Here, al-Ghazali implies that virtue is expressed outwardly in the physical appearance of a person; put differently, he provides a rationale for the connection between looking good and being good. Of course, one could argue that the aesthetic and the ethical good do not have the same meaning, but in both cases the good is praised. As we will see in the chapters to come, there is a slippage between these two goods, especially in the assessment of women's clothing: pleasing forms of modest attire are often interpreted as the outward sign of a good character, while fashion failures are presumed to be the sign of a flawed character.

But there is more at stake here. For al-Ghazali, the connection between inner virtue and outer "luminescence" has to do with *dhawq*, a transcendent aesthetic sensibility that he regards as the basis of autonomy. The purpose of aesthetics for al-Ghazali is to help us access intuitive knowledge that we cannot come by through other means, such as Islamic jurisprudence.[23] This raises the question of the role of aesthetics in the process of moral discernment that is necessary for ethical actions. It is not enough to proclaim, "Muslim women should wear modest clothing." Even more important are the choices that follow, in which a woman has to discern which items of clothing should be worn and which ones should not.

One of the central arguments of *Pious Fashion* is that the meaning and expression of virtue depend on local aesthetic norms. Even when there is agreement about the importance of a virtue, the content of that virtue can still be open to debate or can be expressed in different ways when put into practice. Modesty, the virtue most people associate with Islamic dress, looks different in different locations and also entails a different constellation of aesthetic and moral values.[24] This is why the same outfit that reads as modest on a U.S. college campus reads as immodest on the streets of Riyadh. In other words, the dazzling diversity of pious fashion suggests that "there is no non-cultural way to perform modesty."[25]

The Politics of Clothing

Although some Muslim women have covered their heads since the time of the Prophet, the modern significance of pious fashion is related to more recent political history. Iran, Indonesia, and Turkey all became nation-states in the last hundred years. As part of their respective nationalist awakenings and subsequent nation-building, the boundaries between Islam and the state were established and redrawn, often as part of negotiations between colonizer and colonized. This process turned Islam into fodder for political debate. And since Muslim women were regarded as the receptacles and conveyers of religion, they disproportionately bore the burden of national projects promoted by various stakeholders. The headscarf, as the most visible symbol of Muslim women, became the target of political reform as part of agendas that often had very little to do with Muslim women themselves.

In all three nations, not only Muslim identity but also Muslim character was identified as something that had to be managed as a way to unite the citizens and move them forward through development and modernization programs. Depending on the location, a Muslim character was cultivated (Iran), acknowledged and controlled (Indonesia), or transformed (Turkey). Women were assumed to be particularly vulnerable to moral corruption, and their character was doubly important because as mothers they were responsible for the moral education of future citizens. This education was increasingly conceptualized as a political responsibility, while the state pondered what forms of Islam it wanted to promote or suppress.

On the one hand, this focus can be seen a burden for women, an example of the institutionalization of patriarchy through the regulation of women's bodies and femininity. But on the other hand, it provided an opportunity. Before the twentieth century, political discourse largely ignored women. Increased attention to women during the nation-building process raised their profile, their visibility, and thus their political capital.

Did nations succeed in using women's dress for political ends? Only partially. They certainly made women, bodies, and clothing political concerns and used them to create emotional investment in the idea of the nation. But they have not been able to remake citizens through dress codes as perfectly as they had hoped. The brief political histories provided in the chapters that follow show that clothing has also been used in resistance movements, whether against the shah and the West during the 1979 Revolution in Iran, as a critique of corruption in Suharto's New Order, or as part of a stance against the perceived elitism of Kemalism in Turkey. These rebellious political deployments of clothing likewise had mixed results. Pious fashion always involves some amount of conformity and accommodation of the status quo, through, for example, its reproduction of gender ideologies.

The clothing of Muslim men also plays a role in national politics.[26] Just to name a few of these styles, the black-and-white checkered head cloth (*keffiyeh*) is a symbol of Palestinian nationalism, while a red-and-white version is associated with Jordanian culture and history, and turbans became part of the unofficial dress code of Taliban leaders and supporters in Afghanistan in the 1990s. In the chapters that follow, I provide brief descriptions of Muslim men's clothing and style as a way to emphasize the distinctness of styles and debates about women's clothing. What is most notable about Muslim men's fashion in the three countries is the widespread adoption of Western dress norms, such as trousers, shirts, and jackets. In Iran, men often wear short-sleeved shirts and T-shirts as part of casual wear. Formal attire is similar to what is worn in the United States and Europe with one exception: the necktie. After the 1979 Islamic Revolution, the tie became a symbol of Western oppression and was called "the leash of America." Although never explicitly outlawed, ties are still not part of mainstream business attire. In Indonesia, the nationalist leader Sukarno promoted the Western suit, stating in his autobiography: "The minute an Indonesian dons trousers, he walks erect like any white man. . . . Let us demonstrate we are as progressive as our former masters. We must take our place as upstanding equals. We must put on modern clothing."[27] For Sukarno, wearing a Western suit proved that an Indonesian man was as civilized as his former Dutch colonizers. In Turkey, Mustafa Kemal Atatürk thought that for the Turkish man to be modern, he had to be thoroughly European in his dress. For that reason he banned the fez, a brimless hat made of red felt worn by men during the late Ottoman Empire, and favored European-style brimmed hats.

Men in these locations are almost as covered as women, so in that way their dress is also modest. But men's clothing does not have to be "pious" in the same way. Men's clothing is the marker of the nation's power and modernity; women's clothing is the marker of its morality, honor, and ethnic identity. In fact, one reason the male Muslim citizen can dress in standard Western clothing is because the woman at his side is dressed in local, religiously encoded garb.

This book focuses on Muslim-majority nations; however, women's clothing has been politicized elsewhere, from corsets, to high-heel shoes, to pantsuits. These examples help remind us that non-Muslim women also deal with social and political pressures to dress a certain way but can nevertheless use clothing for their own agendas, such as the pink "pussy hats" that became a sign of resistance to misogyny in 2017. Muslim women are not so different, although the pressures on them may be different. In the chapters that follow, we will see why and how Muslim women's clothing matters by examining trends within the context of local political histories, cultures of style, and aesthetic authorities.

ᥱᡐ ONE ᥱᡐ

Hijab in Tehran

AUGUST 13, 2004 (TEHRAN, IRAN)

I spent the day shopping with my friend Ziba and her cousins while Ziba's aunt stewed a goose with pomegranates and walnuts for dinner. In one clothing store, Ziba's oldest cousin, Homa, noticed a woman and immediately turned to me and whispered: "This is a good example of *bad hijab* for you." The cousins gathered around me, pointing, sighing, and shaking their heads, expressing outrage. I asked Homa what the problem was exactly, and she hissed: "*Hijabi-ou, bibin. Khayli shuhrati!*" ("Look at her *hijab*. It is so slutty!") When I asked her to explain what she meant, she responded: "Her ankles are showing, her pants are rolled up, they are made of denim and tight. Her *manteau* is short, slit up the side, tight, made of thin material, and exposes the back of her neck and her throat. And her *rusari*, look at her *rusari*. It is folded in half so that her hair sticks out in front and back and tied so loosely that we can see all her jewelry. Plus her makeup is caked on."

◆　◆　◆

THIS WAS MY FIRST EXPERIENCE with the infamous *"bad hijab"* of Tehran. I had known that the Iranian authorities complained about it, and that women were arrested for it, but I had never known for sure that I had seen it until Homa declared this woman's outfit to be not only "bad" but also "slutty." I learned that day that what is classified as appropriate or inappropriate is defined by local cultures of style. In the United States, this woman's outfit would not be considered slutty, but in Tehran, its tightness and the amount of exposed skin made it appear sexually provocative. I also learned that it was not only the Iranian authorities who regulated women's clothing. The tenor of Homa's reaction to and commentary on this outfit demonstrated that women were also policing each other through their aesthetic and moral judgments of one another.

I begin this book in Tehran, since the capital of Iran holds an important place in Western ideas about Muslim women's modest clothing. Baby Boomers and people of earlier generations will likely remember the images broadcast in the West of the 1979 Islamic Revolution: mass protests of women in *chador*, a traditional full-body black covering, and *chadori* commandos rappelling down buildings with machine guns strapped to their backs. This image of women as "black crows" is still what comes to mind for some people who are unfamiliar with Iranian fashion. In fact, I was told by a number of women in Indonesia that everyone in Iran wears *chador*. This is simply not the case. While it is true that women's modest dress is compulsory in Iran, pious fashion comes in a remarkable range of styles, no less diverse or stylish than in locations without enforced dress codes. In Tehran, we see the ability of fashion to endure, flourish, and even surprise—as with the case of the slutty *hijab*—despite conditions of intense social control and scrutiny.

Iranian Politics of Modest Dress

In June 2011, the Iranian and Jordanian national women's soccer teams were warming up in Amman, Jordan, before a prequalifying match for the 2012 Summer Olympics. But the game never took place: right before kickoff, the Iranian team was disqualified because officials declared that the players were breaking the dress code of the International Federation of Association Football (FIFA), which did not allow head coverings. Three Jordanian players were also banned from participating that day because of their head coverings, but most members of the Jordanian team were bareheaded by design: coaches favored women who did not wear headscarves so that there would be no trouble playing internationally. This recruitment tactic was not possible for the Islamic Republic of Iran, since all Iranian female athletes are required to cover their hair and neck (as well as their arms and legs) even when traveling or participating in sports abroad. "This ruling means that women's soccer in Iran is over," declared Shahrzad Mozafar, the Iranian team's coach. "Headscarves are simply what we wear in Iran."[1] Eventually, FIFA gave in, lifting the ban on headscarves and other head coverings in 2014, but Mozafar had been quite right: Iranian women's soccer could not have survived a ban on headgear.

As the soccer controversy demonstrates, Iranian women's dress is strictly regulated even outside the country when women represent Iran in some official capacity. It would be easy to attribute the politicization of Muslim women's dress to the 1979 Islamic Revolution, but Iran has a much longer history of attempts to control its population through enforced dress codes. What is striking is that these clothing regulations have not always had the effect on women or on Iranian politics that their architects intended.

When the Qajar Dynasty ruled the area that is now Iran from 1796 to 1925, many women wore *chador*. The *chador* ("tent" in Persian), which is made of a single, large semicircle of fabric, dates back to at least the tenth century. In 1925, Reza Shah Pahlavi assumed the throne as the first shah of the Pahlavi Dynasty. Part of his vision for development included a citizenry that looked modern: men and women should dress in European-style clothing, and women should appear in public without head coverings. The *chador* was banned in 1936 for all teachers as well as for wives of government officials. This unveiling edict was violently enforced, and as a result, some women who wished to remain veiled voluntarily secluded themselves to avoid harassment. Others shifted from wearing a *chador*, which at the time was the most common form of Islamic modest dress for women, to a loose cloak (*manteau*) and headscarf (*rusari*), an early version of the contemporary combination favored by fashion-conscious women in Tehran today. In short, when the state tried to impose a dress code on women as a way to control the direction of modernization and development, women created new styles of dress that would allow them to remain publicly Muslim while still abiding by new political restrictions on full-body covering.

In 1941, Mohammad Reza Pahlavi replaced his father as shah. During his reign, conflicts between the clergy and the Pahlavi Dynasty increased and were played out in part through women's dress. For instance, the clergy took a stand against the throne in 1948, when religious authorities issued a *fatwa* forbidding women to shop while unveiled. Despite the state's continued coercive measures, the *chador* reappeared on the street. The shah only increased his attempts to westernize and secularize Iran, such as through a series of reforms, known as the White Revolution, that were undertaken throughout the 1960s and 1970s.

Dissatisfaction with the Pahlavi monarchy came to a head in the 1979 Islamic Revolution, and women's dress played an important role in the symbolic politics of that time, as well. When women joined mass street protests, they often wore *chador*. This style symbolized an alternative vision of Iran's future: the shah had wanted women uncovered, so revolutionaries, including secular revolutionaries, used Islamic dress to indicate their resistance to government control. For some, it was a sign of religious identity; for others, nationalism; and for yet others, political populism. What these politically diverse *chador*-wearing women shared was not a level of religious devotion but rather a commitment to revolution.

Protests culminated in the collapse of the Pahlavi Dynasty and a national referendum in which the majority voted to establish an Islamic republic. Ayatollah Ruhollah Khomeini presided over the transitional period and rapid Islamization of the new republic. As his first task, he oversaw the writing of a new constitution based on the Quran, which declared that all "laws and regulations [in Iran] must be based on

Islamic criteria" (Art. 4). In order to guarantee that every decision made by the executive, judiciary, and legislative branches was indeed compatible with Islam, the position of supreme leader was created. The authority for this position derives from the Shii concept of guardianship of the Islamic jurist (*vilayat al-faqih*). Khomeini held the position until his death in 1989.

Because of Khomeini's position as supreme leader, his opinions on a range of issues became the basis for legislation and various nation-building policies. For instance, he believed that creating a public space governed by the principles of Islamic morality was crucial to the survival of the Islamic Republic, and women's modest dress, along with gender segregation, was part of that vision. Within a month after the Islamic Republic was established, all women in government offices were required to wear *hijab*. (However, as we will see below, *hijab*, or modest dress, was never clearly defined.) By 1983, Islamic *hijab* was mandated throughout the republic with the intention of creating and protecting an Islamic social space based on the regulation of gender norms in public. This dress code remains in place today.

Iran also has a popularly elected president, but this position holds very little power. Abolhassan Bani-Sadr, an anti-shah exile, was the first president of Iran. His brief term (1980–1981) ended with impeachment over tensions with conservative clerics. Ali Khamenei, the next president, served two terms (1981–1989). A former student of Khomeini, Khamenei became the supreme leader after Khomeini's death in 1989 and has held the position for almost three decades. During his term as president (1989–1997), Akbar Hashemi Rafsanjani loosened the enforcement of some cultural and social restrictions. Art galleries reopened. Previously banned satellite dishes reappeared. The Iranian film industry thrived. Women began to wear more color and show a bit of hair, especially bangs. Political restrictions, however, remained strictly enforced, and thousands of dissident intellectuals were killed during Rafsanjani's presidency, through a variety of mysterious means—such as stabbings and car crashes—or while in police custody.

Mohammad Khatami's stunning electoral success in 1997—when he won 70 percent of the popular vote—began a period of political liberalization. This was reflected in clothing styles: brighter colors, shorter sleeves, and capri pants started showing up on the streets of Tehran. However, Khatami's reformist agenda created tension with the hardliners in the supreme leader's office and the parliament. By his second term it was clear that the hardliners had gained the upper hand, as another wave of arrests of journalists and intellectuals took place.

In 2005, the conservative mayor of Tehran, Mahmoud Ahmadinejad, succeeded Khatami as president and held office until 2013. He ran as an anti-establishment political outsider who was controversial both within Iran, for his aggressive economic policies and his indifference to civil rights, and internationally, for his hostility toward other nations and support for Iran's nuclear program. His liberal import policies, which hurt domestic industries, allowed items like inexpensive Indian clothing to enter the Iranian market. As we will see later, this contributed to the availability of popular "ethnic chic" styles of *hijab*.

When Ahmadinejad ran for a second term in 2009, official results showed him as the winner, but his opponent, Mir Hossein Mousavi, claimed victory. Many believed the results were fraudulent. The largest resistance movement in Iran since 1979 ensued—known as the Green Revolution—and violent clashes broke out between police and protesters. *Hijab* became an issue during these political protests, if only in a tangential way.

In December 2009, a student activist named Majid Tavakoli was arrested after giving a speech at Tehran's Amir Kabir University during a demonstration. The semi-official *Fars* news agency then posted a picture of Tavakoli in a headscarf in an attempt to embarrass and discredit him; it reported that he had dressed as a woman in an unsuccessful attempt to escape arrest.[2] The smear campaign backfired, as Iranian men began posting pictures of themselves in *hijab* on Facebook. Neither side questioned the ethics of compulsory *hijab*. Instead, both sides deployed *hijab* for their own political agendas: the authorities used *hijab* to try to make Majid look weak, while his supporters tried to revive *hijab* as a symbol of revolution by using it as a form of drag.

Attempts to officially regulate women's dress have not always had the intended results. The 1936 ban of the *chador* was a Western-looking shah's attempt to undermine the authority of the Shia clerics and to modernize Iranian women. But because it was not accompanied by more substantive reforms, such as improving access to education, it did not remake Iranian women in the way officials had hoped it would. In fact, the opposite occurred. Devout women stayed indoors rather than uncovering. Others merely switched the full-body covering of the *chador* for a more updated version of modest dress. The dress code established following the 1979 revolution did not necessarily work in the way it was intended, either. The fact that women's dress still needs to be enforced demonstrates that the goal of establishing an Islamic social space through clothing and public gender segregation was not entirely successful. Contributing to this lack of success is the fact that although Iranian law still requires *hijab*, it does not specify exactly what that entails. Thus, today's Iranian women have some choice in what they wear even if multiple authorities—individuals, institutions, organizations—attempt to influence or coerce that decision.

Style Snapshot

Since there are a number of Persian words used to describe items of clothing used for *hijab* in Iran, a short primer may be helpful before we delve into the details of a particular season's trends. The *chador*, the traditional form of Iranian dress, is a floor-length outer covering that is draped over the hair and shoulders. Because a *chador* does not have any fasteners or even sleeves, one hand is devoted to holding it in place. If both hands are occupied, the edges of the fabric can be held with the teeth. Many people unfamiliar with Iranian dress, including Muslim women from other regions, are under the impression that *chador* is the only form of legal dress in Iran.

The alternative to *chador* in Iran is a *manteau* with some sort of head covering. A *manteau* ("coat" in French) is a loose, knee-length or longer coat-like garment with sleeves that is meant to hide a woman's shape. *Manteaus*—also referred to by the Persian word *rupush*—allow for many varieties of *hijab*, since secular fashion trends and personal taste can be expressed through variations in color, pattern, cut, and embellishments.

There are two popular head coverings to pair with a *manteau*. One is a sort of balaclava, called a *maghneh*, consisting of a piece of fabric that fits tightly around the head, covers the entire neck and chest, and has an opening for the face. *Maghnehs* are integrated into many work uniforms in patterned fabric that visually references specific employment situations or employer values. During a visit to Tehran's Planned Parenthood offices in 2004, for example, I noticed that the junior female staff wore pink-and-white striped matching *maghnehs* and *manteaus*, a *hijab* version of the Western candy-stripe uniform. Both medical and Muslim, this uniform indicated that the staff were involved in the provision of health services within an Islamic society, rather than emphasizing the reproductive rights agenda of Planned Parenthood, which might have raised the eyebrows of Iranian authorities. However, most *maghnehs* are a solid color, often black or navy, and are associated with an "unfashionable" form of *hijab*, especially when paired with a long loose *manteau* in black, navy, or beige. The *maghneh* can appear not only as old-fashioned but also as juvenile, since it is integrated into most school uniforms—the equivalent of a plaid kilt and knee socks in the United States. It is worn by those who are not yet fashionable (primary school girls), those who may no longer be fashionable (older women), and those who are uninterested in being fashionable (such as the Planned Parenthood staff).

As an alternative to the *maghneh*, the fashionable women of Tehran wear a *rusari*. *Rusari* is a generic term for any scarf, either square or rectangular, that is draped over the head and knotted under the chin or wrapped around the neck. A *rusari* often shows more hair and skin than a *maghneh*, which is ironic, since *rusaris* began as a style innovation by very pious women (who wore it in a way that covered up their hair and skin) when the shah banned the *chador* in the 1930s. Today, the *rusari* provides an opportunity to integrate tremendous stylistic diversity into *hijab* through varied fabrics, colors, patterns, and styles of drape.

The large weave of this coat, which doubles as a *manteau*, creates graphic interest. The small, delicate cream handbag contrasts with ripped skinny jeans, rolled above the ankle to show off cuffed suede booties. The salmon-pink color of the loose *rusari* completes a soothing color palette. Courtesy of *The Tehran Times* fashion blog. Photograph by Donya Joshani, January 3, 2017.

Summers 2004 and 2011

I had traveled to Tehran in 2004 with only one *hijab*-appropriate outfit—the loaner from my friend, described in the Preface—so one of the first things I had to do was go shopping.[3] Unfamiliar with Tehran though I was, it was still easy to locate places to purchase *hijab* items. The three-mile walk up Valiasr Street from my all-female boarding house near Vanak Square to Dehkhoda Institute, where I was studying Persian, was lined with shops. Scarves were particularly easy to purchase. I saw them for sale everywhere, from street stalls to upscale boutiques in Tajrish Square. I could buy them without trying them on, and then in the privacy of the boarding house figure out how to wear them, sometimes with the help of my sixteen-year-old roommate.

Rusaris come in a wide variety of fabrics and patterns, and in 2004 the most popular way to wear them was loosely crossed at the front of the neck. Another style involved folding a square scarf into a triangle and tying it under the chin by two of the three points. Various techniques for creating volume under the scarf were used, from piling hair on top of the head with a large clip to using a scrunchie made of fake hair to create the illusion of a hidden mass of hair. These bumps can be very large; Parissa, a thirty-four-year-old biology graduate student, described one as looking "like the woman is hiding a baby watermelon under her shawl." I confess that I purchased my own fake-hair scrunchie, since I had fine, chin-length hair that did nothing to create volume under my headscarf. Although I only wore it once, I did find the overall look more attractive.

Since scarves and *manteaus* are rarely purchased as a set, and *manteaus* can be designed in many different styles, they tend to be the clothing item that most reflects fashion trends. But shopping for a *manteau* was more stressful for a *hijab* newbie like myself than shopping for a *rusari*—I would have to enter a shop to buy a *manteau,* and I would have to try it on.

After my third day of classes, I worked up enough nerve to enter a shop with a huge display of *manteaus* in the window. I went right to the section of black *manteaus* and tried to figure out what my size would be. A male salesclerk sauntered over, dressed in tight jeans and a button-down shirt. He looked me up and down, followed me around the shop, and commented on every *manteau* I tried on, encouraging me to try more fitted versions. "How ironic," I thought. "In order to purchase clothing meant to prevent male scrutiny, I have to endure this." Despite that young man's efforts, or perhaps because of them, I purchased a very loose, knee-length *manteau* that day, in a size too large. By the end of my stay, when I had acquired a number of more fashionable *manteaus*, I rarely wore my first purchase.

In the summer of 2004, *manteaus* in a wide range of styles were available in Tehrani boutiques, in various lengths, made of various fabrics, and with various sorts of fasteners down the front. There were a number of styles that storekeepers insisted were "of the season" and that women were excited to point out to me as new. I referred to one of these styles as "cowboy." *Manteaus* in this style were embellished with stitching on the back and on the pocket placards. The sleeves had buttoned or snapped cuffs, like a tailored shirt, and they were made of a cotton and Lycra blend to ensure a snug fit. They reminded me of the cowboy shirts that were all the rage when I was in elementary school and that hipsters wore in the late 1990s. Another style, embellished with buckles and snaps and made of khaki or olive-green fabric, I dubbed "military." "Mod" *manteaus,* with white piping and shaped like a Twiggy-inspired minidress, were a fun surprise. It was easy for me to label these forms of dress because they were so similar to Western styles I was familiar with. If these Iranian styles drew on Western fashion, however, they did not merely imitate it. Instead, street style in Tehran reinterpreted Western trends in an Iranian cultural context. Cowboy *manteaus,* for instance, were worn not with jeans, pigtails, or cowboy hats but rather with long, wide-legged linen pants and gauzy, colorful *rusaris*. Military jackets were combined not only with combat boots but also with bright floral pants and patent-leather handbags.

In this urban casual look, the hardware on the Dr. Martens boots echoes the studs on the Valentino crossbody bag. The Topshop floral leggings are the stand-out item, made even cooler by being paired with utilitarian items like a black scarf and a military jacket. The graffiti in the background is of a dish-soap bottle. Courtesy of *The Tehran Times* fashion blog. Photograph by Anita Sepehry, February 7, 2017.

Overall, fashionable *manteaus* in 2004 were tighter and shorter than they had been in years past. Hemlines of *manteaus* were creeping up above the knee. The daring wore capri pants with them. Sleeves were sometimes three-quarter length and were often rolled up to expose even more of the forearms. Many *manteaus* contained Lycra for stretch and were sometimes worn so tight that the outline of pants pockets underneath could be seen. It was hard not to think that this tightness was a form of rebellion, since it read as "sexy." I owned one tight cowboy *manteau,* in deep bordeaux, that snapped up the front. I wore it often to socialize. It was 10 percent Lycra and tight enough that I was worried those snaps might burst open when I sat down. It also hugged my hips, almost like a pencil skirt, which caused me to exaggerate the sway of my hips when I walked.

On the streets, "punk" *hijab* was a distinguishable style in 2004; it included jeans, messy gelled hair peeking out of headscarves, heavy eyeliner, and visible piercings. Young men also wore a punk style, with T-shirts and tight jeans. On Tehrani women, punk *hijab* reminded me of the styles of music icons Joan Jett or Siouxsie Sioux, since it conveyed darkness and hardness, rejecting female beauty ideals of lightness and softness. Sometimes it incorporated pigtails, which might not seem particularly countercultural in a Western-style culture, but in Tehran, pigtails emerging from under a headscarf provided a way to reveal the hair. These styles were a little sloppy and had a definite grunge look.

To my eye, the most obvious fashion trend for Tehrani women in the summer of 2004 was the prevalence of particular colors. The mannequins in store windows in trendy areas like Vanak Square and Tajrish were all dressed in neon lime green and bright turquoise hues, colors that looked surprisingly nice against some skin tones. Even though these same colors did not dominate boutiques in the United States or the pages of Western fashion magazines, from what I was told by a number of Iranian women, this trend might have been influenced by Western literature on the psychology of color that had permeated Iran. This literature argues that dark colors lead to depression, while bright colors are the expression of happiness. Women used this psychological discourse to explain their own colorful dress. "By wearing various bright, cheerful, or beautiful clothes I show that I am not a cold person and I'm friendly," explained twenty-six-year-old Fatemah. Pious fashion has changed considerably with the availability of more colors. After the revolution, women were extremely limited in their clothing palettes; fashion was dominated by solemn blacks, navy blues, and grays. But in recent years, the concept of an "in-season color" has been introduced and embraced, adding to the repertoire of acceptable colors.

Pious fashion in Tehran changed significantly from 2004 to 2011. In part this had to do with the availability of different clothing items. An imported fit-and-flare *manteau* was popular in 2011, with a long, full bottom that resembled a skirt. Leggings were everywhere that year, as they were in the United States. So were brightly colored skinny jeans and slim-fit, "cigarette" pants. The 2004 trend of tight, short *manteaus* had not endured. By 2011, *manteaus* were generally longer and looser, though both long and short *manteaus* with belts were popular. Overall there was a move toward more casual, even sloppy, attire—sneakers, sweatshirts, and T-shirts with phrases or images on them were prominent in street style. The Tehrani elite also began to wear these markers of laid-back global fashion, often combined with designer items.

Three new and distinct forms of women's dress had emerged between 2004 and 2011. One of these styles integrated traditional motifs, cloth, and embroidery, whether Kurdish, Turkoman, or Indian. In Persian this style is called *lebase mahali*, meaning "local clothing," where "local" is a reference to villages. Embroidery of black thread on black fabric was common in earlier decades, but bright colorful embroidery was everywhere in Tehran in 2011: on the fronts of *manteaus*, and in details on sleeves, hems, and other edges. Intricate patterned cloth, with intense greens and reds, was used to make everything from *manteaus*, to the loose pants that women called "Indian pants," to handbags. These kinds of patterned clothing and accessory items, which had previously only been available in expensive boutiques, had become

This outfit combines a high-end Baume & Mercier watch and Tom Ford sunglasses with a fuzzy and affordable Zara overcoat. The stunning gold earring is a copy of a design from the Persian Empire. Red lipstick nicely sets off the lime color of the headscarf, a color first popularized in 2004. Courtesy of *The Tehran Times* fashion blog. Photograph by Anita Sepehry, March 7, 2017.

readily available in stores and street markets in Tehran as a result of President Ahmadinejad's liberal import policy. "Wearing these ethnic styles, like colorful clothes with traditional patterns, is considered artsy, and everyone is trying to keep up with it," twenty-year-old Faraz wrote on her survey. Women created additional visual complexity by wearing multiple intricate prints at the same time, linking them together through complementary color palettes.

This "ethnic" style challenged existing aesthetic standards by asserting the value of the taste and style of minority groups over that of the dominant tastemakers. However, this valuation of minority taste or village life only pertains to fashion. "Village chic" can be adopted by fashionable women in Tehran because there is an immense distance between these women and the poor rural people they are imitating.[4] Wearing what might otherwise be seen as provincial clothing also demonstrates a certain level of confidence. The fashionable woman asserts her sophistication and design savvy when she successfully incorporates traditional cloth and patterns into a cutting-edge outfit. She is so modern that she takes no risk in wearing village chic—there is no chance that she will be mistaken for an actual villager.

I observed the incorporation of so-called ethnic elements into pious fashion in all three locations I studied. In Tehran, this style included the disruption of local religious aesthetics through the combination of red and green embroidery. Red and green have symbolic meanings in Shiism, the dominant branch of Islam in Iran: green is positive, while red has a number of negative connotations.[5] For instance, in a passion play (ta'ziyeh) that reenacts the Battle of Karbala, green represents the hero, Imam Hussein, who is violently martyred. Red, on the other hand, represents his killer, Shemr, and Hussein's blood sacrifice. In the 1979 referendum on establishing the Islamic Republic, the ballots were color-coded: ballots in favor of the Islamic Republic were green, while those against it were red. In Tehran today, the strict dichotomy of this symbolism is contested when red and green are incorporated into the same textile or combined in the same outfit. A new appreciation for the aesthetic value of these color combinations has made possible what

Layers, ethnic patterns, and natural fabrics give this outfit a boho-chic vibe. The headscarf, which displays a Turkoman style of embroidery, is combined with a denim *manteau* and trendy culottes. The shoes mix menswear fringe with geometric beadwork. Photograph by Donya Joshani, January 4, 2017.

would have seemed unthinkable a couple of decades ago: *hijab* that breaks the rules of Shiism's color symbolism.

A second major trend in 2011 was a popular new cut of *manteau* called an "Arab *chador.*" The traditional *chador* has not changed in eleven centuries, and it can be quite difficult to wear. Perhaps in acknowledgement of these stylistic difficulties, or concerns about the *chador's* waning popularity, in May 2006 the Iranian parliament passed a bill to promote an updated form of national dress. Eight months later a government-sponsored fashion show made public the designs selected by an official committee. As at any fashion show, not every style was equally successful, but the Arab *chador* quickly gained traction among Tehrani hipsters and artists. This was not a new style, having been worn previously in religious cities like Mashad and Qom. Nonetheless the Arab *chador* became adopted as a fashionable form of *hijab* in Tehran around 2007. In 2004 I did not encounter a single woman wearing this style in Tehran. By 2011, it was one of the most popular forms of *hijab.*

Other than in name, the Arab *chador* bears little resemblance to the traditional *chador.* Like a traditional *chador,* the Arab *chador* is long, extremely loose, and does not have a fastener. However, unlike a traditional *chador,* it is meant to fall open and comes in a rainbow of colors. Its major practical improvement is that it has long billowing sleeves. One popular style among upper-class Tehrani youth is to wear an Arab *chador* with a very big *rusari.* The Iranian authorities endorse this type of overcoat in part because it is long and loose, and in part because its name links it to the culture and geography of Islam. But the women I interviewed described the Arab *chador* as a "bohemian" form of dress, popular especially among "artist types." Many women who participated in my 2011 survey mentioned that they admired this style as creative and colorful. Marziyeh, who declined to give her age, wrote that the Arab *chador* provides a way to rebel against *hijab* rules without explicitly breaking them, through "innovative design." In this case the rebellion does not break the law but rather challenges the notion that *hijab* is a traditional form of clothing that never changes.

Thus, the Arab *chador* succeeded as a style by being both more religious and more modern than the traditional *chador.*

A third trend in Tehrani pious fashion that was identifiable in 2011, especially when compared to clothing in Yogyakarta and Istanbul, was what might be called urban-edgy *hijab.* In 2004, there was a style that gestured at 1980s punk rock in the West. It was dark, a little angry, and had a grunge look. It was also rare, which is what made it seem "cool." But by 2011, a fresher form of edgy *hijab* was popular, one that incorporated bright colors and large graphics. In 2004, I would occasionally spot a young teenage girl who looked punk, but by 2011, twenty-somethings everywhere were wearing T-shirts with large images of skulls over sleek leggings, with stiletto lace-up booties. People wore spikes on their heels instead of spiked hair. There was an edge to these styles, but they were not grunge, even when incorporating ripped jeans. They were fierce insofar as they were assertive and bold, but these ensembles were also glammed up, highly stylized, and decisively feminine. Less Joan Jett, more Alexa Chung or Santigold.

One thing these three fashion trends—ethnic chic, Arab *chador,* and urban-edgy *hijab*—have in common is that they invoke a feeling of movement and volume. The embroidered cotton *rusaris* that were popular in 2011 were more flowing than the silk Hermès scarves of 2004. The billowy Arab *chador* also lacks structure and tailoring in comparison with the *manteau.* Even the edgy *hijab* style played with volume, with design elements like shoulder pads, and movement, with loose, layered graphic tees over tight pants. This shift in Iran is even more striking when compared with the Turkish fashions in 2011, which tended to be structured and tailored.

It might seem as if there is nothing connecting 2004 and 2011 *hijab* fashion. Both seasons, however, featured styles of clothing that allowed women to critique the norms promoted by the Iranian authorities. In 2004, this critique was conveyed through tight clothes and exposed forearms, ankles, calves, and hair that pushed the limits of acceptable modesty, privileging fashion over piety. In 2011, the critique had shifted. *Hijab*

This outfit is a glam version of edgy *hijab*. The Alexander McQueen–style skull-patterned scarf, fur vest, and Givenchy Rottweiler-print clutch give the woman a rock vibe. Courtesy of *The Tehran Times* fashion blog. Photograph by Donya Joshani, January 27, 2017.

became less formal. Trends were toward laid back, flowing, drapey layers that felt fresh—because they were casual and unstructured—or fierce—because they were assertive and highly stylized. This was a rebellion not against modesty but against the theocracy's vision of how Muslim femininity should be publicly expressed. A woman in ethnic *hijab* or Arab *chador* did not primarily communicate either allegiance to the government or submission to traditional gender ideologies.

Iranian men's clothing also reflects political and religious values, even if less obviously than women's clothing does, and I made some observations about men's dress in the same seasons. In 2004, Mohammad Khatami was almost at the end of his term as president. To the untrained eye, it appeared that Khatami was simply wearing traditional clerical garb: a turban, a high-neck tunic, and a long robe. But in Iran, Khatami was known to be a bit of a dandy. For his robe, he favored the structured *labadeh*—considered more modern and stylish, with its high collar and semifitted sleeves and torso—over the loose and flowing *qaba*. He wore luxurious fabrics, such as tightly woven twills with a silky-smooth finish and refined drape. He was especially known for bold color choices, including a cream cloak that quickly became adopted by other prominent clerics in the government.[6] Khatami's "chic mullah" style was the material expression of his reformist agenda, combining traditional Shii garb—which conveyed clerical rank—with modern fabrics and meticulous tailoring—which conveyed a desire to innovate.

In 2011, Mahmoud Ahmedinejad was in his second term as president of Iran. During his campaign, he became well known for his light beige polyester Members Only–style windbreaker, worn over a white button-down shirt and slacks. Once elected, he traded his windbreaker for poorly tailored suits, always worn without a tie. The intentional casualness of his windbreaker and the cheapness of his suits was a way of claiming that he was of the people rather than part of the ruling elite. Going without a necktie was a clear sign of allegiance to the aesthetic values of the theocracy. This leader was pious in a much different way than Khatami, signaling class consciousness instead of clerical status. These two presidents did have one style choice in common, however: a full beard. Although there was some flexibility in how piety could be expressed in men's clothing, aesthetic and moral values dictated facial hair for the highest elected official of Iran.

The standard business attire for Iranian men in both 2004 and 2011 was Western slacks, a button-down shirt, and a tailored jacket. The only real difference between a banker in Tehran and one in New York was the lack of a tie and the tendency to wear facial hair. Pants, jeans, and T-shirts have remained the foundations of male street style. By 2011, a male version of urban edgy street fashion had emerged, and mustaches were sported as a sign not only of traditional Persian aesthetics but also of hipster coolness.[7]

Location Matters

Even in a country where the same legal dress code applies everywhere, location and social context matter. I noticed this in making my own clothing choices. During Persian class I wore a simple knee-length *manteau* and loose *rusari*. To socialize, I followed my Iranian friends' lead and favored more tailored and embellished *manteaus*. During interviews, I tried to dress in a way I thought would be perceived as more conservative: dark colors, long loose *manteaus,* and baggy pants. I purchased a *maghneh* and sometimes wore it for these interviews, although I disliked this style. When I visited Shii shrines, I wore a long black *chador*. I learned to practice what I observed others doing: using specific forms of *hijab* within specific contexts to signal status, respect, or identity.

When I traveled outside Tehran, it became clear that *hijab* looked very different in different regions, whether south of the capital in Qom, where the majority of women wore *chador,* or in the north, where it was possible to wear a blouse or a tunic in lieu of a *manteau*. Dress norms are tied so closely to location that Tehran-born Zahra pointed out that traveling from one place to another temporarily suspends these norms: "During road trips, because you're far away from formal settings or maybe because you are traveling, wearing more comfortable clothes wouldn't cause any trouble." She confirmed that she would "step down" her *hijab* while traveling, opting for a casual long tunic instead of a buttoned-up *manteau*.

Within Tehran, *hijab* norms vary by neighborhood as well. Yasmin, an art student whom I interviewed in 2011 over email, explained this as follows:

> When I go to the central or southern parts of the city I realize that people are staring at my clothes, whereas if I wear the same clothes in the northern parts of the city no one will stare at me. Women in the southern districts wear loose dark clothes without makeup, and they wear *chador*. But it's not that way in uptown.

Yasmin is describing what everyone in Tehran knows: the most fashion-conscious forms of *hijab* are worn by women in the northern sections of Tehran, like the affluent Tajrish neighborhood where my Persian school was located. This variation is an expression of socioeconomic class, since the latest styles of *manteaus* and *rusaris* are too expensive for people with working- or middle-class incomes. These financial reasons aside, there are additional reasons why fashion is emphasized over piety by some groups, rooted in ideas about how status is gained in Iran.

Immediately after the revolution, public displays of piety were used as a strategy for upward mobility, such as procuring a government job, or joining the political elite, who had enormous power and incomes. *Hijab* that emphasizes piety over fashion is still considered necessary for achieving economic prosperity within the lower and middle classes. In contrast, upper-class Iranians do not particularly benefit from public displays of piety. This class consists of some of the same social groups that made up the pre-revolutionary elite, including landowners, financiers, and merchants. These groups did well under the shah's monarchy, and those who stayed after the revolution did not necessarily support the Islamic theocracy or its promotion of an Islamic public space. As a result, public displays of piety are not a means toward social and political capital within this class. Some elite women wear *hijab* only grudgingly, happy to push the boundaries of acceptability in the pursuit of style.

Differences in clothing also depend on the type of "public" a woman is in. Many government offices have explicit dress codes for women, requiring dark colors and a *maghneh*. Many universities have their own dress codes as well. Thirty-one-year-old Nasrin described some of these codes in her survey: "Universities like Allameh Tabataba'i have ridiculous restrictions and would measure the length of your *manteau*. Some other universities, like Tehran University, are more laid back." On university campuses, students in different groups tend to wear similar *hijab*. My interlocutors told me, for example, that technical and engineering students tend to wear a "sporty *hijab*," a casual style, as a sign that they are studious. In this way, forms of dress, as on any college campus, demonstrate group membership.

Parks are another space with their own implicit dress code. Although parks are technically public spaces, *hijab* tends to be more casual here: some women wear tracksuits with a headscarf when they exercise. Dress requirements can be suspended in semipublic spaces such as the courtyards and hallways of apartment buildings. Fatemah, a twenty-one-year-old college student, explained on her questionnaire that "in some apartment complexes, in spite of not knowing each other and not knowing each other's beliefs, people socialize without wearing the *rusari*."

These examples show that it is impossible, even within one city, to define a single Iranian *hijab* style. The meaning of a particular form of dress, whether political, ethical, or religious, is determined in part by where it is worn and what the social context is, and women must understand local aesthetic expectations when deciding what to wear.

Chador *as Distinction*

Chador is symbolically rich, conveying a number of meanings in Iran. The *chador*'s primary modern association is with the 1979 revolution, during which it was promoted as a symbol of a new era of Muslim politics that rejected Western forms of modernization. For several decades after 1979, when revolutionary credentials were required to gain entry into the political elite at the national or provincial level, the association of the *chador* with the revolution meant that women could signal their commitment to the Islamist regime by choosing to wear a *chador* in public rather than other versions of *hijab*, such as a headscarf and overcoat. This association is one reason we find more use of *chadors* among government bureaucrats and high-ranking government officials.

A controversy that occurred in 2000 shows how the unofficial preference for *chador* was used to discourage certain women from running for elected office. That year Elahah Kulai, a prominent academic and expert in international relations, was elected to the Majles (Iranian parliament) and attended the inaugural session wearing a *rusari* and a long *manteau*.[8] While there is no specific dress code for the parliament, since the 1979 revolution no woman had ever sat in the Majles without a *chador*. Kulai was harshly criticized and even received death threats for her outfit that day.

The flip side to this imposition of *chador* is that women figured out how to use this style to gain access to leadership roles in the government. For instance, built into the structure of the Iranian government are numerous advisory roles for women: the president has a special adviser on women's affairs, as does every governor. Within the parliament and the judiciary, there are special advisory bodies that deal with women's issues. A woman I interviewed in 2004 who held one of these appointed government positions told me that wearing *chador* was a requirement of her appointment. On one hand, such requirements might seem to limit who can have access to these forms of political power, since someone who supports the current regime might be more likely to wear *chador*. But on the other hand, women are able to take advantage of the symbolic meaning of the *chador* to mark themselves as supporters of the theocracy, independent of their actual political views. Dress therefore becomes an important way to access governmental power, as well as a sign of holding that power.

Chador among government representatives made sense, but I had not expected to find this style of pious fashion among activists working on issues of democratization and women's rights. My ignorance caused a significant amount of embarrassment on one occasion. I was invited to give a lecture at the governor's mansion in Isfahan to leaders of non-governmental organizations focused on women's affairs. I showed up in a form of stylish *hijab* I had been wearing in Tehran while doing work in the Khomeini archives: a light-blue linen *manteau* and silk embroidered *rusari*. Almost every one of the forty or so women in the room was wearing *chador*. I knew immediately that I had grossly misjudged what appropriate *hijab* would be in that setting, and I felt the acute sting of a fashion failure.

My faux pas at the governor's mansion had a silver lining: it made me aware of an implicit *chador* dress code among leaders of civil society, especially when they meet with government officials or in government offices. I began to note that various prominent leaders of the Iranian women's movement wore *chador*, even those who would admit to me off the record that they were critical of mandatory veiling. These sartorial practices were strategic: they allowed activists to visually signal that their work was about the common Muslim good, not about resisting religious norms. By nodding to the government preference for *chador*, activists avoided having to defend their activities as Islamic.

Chador can also be a marker of social distinction in Tehran. But this meaning is complicated because it varies according to social class: there are both upper-class and lower-class women who wear *chador* predominantly because of their socioeconomic status. Political scientist Norma Claire Moruzzi analyzes this phenomenon within universities, arguing that *chador* can play three distinct roles: (1) as a form of dress for young women from outside Tehran, who will eventually transition to other forms of *hijab*; (2) as a marker that a student is from a poor or traditional family; or (3) as a claim to social distinction for an upper-class Tehrani student.[9] Distinguishing among these meanings can only be done by knowing a woman's background or by determining the quality and cost of the black fabric of her *chador*, which can range from inexpensive polyester to luxurious silk crepe. This means that although wearing *chador* is often tied to class, one cannot immediately decipher which class it is reflecting.

To complicate things further, interpreting *chador* as a signal of low or high economic class depends to a great extent on the viewer's, not the *chador*-clad woman's, own social location. For instance, thirty-three-year-old Sara wrote on her survey, "In lower-income neighborhoods or religious neighborhoods, more people tend to wear *chador* than in other neighborhoods, and you do not see *manteaus* that are in style in those neighborhoods. It is a matter of affording to buy those *manteaus*." Sara noted that she never wears *chador*, and she herself is from an affluent family that lives in Tajrish. Her interpretation of *chador* as a sign of lower income is a function of her own social location. In fact, a *chador* made of expensive fabric can easily cost more than a *manteau*.

Rather than a simple indication of Islamism, the *chador* can indicate political allegiance to the Islamic Republic, create political capital, or demonstrate social distinction. And which of these meanings it conveys depends not only on the intention of the wearer but also the viewer's presumptions about the role of piety and class in Iranian social and political life.

Bad Hijab

I began this chapter with an account of my first experience with the infamous *bad hijab* of Tehran, an amusing oxymoron that highlights the rebellious potential of an apparently conservative dress style. The Persian word for bad is *bad*, and *bad hijab* is the phrase commonly used in Iran to refer to styles of clothing judged to violate public dress codes. However, it is a very odd grammatical construction, even in Persian. Technically, *bi hijab* ("without hijab") would be more accurate to describe improper *hijab* in Persian. If wearing *hijab* is a pious act that demonstrates virtuous character, then *bad hijab* is an oxymoron: by definition, *hijab* is moral, not immoral. However, as I learned during the shopping trip with Homa described at the beginning of this chapter, an egregious aesthetic failure changes *hijab* from a moral to an immoral display. Even more striking is how the wearing of *bad hijab* is interpreted as a sign of an inner defect of character, based on the assumption that a woman's outer style reflects the status of her moral formation.

Identifying *bad hijab* is not an easy task for an outsider. *Bad hijab* in Tehran depends on Tehranis—whether regular citizens like Homa or the morality police we will discuss later—judging the outfit to be an extreme failure. Not only do aesthetic and moral norms change from season to season but the same outfit might be acceptable to one person and offensive to another. In general, *bad hijab* applies to any form of dress that calls attention to an individual, such as bright colors, tight *manteaus*, flashy embellishments, or heavy makeup. But for these things to be deemed *bad hijab*, the attention they draw must be inappropriate in some way, such as violating taste by being too garish or violating moral norms by being sexually provocative. On a deeper level, *bad hijab* is defined by men, whether actual male viewers, or the hypothetical men whom Iranian authorities think they must protect women from, or even the male gaze implied in women's scrutiny of each other.

Homa's determination of *bad hijab* was based primarily on fit and fabric. The woman's "slutty" outfit exposed her ankles, the back of her neck, and her throat and hair, parts legally required to be covered. The fact that this display seemed intentional, because the woman's pants were rolled up and she had draped her *rusari* to achieve maximum exposure, made the displays all the more egregious. Specific articles of this woman's clothing caused another sort of exposure. For instance, her pants were tight, and her short, slit *manteau* was made of gauzy fabric, exposing the outlines of her body.

Disapproval of the woman's jeans was based in part on the material. Denim is considered improper for women to wear in Iran for both aesthetic reasons (as a fabric that is too casual or sloppy) and political reasons (as a Western fabric that might infect the individual with Western ideas). Other items, such as cowboy boots, receive scrutiny from Iranian authorities for similar reasons.

Aside from the headscarf, this outfit could be seen on any American college campus: skinny ripped jeans, a long button-down shirt, a parka with a fake-fur-rimmed hood, and Timberland boots. The loosely draped peach headscarf balances the look. Black fingernail polish and mirrored, oversized sunglasses amp up the cool factor. Courtesy of *The Tehran Times* fashion blog. Photograph by Donya Joshani, January 24, 2017.

Homa spent considerable time describing for me why this woman's *rusari* was so inadequate. In this case, the violation depended in part on the scarf's material, which was translucent and allowed us to see her hair. The way the scarf was worn was also a problem: by folding the *rusari* lengthwise, the woman created a demi-*rusari* that only covered half as much hair as normal. Homa had also criticized the woman's heavy hand with makeup. Cosmetic use in itself was not a concern. Kohl has traditionally been used as an eyeliner and is widely accepted in Iran, and cosmetic stores are extremely common throughout Tehran. There is little anxiety about makeup that hides imperfections or imparts a sense of symmetry to the face. But this woman's heavy makeup was judged to be a *hijab* "failure" because it sexualized her by making her appear more alluring to the opposite sex.

The five perceived violations of proper dress that Homa identified—exposure, sloppy dress, Western clothing, improper head covering, and heavy makeup—also turn out to be an accurate summary of the types of violations that morality police arrest women and girls for, as we will see below. Homa's judgment of this woman's dress indicated that she had internalized the Islamic Republic's aesthetic of body concealment, a dynamic I will discuss further in the conclusion of this chapter.

Some Western journalists and scholars have portrayed *bad hijab* as a counter-movement, an act of resistance to the regime's authority. This interpretation is problematic for a number of reasons. For one thing, what looks like rebellion in one political context might not look the same in another. We are quick to see expressions of agency in Muslim women's clothing that includes elements of secular fashion: high heels, side slits, glamorous makeup, denim. In Iran, however, these items might signal that an outfit is an aesthetic or moral failure, not a successful act of women's empowerment. In addition, the very definition of *bad hijab* depends on the regime's authority, specifically its various forms of regulating public dress. In this way, *chador* and *bad hijab* have much in common. Both styles can signal or create social distinction by taking advantage either of religious institutionalized aesthetic authority or of Western aesthetic authority.

Finally, it would be difficult to conclude that *bad hijab* is part of a coordinated feminist revolution. When I asked Leila—who works in a government office but pushes the boundaries of *hijab* with heavy makeup and tight *manteaus* when not at work—if clothes give her a political voice, she replied, "to some extent." When pressed to explain, she conceded that "sometimes refusal to obey the regime's dictated rules related to *hijab* is a form of civil disobedience." She insisted, however, that "sometimes it is not political at all, but only an attempt to stand out from the crowd. But the regime itself insists on always interpreting the disobedience as political." *Bad hijab* does not constitute resistance in the sense of a social movement with specific goals and widespread coordination. But it is political insofar as it challenges existing aesthetic preferences and officially promoted moral values, even if only on an ad hoc basis.

Authorities

Of the three cities featured in this book, Tehran is the only one where women are legally required to wear Islamic dress in public. But the pressure to dress a certain way is only partially explained by these laws. A combination of political, social, cultural, and religious institutions, as well as some influential individuals, collaborate and compete for aesthetic authority, resulting in a multilayered management of women's dress in Iran. Five authorities that shape and regulate pious fashion are religious experts, the morality police, visual propaganda, fashion designers, and fashion blogs. These authorities sometimes reinforce each other, but at other times they offer alternative visions of women's public appearance.

Religious Experts

Male legal experts produce a tremendous amount of *fiqh* (Islamic legal jurisprudence) on the topic of women's clothing, which reflects male bias about women in general and women's bodies in particular. This bias no doubt explains why women's modest clothing is more often discussed than men's in the jurisprudence, despite the fact that the Quran states that Muslim men also have a duty to be modest.[10] Especially important in Iran is a strand of legal thought that emerged in medieval legal scholarship and viewed women's modest dress as a way to prevent *fitna*, or worldly disorder. The disorder at stake is the chaos of sexual desire outside of marriage, and the assumption is that the exposure of women's bodies causes arousal in men. The way to prevent it? Cover women.

In Iran, religious arguments for mandatory Islamic dress in public are also based on concerns about combating *gharbzadegi*, often translated as "Westoxication." A term popularized through the widely circulated work of the Iranian writer Jalal Al-e Ahmad, *gharbzadegi* refers to the loss of Iranian culture through the adoption of Western norms and practices. Al-e Ahmad describes *gharbzadegi* as a disease, worse than cholera, that infects from the inside out, leaving only a surface shell "like a cicada on a tree."[11] Shii Islam, identified by Al-e Ahmad and others as one element of Iranian life uninfected by the West, becomes a safe place to look for authentic norms and practices. Women's dress is an acute political concern within the logic of *gharbzadegi*. A bareheaded woman dressed in a miniskirt represents all Iranian social ills, while a woman in modest clothing is an antidote against past Western cultural invasions, as well as an inoculation to protect against future ones.

The book *The Question of Hijab (Masaleyeh hijab)*, based on a series of lectures by Ayatollah Murtadha Mutahhari in 1966, is still among the most influential texts in Iran on the topic of *hijab*. An important intellectual architect of the 1979 revolution, Mutahhari argued that Islam is a complete system of life and can ground all dimensions of a modern nation-state. A supporter of *hijab*, Mutahhari understood sartorial practices to have powerful psychological, economic, and social effects. In his book he claimed, first, that a women's dignity is protected by wearing *hijab*: "[If] a woman leaves her house covered, not only does it not detract from her human dignity, but it adds to it" because "there is nothing which would cause others to be stimulated or attracted toward her."[12] Second, *hijab* creates "social dignity" by helping to establish a particular kind of social interaction between men and women. In Mutahhari's words, "the well-being of society demands that a man and a woman commit themselves to a special kind of association with each other" for "the tranquility of the spirit of society."[13] This association consists of what we might call a form of public chastity, where men and women can interact in public but only in ways that avoid any sexual impropriety. For Mutahhari, dress codes are a mechanism for creating and maintaining this public chastity.

If Mutahhari conceptualized compulsory public *hijab* within an Islamic social context, Ayatollah Ruhollah Khomeini, the first supreme leader of Iran's new Islamic government, helped to establish it within the government structure. For Khomeini, mandatory Islamic dress for women was part of articulating and sustaining a distinctive Muslim public morality. The stakes for this ethical project were high for Khomeini, because he saw it as necessary for stabilizing the new form of Islamic government he was creating. However, by leaving unanswered the question of what proper *hijab* entailed, Khomeini left the decision about what to wear up to Iranian women. Take, for example, his statement in a 1978 interview, before the revolution: "In Islam women must dress modestly and wear a veil, but that does not necessarily mean she has to wear *chador*. Women can choose any kind of attire they like so long as it covers them properly and they have *hijab*."[14]

Today, the majority of Iranian legal experts agree that mandatory *hijab* is necessary, but the diversity of their legal opinions (or *fatwas*) on what *hijab* requires is astonishing. Each jurist seems to have a particular concern about women's appearance. Some focus on bare ankles, others on gold rings, makeup, or poofy hair. This variety of concerns is reflected in a wide range of definitions of proper *hijab*, each one emphasizing a different aspect of women's clothing: one jurist will require socks, another will specify colors for *manteaus*, yet another will prohibit certain styles as too masculine or aggressive, or even ban sequins or shoes that make noise when a woman walks. Despite this diversity, three major concerns are widely shared.

The most common set of concerns has to do with women's dress that attracts attention, sometimes referred to as *shoreh* clothing.[15] This is a broad category that covers two different types of attraction. One concern is with clothing that stands out, grabbing and keeping someone's attention. This is seen in the focus on discouraging flashy clothes (e.g., items that glitter or sparkle, are embellished with sequins, or are brightly colored) or clothing and shoes that make noise (e.g., stiletto shoes). The other concern is with any form of dress that could be perceived as attracting sexual attention from men. This might include a short tight *manteau* that emphasizes the shape of a women's body, or makeup that accentuates facial beauty. This style is interpreted as overly feminine and is seen as potentially creating social disorder by arousing the powerful passions of men.

The flip side of too much femininity is not enough, and a second set of anxieties centers on forms of women's dress that are perceived as masculine. This concern is why some legal experts warn against clothing with images of animals like wolves and foxes. These animals symbolize aggression and sneakiness, which are considered inappropriate character traits for women to possess or express.[16] Women are also not supposed to wear male-inspired business suits, which could encourage androgyny and the blurring of gender lines.

The third category of concerns is with clothing that is regarded as Western. Denim jeans, cowboy boots, clothing with graphics of pop icons—these are all items that religious experts interpret as un-Islamic because they are considered as signs of dependency on the West, cultural imperialism, and consumerism. This is an interesting place to see the slide between the ethical and aesthetic values associated with clothing. Western-influenced clothes are linked to moral corruption, and by wearing them, an individual presumably displays a poorly formed character. These items are thought to lead to the demise of social norms as well, by infecting society with foreign values.

Morality Police

During my visit to Tehran in 2004, I interviewed Ayatollah Hossein Boroujerdi, a well-known critic of the Iranian government. Despite having a reputation as a liberal cleric, he was still an ayatollah, so, out of respect, I took pains to construct a modest outfit on the day I was to meet him. I decided my *chador* was overkill and chose instead the oversized black *manteau* I had purchased during my first few days in Tehran, long wide-legged navy linen pants, and a black *rusari* with a small amount of embroidery around the edge. As I left to meet my taxi, my roommates teased me that I looked old and dowdy, to which I shot back, "That is the point!" I was still smiling over their teasing as I was stepping into the taxi. Suddenly someone grabbed my elbow and pulled me out. I stood facing a large, imposing woman in her fifties, wearing a black *chador*. She began to scold me for my *hijab*. "We worked so hard for the revolution," she began in Persian, "and you young girls, you have no respect." She realized very quickly that I was not Iranian. I was also not "young," but thirty years old at the time, almost twice the age of most of the girls living in the boarding house. She dropped my elbow but recovered quickly and continued her rant. "I know, I know, you are just a visitor," she continued, "but this is unacceptable. You must wear socks." "Socks?" I thought, looking down at my sandal-clad feet. I thought I had misheard the Persian word, *jurab*. No one wore socks in Tehran in the summer, at least not that I had noticed. And the forecast that day was for temperatures in the upper nineties. She saw my expression and grabbed my arm again, excitedly gesturing at my ankles. "Ankles should not be exposed. Cover yourself up." At that point, adrenaline kicked in. I did not like being accosted by a stranger, and I did not like being told to cover up, especially when I was making my best attempt at pious frump. I said "*bashi, bashi* (okay, okay)," pulled away, got back into the taxi, and left.

By the time I arrived at Boroujerdi's office, I realized that I had just had my first run-in with a member of the Basij, Iran's infamous morality police. The enforcement of *hijab* in Iran is carried out by this paramilitary force whose full name is Sazman-e Basij-e Mostaz'afin (The Organized for Mobilization of the Oppressed). Established by Ayatollah Khomeini and supervised by the Iranian Revolutionary Guards, today the Basij is primarily a domestic security force made up of volunteers. Its mission can be broadly defined as helping maintain law and order by enforcing Islamic values in public, including the wearing of *hijab*.

Who are the members of the Basij? Official reports, which are probably grossly inflated, claim that there are 13 million active members, which would be a stunning 20 percent of Iran's population. A more conservative estimate puts the number closer to 1.5 million. By some estimates, women make up over one-third of the Basij. Ordinary citizens also collaborate with the Basij by reporting violations of public morality. As twenty-year-old Suri notes, "If someone provides photos of a person sitting in a car with *bad hijab* for the cops, the Basij will follow up on the case."

Even though the Basij is considered a military force, its members are poorly trained and only occasionally armed. But what they lack in firepower they make up for in techniques of intimidation. Basij enforcers harass and shame women and girls they consider to be violating the Islamic dress code. "The morality police are vulgar," twenty-six-year-old Fatemah told me. "Sometimes they even humiliate and brutalize people." Twenty-year-old Faraz called their behavior "rude and disgusting" and thought they treated people like criminals. A clash over class in part drives outrage about the morality police. When a van pulls up in a popular shopping district in northern Tehran, it is often wealthy girls who are rounded up. In that neighborhood there are many families who consider themselves part of the secular elite, and thus their daughters, who are more interested in the pursuit of fashion than the expression of piety, are likely to be wearing barely passable *hijab*. In contrast, the vigilantes doing the harassing and arresting are more likely to be from the lower or merchant classes, who have more to gain by allying with the theocratic authorities.

Women reported to me that the Basij threatened to file official charges or to put violations of dress on their permanent records in other ways, such as contacting a college student's dean. In addition to harassment, Basij members arrest women for improper Islamic dress in various times and locations. "They are sometimes even stationed in an area and detain everyone, no matter what they are wearing," Fatemah says. "They pretend that they just want to warn you, then they take you to their car with lies and tricks, then force you into their car and take you to the police station." Women are then detained, often until their family comes to the station. They can be fined, and some women report that additional bribes are extracted. That day in front of my boarding house, I had gotten off easy.

Not only clothing but also makeup use can be cause for arrest, as recounted by a woman interviewed by the Iranian women's rights activist Shadi Sadr. "When they arrested us," the woman told Sadr, "one woman in the minibus with a bag of cotton balls came and one by one rubbed the cotton on different parts of my face." These stained cotton balls were then put into a bag as evidence to be used in court.[17] I was told that fines are doled out for each painted fingernail (up to 150,000 rials, or $5, per nail) and for certain accessories (500,000 rials, or $15, for sunglasses).

Some women advised me that the best way to avoid arrest was to resist. Of the twenty-seven women who responded to my 2011 survey, only Marziyeh admitted to a first-hand encounter with the morality police, and she credited her release to her attitude: "I personally got serious warnings from them twice, but I was able to escape detention by protesting and defending myself." Twenty-year-old Suri believed that "the more saucy and bold you are, the more likely that they will release you."

When I was in Iran in 2004, a number of rumors were circulating about the morality police. A common story was that the Basij would arrest girls for improper *hijab* and then force them to put their feet in a bucket of cockroaches. In 2011, I heard similar outlandish stories, such as reports that Basij members were having sexual affairs with the women they detained. Many of the rumors are so far-fetched they are difficult to believe: How exactly could a girl be arrested for not wearing undergarments? However, these rumors do not necessarily have to be true for them to have an influence on women's public appearance. Even the remotest of possibilities that your feet will end up in a bucket of cockroaches might be enough to encourage you to abide by a stricter interpretation of *hijab* than you would otherwise.

However, something shifted between 2004 and 2011. By 2011, most women insisted that the stories about the morality police were all true, despite the fact that only one woman surveyed had firsthand knowledge of Basij tactics. "I heard there have been clashes between the morality police and people that wear *bad hijab*," thirty-five-year-old Jasmine told me. "I thought perhaps it was a rumor, but when I keep hearing it from my friends, and when I saw the morality police cars in city squares, I realized that it wasn't a rumor." As twenty-eight-year-old Kiana put it,

> In the past—ten or fifteen years ago—there were more rumors. I remember I heard that the morality police would paint a girls' hands whose sleeves were short or paint the girl's lower legs if she was wearing short pants! But now there is no need for rumors. There are so many pictures and videos of clashes between the morality police and the people that there would be no need for imagination and making up rumors. We witness everything ourselves.

This shift might indicate that the actual public presence of the Basij is increasing, but more likely it is the result of sharing stories of encounters with the Basij on social media. However, the movement from the realm of rumor to fact in Iranian consciousness also suggests an implicit, if reluctant, acceptance of the Basij as an aesthetic authority in Iran. There are occasional reports of Basij forces being attacked by mobs of angry citizens, but these are not common. For the most part, even if the authority of the Basij is not approved of, it is accepted as part of Iranian life.

Visual Communication

Images and slogans in public spaces play an important role in establishing aesthetic authority and teaching women about proper dress. Describing modest fashion is one thing, but visual representations make the underlying moral values concrete and thus more readily apparent to all. Fatemah said that Iranian women learn the unspoken rules of *hijab* from seeing what others are wearing: "Usually we become aware of these rules by going to the street and observing how people dress." Other women expressed similar ideas about the important role of observing others when deciding what one should wear. Thus, "good dress" becomes "commonly worn dress," and *bad hijab*, as eighteen-year-old Afsaneh put it, is "anything that makes you stand out from everyone else."

Visual communication can also be used to teach women what to wear in a direct way. Consider the manner in which Persian slogans, first promoted by the government after the revolution and plastered on everything from doors of restaurants and shops to the brick walls along busy streets, work to continuously remind and cajole women to dress a certain way. Slogans that I saw in Tehran in 2004 or heard reports of include:

> A woman in *hijab* is like a pearl in her shell.
> The veil on a woman's face is like the drops of water
> on a rose.
> My sister, your *hijab* is your grace.
> *Hijab* is dignity.
> My sister, your veil is more powerful than my weapons.
> [This slogan is attributed to the martyrs.]
> A woman without *hijab* is like a man without honor.
> *Hijab* is the command of God.
> Women must be veiled or they will be assailed.
> A woman in *bad hijab* is a toy of Satan.
> Death to the unveiled.

Even in this small sampling, we can see the range of positive and negative reinforcement that characterizes this form of public inscription: in some slogans, women are praised for displaying qualities associated with femininity, such as grace and beauty, through their dress; in other slogans, sartorial failure is associated with Satan, and offenders are threatened with violence.

In an article published in Iran that resulted in her suspension from her teaching post at the Islamic Azad University of Karaj near Tehran, Fatemeh Sadeghi described the underlying message of such slogans. She focused on the common public inscription "A woman in *hijab* is like a pearl in her shell." This is "the most humiliating sentence about *hijab* which I have ever heard," Sadeghi wrote. "Without having met the creators of this sentence, I can tell that they were experts in the psychology of personality disorders. Can you guess why? This sentence combines praise and humiliation. A woman is praised but only as a being who must be beautiful."[18]

Some slogans are accompanied by images. "*Chador* is the higher form of *hijab*" is printed on posters showing women in *chador* alongside women in presumably less desirable navy *manteaus*, pants, and *maghnehs*. A recent government propaganda poster presents a more extreme version of this strategy of visual pedagogy. Two women standing on the left side of the poster represent *bad hijab*. They are wearing *manteaus* in bright turquoise and fuchsia, nipped in to show off their waists, extending only to the mid-thigh. Their sleeves are rolled up to their elbows. Both women wear tiny *rusaris*, barely covering six inches of their hair. Spiky bangs poke out the front and choppy hair sticks out the back. These women's head-to-toe looks are meant to represent cases of *bad hijab*, especially when compared with the two women on the right who represent good *hijab*. One of the pious women wears a camel-colored *maghneh* over a long brown *manteau*. The other wears a *chador* with a blue headscarf. In this poster, *bad hijab* is much more than a lack of modesty. The women wearing *bad hijab* are not attractive. Their features are angular, their hair messy, their makeup extreme. Despite the telltale sign of a nose job on the fuchsia-wearing woman (a bandage across the bridge of her nose), it is the women wearing proper *hijab* who have the idealized cute button noses. In other words, the moral failure of *bad hijab* is manifested in physical ugliness. And to add insult to injury, the Persian text on the poster reads, "Psychologists believe that women who wear tacky clothes and makeup have personality disorders." Thus, aesthetic failure is a symbol not only of a poorly formed character but also of mental illness.

Other slogans, such as "Do good deeds, and stop the evil" and "Commit the right and forbid the wrong," encourage ordinary citizens to remain vigilant about perceived abuses of Islamic norms, including improper dress. This reflects how the establishment of the Islamic Republic changed the nature of religious and moral authority, especially for women. Ordinary citizens are encouraged to police others on behalf of the state, in order to enforce the state's vision of what personal and social Islamic morality should look like.[19]

Fashion Designer

In Tehran, it is easy to find tailors who will copy the latest fashions right out of a foreign magazine. There are also a small number of independent designers who create fashion-forward versions of *hijab*.[20] For the most part, they operate on a small scale, holding fittings and fashion shows in their workrooms and private residences. One important exception is Lotous House, run by Mahla Zamani. "I decided that since the Revolution 23 years ago, nothing had been done to change the way women dress," Mahla told a reporter for the *Christian Science Monitor* in 2002. "This is not normal. In every modern society fashions change, yet most women in Iran still wear the same outfits they did two decades ago. And so I have decided to do something about it."[21]

When I visited Mahla's workroom in 2004, perusing her over-the-top couture designs was a real treat. There was a rack of showpieces I was especially drawn to: dresses embellished with large cutouts in organic shapes and gatherings of fabric down the sides, paired with dramatic capes and large headdresses. "Those are not for sale," she joked. But there were also ready-to-wear styles, such as reversible tunics, long skirts, and flowing pants, all made to be worn outside the home with a head covering. Lotous House produces everything from couture evening gowns to school uniforms. Mahla's clients include wives of Iranian diplomats, the Iranian airline Mahan Air, for which she designed flight attendant uniforms, and a luxury hotel. She favors volume and plays with a mixture of fabrics, some embroidered using traditional techniques, drawing inspiration from ceremonial costumes of Turkmenistan, as well as elaborate dress of the Qajar Period.[22] Other designs are sleek and modern, using smooth silks and satins.

In 2001, Mahla obtained permission to launch *Lotous: A Persian Quarterly*, which became the first Iranian magazine since the establishment of the Islamic Republic to show the faces of women.[23] The direct impact of *Lotous* on Iranian fashion is debatable. I could not find the magazine on newsstands in Tehran in 2004, nor did any woman I interviewed about fashion in 2011 bring it up. But the very existence of *Lotous* is intriguing, considering how heavily regulated and censored images of women are in the Iranian press. Through a visual balancing act of compliance and critique, Mahla manages to propose new styles and market them through her publication while simultaneously abiding by official norms of dress. While her clothes are certainly modest, with high necklines, volume that hides a woman's curves, and long sleeves, her styles at the same time serve to unsettle the government's authority.

For instance, *Lotous*'s cover declares it a "Persian" quarterly. The styles of the photography, clothes, and positions of the models invoke the Qajar period of Iranian history, all of which contributes to the impression that *Lotous* is authentically local. But by emphasizing Iran's links to Persia rather than its Islamic identity, it offers a subtle critique of official governmental aesthetic authority. As anthropologist Alexandru Balasescu cleverly puts it, *Lotous*'s Iran is grounded in Persepolis, not Mecca.[24] In a country whose government couches its legitimacy within the Islamic tradition, it is not hard to see why this is a bold move.

Mahla performed a similar tightrope walk in naming her label and magazine. *Lotous* is not only a flower but a symbol in Zoroastrianism meaning "good acts and thoughts." Flowers might be politically neutral in Iran, but Zoroastrianism is not. For one thing, this ancient religion has a longer history in the region than does Islam. In addition, Zoroastrian intellectuals have presented themselves as alternatives to the local *ulama* (Shia intellectuals) in important moments in Iranian political history, such as the 1906 Constitutional Revolution. Mahla has thus symbolically aligned herself with a political vision that is not particularly supportive of, or even compatible with, the current regime.

Mahla's designs are very modest in terms of coverage, but they are not demure. They are highly embellished, with ruffles, brocade, and embroidery. Many are saturated in color. Always the careful politician, she justified her colorful designs to me by referring to a government study of women in the Iranian city of Qom. The study, Mahla said, found that women in Qom, who are more likely to wear *chador*, are more depressed than women in Tehran. "In our culture," she told me, "black is associated with sadness and mourning. Obviously, their black clothing is to be blamed." She went on to argue that wearing black has contributed to depression and even suicide rates throughout Iran. This was a clever reshaping of the official propaganda that *bad hijab* is a sign of psychological problems. Mahla argues that it is actually black clothing that causes these illnesses. Color is the treatment Mahla prescribes.

Mahla's brand is based on modernizing ancient Iranian clothing to suit the demands of modern life. She insists that designs like hers help prevent women from choosing less appropriate Western styles. "We should get rid of the Western designs which are not appropriate for Iran," she told a journalist for the *Globe and Mail* in 2003. "If we provide fashion for our women they will never have to resort to Western fashion."[25] She redefines fashion as a form of local national dress that is not driven by global trends but instead is derived from aspects of Iranian history and culture that are neither Islamic nor Western.

Blogger as Curator

Of the twenty-seven women who participated in my 2011 survey, only one had ever attended a fashion show in Tehran. Twenty-five-year-old Anita told me she had never gone because the styles on the catwalk were so similar to what was already in the stores. Golnaz, who declined to give her age, had a theory about why the fashion presented at such shows is not particularly innovative. "Of course all of these fashion shows try to be consistent with the current customs of the society," she said, "and they are less likely to be innovative and creative because they want to get a permit from the government." Numerous women mentioned blogs and Facebook, rather than established designers and fashion shows, as important local tastemakers. In her survey, twenty-year-old Faraz suggested that social media was the platform that had the most impact on fashion "because fashion designers can show their products under less restriction and can attract more fans and followers."

A fashion designer named Araz Fazaeli founded the first Iranian blog of street fashion, *The Tehran Times* (http://thetehrantimes.tumblr .com). A portrait of Araz posted on his blog shows a young man with a handlebar mustache and light stubble. His own fashion flair is conveyed through dramatic sunglasses, a feathered pin on the chest of his jacket, a scarf over his right lapel, and a large watch. "It's not about our taste," he tweeted in August 2016, "it's all about those who tastefully dress their taste." His blog is certainly popular. Established in 2012, today *The Tehran Times* has almost 24,000 likes on Facebook, and nearly 74,000 Instagram followers. The photographs of Tehran street style throughout this chapter are taken by two frequent contributors to this blog, Donya Joshani and Anita Sepehry.

Although the blog includes essays and some videos, most of the posts fall under the tabs "Street style" and "Artworks." In the first years of the blog these two topics were combined. Candid photos of stylish young women and men were juxtaposed with images of contemporary Middle Eastern art. Art was "inspiration" for fashion, Araz claimed, and viewing the art and the fashion at the same time encouraged his readers to associate the clothing with aesthetic values. This juxtaposition also established Araz's aesthetic expertise. Since the artwork he featured was decisively avant-garde, the fashion he showcased seemed even more cutting edge.

The decision to feature artworks is also a form of social criticism, especially against the standard portrayals of Middle Eastern women in art. "I see too many artists portraying women as isolated," Araz told the online journal *Atlantic Post* in a 2013 interview, "and maybe in that way they can get more attention from the West."[26] Araz's comments helped me put into perspective an exhibition that ran that same year at Boston's Museum of Fine Arts. "She Who Tells a Story" featured women photographers from Iran and the Arab world. The exhibit's curator, Kristen Gresh, tells us the exhibit "is intended to break down ideas of a nostalgic, Orientalist, traditional, or exotic world through showing contemporary visual media."[27] However, as I stood in front of these photographs, which often featured women in some sort of headscarf, the comments I heard from other viewers were mostly along the lines of, "Oh, those poor women." In part this was because the photographs did not show women's actual sartorial practices, so viewers' preexisting assumptions of Muslim clothing were not challenged. In contrast, *The Tehran Times* exposes the gender and racial stereotypes reproduced in art from the region through visual juxtaposition: if some of the art occasionally represents Muslim women as silenced, hidden, and weak, the street-style women are always assertive, confident, and strong. As Araz puts it, "There are different sides of the society and you shouldn't only concentrate on one but show all sides."

In the *Atlantic Post* interview, Araz asserted, "The main issue in Iran is not the dress code. Fashion is creative enough to make its way through any restrictions." The dazzling range of pious fashion on his blog confirms this claim. Araz posts five to six shots of the same outfit from different angles. Two images from 2012 and 2013 show the range and evolution of the ethnic chic style. In an outfit featured in October 2012, the ethnic element appeared merely in the colorfully embroidered border on the hem of the *manteau*. Coupled with a Louis Vuitton handbag, patent leather loafers, and sunglasses, this version of ethnic chic was structured and polished.[28] A post from November 2013, a couple of years after this trend first emerged, displayed an outfit that was much more assertively ethnic. It utilized batik cloth in indigo and earth tones in multiple ways. The loose *manteau* was a neutral beige, but there was a lot going on under it. The pants had a dropped crotch and were pieced from different hand-dyed fabrics. The *rusari* was bright blue and white, draped loosely over the woman's chest to display as much as possible of its paisley pattern. Even the espadrilles were tie-dyed.[29] Ethnic chic by this point had become so mainstream that in order to be considered fashion forward, an outfit had to be over the top.

Although the 2011 trends I identified are all found on Araz's blog, he favors the urban-edgy *hijab* style, especially the use of graphics on T-shirts, scarves, and pants that add a decisively sleek and cosmopolitan feeling to the outfit. In an edgy combo of Mickey Mouse and skulls posted in September 2012, three black-and-white patterns are combined and topped with a bright red cape-like *manteau*. This outfit displays multiple aspects of Western pop culture. A little Walt Disney, a little Alexander McQueen. One reposter titled the outfit "bitchy mouse."[30] A post later that month features a white T-shirt with a large image of what looks like Grace Jones in sunglasses, smoking a cigarette. The T-shirt is worn over tight black shiny leggings, and the shoes are black velvet loafers with white skulls embroidered on the toes. It is aesthetically aggressive. But in anticipation that it might draw the attention of the morality police, the outfit is covered with a loose red Arab *chador* and a dusty blue linen *rusari*. With the *chador* held closed and the *rusari* tightly wrapped, only the shoes and about twelve inches of the leggings hint at what lies underneath.[31]

From the hashtags Araz provides for every outfit, we can see that some of his hipsters construct their outfits almost entirely of expensive items from European designers such as Roberto Cavalli, Versace, Hermès, Salvatore Ferragamo, and Burberry.[32] Araz also shows women wearing affordable brands like Zara and H&M, but he decidedly favors an upper-class view of what is considered fashion.

Compliance, Creativity, and Critique

After the Islamic Republic was established in 1979, a process began of institutionalizing two types of Iranian citizens, male and female, with different rights and duties. The code regulating women's dress is just one example of the many laws that treat men and women distinctly. But this gender dualism has also created unintended opportunities for women to contribute to politics. Because sharia-based *hijab* is a legal requirement, every woman plays a part in forming Islamic norms as she decides each day what Islamic dress entails for her. These decisions are not completely free, since a number of authorities try to influence what she wears, but, as Araz says, "fashion is creative enough to make its way through any restrictions."

Specific styles of gendered clothing are evidence of a process of negotiation among various forms of aesthetic authority. Take the *chador*. Wearing this form of dress can be seen as submitting to anxieties over the public display of women's bodies; *chador* becomes a way both to combat *gharbzadegi* and to create social dignity. However, *chador* is also a form of social capital that can be used to contest and redefine these moral and social goals, such as when women adopt *chador* as a way to access traditional forms of political power (elected offices) or to convey socioeconomic distinction.

Or take the more recent style of ethnic chic. It does not necessarily push the boundaries of modesty through exposure of skin or body shape, and thus it meets the aesthetic goals set by religious experts and the morality police. And since traditional fabrics are considered anti-Western, they can be seen as combating *gharbzadegi*.[33] On the other hand, something potentially subversive is going on when Persian and Asian aesthetics are privileged over Islamic and Arabic ones. The incorporation of ethnic cloth into pious fashion might be motivated

This outfit—camel wool coat with black leggings, headscarf, and shoulder bag with gold hardware—incorporates timeless wardrobe staples. The expensive Gucci shoes and bag are combined with a more affordable Zara coat. Courtesy of *The Tehran Times* fashion blog. Photograph by Donya Joshani, December 17, 2016.

primarily by the taste of designers and customers, but as a result, this style of clothing promotes local Islamic identity over an identity grounded in Mecca. In the case of Kurdish prints, which involve intricate floral patterns of deep greens and reds, there is an implicit theological critique, even if an unintentional one, since Shii color symbolism is replaced with another tradition of color. Thus, the style of ethnic chic undermines Islamic authority because it draws on sources of authority that predate the Islamization of Iran.

Even if it is neither part of a coordinated feminist social movement nor a sign of secular political aspirations, the concept of *bad hijab* affects how women look and how they are looked at in public. It also shows how a style of pious fashion can become an aesthetic authority by shifting what counts as proper dress. For instance, although Homa harshly judged the woman with *bad hijab,* described in the opening vignette to this chapter, she and her cousins were violating some of the very same cultural norms that they accused this woman of violating. Although the cousins were wearing dark, muted shades of navy, black, and gray, each one had exposed ankles. All had some hair showing from under their scarves. And that morning, everyone had applied foundation, eyeliner, and mascara. My point is not that these fashion critics are hypocrites but rather that moderate or proper *hijab* is defined in contrast with what are perceived as more extreme forms of *bad hijab.*

A second political impact of *bad hijab* is perhaps not intended by the young women but is nevertheless observable to the outside visitor. As mentioned, there are harsh punishments for inadequate *hijab* in the Iranian penal code. But the sheer number of young women wearing *bad hijab* makes enforcement of the law impossible. There are not enough police in Tehran on a hot summer day to arrest every young woman wearing capris, and there would undoubtedly be a public outcry if everyone wearing nail polish was administered the required seventy-four lashes. In this way *bad hijab* has shifted the effective enforcement of sharia. Pious fashion has begun to form, instead of only being formed by, Islamic law and politics in Iran.

In addition to contesting aesthetic authorities through their own sartorial practices, women collaborate with the regime of regulation by judging the dress of others. Putting down another's style in terms of aesthetics (taste) or morals (modesty) shores up one's own status, while at the same time it reinforces structural gender discrimination. Homa's assessment of the mystery woman's *bad hijab* was a way to legitimate her own clothing choices. Women's claim to moral authority comes up elsewhere as well, such as in Marziyeh's insistence that standing up for herself in the face of harassment by the morality police allowed her to escape detention. The assumption here, shared by other women I surveyed, is that women's moral authority has a legitimate contribution to make.

The story of pious fashion in Tehran does not end with the facts of its legal codification and official policing. On the streets of Tehran, in its cafés and places of business, Iranian women find ways to use their clothing to make claims about what counts not only as fashion but also as piety. Within a regime that has attempted for decades to promote dress codes as a way to craft particular types of Muslim citizens, a simple fashion statement against uniformity can be subversive. Under conditions where direct political resistance is dangerous, clothing becomes a form of political engagement that is potentially powerful because it can sometimes slide under the radar as a matter of culture versus statecraft. This power comes with substantial risk. Since clothing is so strongly linked to character, a woman who uses dress for a larger political statement faces the danger that her outfit will be viewed as an expression of bad character.

In the next chapter we move to Yogyakarta, Indonesia, where pious fashion not only looks quite different but has an entirely different set of meanings.

༄ TWO ༅

Jilbab in Yogyakarta

The restaurant set up a special place on the patio for the focus group. Bamboo in front of a concrete wall created a garden-like atmosphere, and rattan screens provided privacy from the street. The sound of a fountain that fed a tank with a few fish competed with the noise of motors and horns just a few feet away. Woven floor mats and a long low table furnished the space. We were eight that day: six female college students who wear *jilbab,* my research assistant, and me.

I knew the students were all either twenty or twenty-one years old, but the young woman who sat directly across from me, Raissa, seemed older. I think this was in part because of the demure way she was dressed: dark blouse and pants, black headscarf. She followed the conversation closely, her brown eyes focused on whoever was speaking. She was one of the most vocal in the group but was respectful of others' opinions.

Unlike most of the other participants in the focus group, Raissa said that she began veiling before college. "My father is an *ustadz* [Islamic teacher], and I started to wear *jilbab* after I finished primary school. My father said that I had to wear *jilbab* right after my first menstrual period." I wondered if this explained her style of dress, which was not particularly chic. Her headscarf was neither colorful nor patterned, like those of many of the others in our group. The fabric, length, and cut of her dress were unexceptional. She was confident and generous in offering her opinions about the role of Muslim dress for the modern Indonesian woman, but she seemed unconcerned with fashion trends in her own wardrobe.

Toward the end of our conversation, I asked each student to explain how she picked her headscarf style. Raissa was the first to offer a response. "I had been trying to wear that style," she said, gesturing toward Tari, who had a chiffon scarf pinned neatly under her chin. "But then I realized I have chubby cheeks. So I picked a style that fits my face. Because I'm so chubby, this style suits me the best." Giggles from the group. Raissa smiled as well.

I was confused. I looked at Raissa and Tari, back and forth. True, Raissa's scarf was plainer, but the style did not seem very different. Both were made of a gauzy chiffon cloth and were pinned under the chin. Both completely covered the hair. My confusion must have been evident, because a couple of the students patted the back of their heads, and one said *"bun ciput."* Raissa explained: "There is a fake bun under my scarf. It helps with my chubby cheeks."

◆ ◇ ◆

THIS SCENE TOOK PLACE EARLY ON in my fieldwork, and I was surprised to learn that Raissa was wearing a fake bun. Especially for Raissa, whose dress was quite modest, an accessory that created the illusion of volume seemed a contradiction. What I learned that day was that a headscarf can be both pious and attractive. This is not an oxymoron. In fact, pious fashion in Indonesia is supposed to be attractive, if done correctly. As Nurul, another student in the same focus group, put it, the decision about how to veil "depends on your face, because it needs to look right." The availability of different styles is what makes finding a suitable style possible in the first place. And suitability includes not only modesty but also a broad range of feminine ideals including, apparently, a large coif of hair, even if that coif is hidden.

The Middle East is the birthplace of Islam, and in the imagination of the West, its geographic center. Yet Indonesia is the world's most populous Muslim nation. Still, scholars who study Islam tend to neglect Indonesia's Muslims. The Islam practiced in Indonesia, especially in Java, is often described as "syncretic," a blend of Islamic belief, Javanese custom, and Sufi spirituality. Both Indonesians and outsiders tend to argue that Indonesian Islam is less rigorous and less orthodox than its Middle Eastern counterparts, and, consequently, more civil and tolerant. Yet even in Indonesia, Muslim women are symbolic representatives of political Islam, and *jilbab,* as pious fashion is called there, plays a role not only in personal moral formation but also in national politics.

Indonesian Politics of Modest Dress

When gearing up for his reelection campaign in 2009, President Susilo Bambang Yudhoyono decided not to select his then vice president, Jusuf Kalla, as his running mate. One reason that has been suggested for this snub is the difference in their wives' dress: Yudhoyono's wife appeared in public bareheaded, while Kalla's wife wore *jilbab.* Kalla decided to make his own bid for president under the Golkar Party and selected General Wiranto as his running mate.[1] Wiranto's wife also wore *jilbab.* In the end, three parties put forward candidates for president and vice president. Only the Kalla / Wiranto ticket had *jilbab*-wearing wives.

The role of *jilbab* in the campaign did not stop with the selection of running mates. In this personality-driven campaign, the three parties covered Jakarta in posters featuring the candidates. But only the Golkar Party also advertised images of the candidates' wives, dressed in head-to-toe pink *jilbab,* including tightly wrapped headscarves that covered their hair, ears, and neck. The press was also invited to accompany Mrs. Kalla and Mrs. Wiranto on a shopping excursion in Tanah Abang, Jakarta's largest textile market. Mrs. Wiranto seemed particularly familiar with the *jilbab* vendors in the market, which was seen by many voters as evidence of her piety. However, this strategy to gain votes among *jilbab*-supporting Indonesians was not enough. The Golkar Party won less than 10 percent of the popular vote—results that help demonstrate the ambiguity of the local politics of modest dress.

We can begin the story of the politics of women's dress in the early twentieth century, when Indonesia's Muslim-majority population was under Dutch colonial rule. For much of the early colonial period, there were customary laws in place that called for different forms of dress for colonists and colonized subjects. A Dutch woman might wear a version of the Javanese *kain kebaya*—a wrapped sarong-style skirt with a blouse—at home, but in public she would wear a European-style dress or blouse and skirt, and cover her head with a hat. Indonesian women did not adopt Western forms of dress until the 1950s.[2] Each subsequent group to come to power followed the Dutch lead in trying to use dress codes to promote its own agenda.

Indonesia's first president, Sukarno, led the resistance movement against the Dutch and governed the newly independent nation of Indonesia for two decades (1945–1967), a period known as the Old Order state. President Sukarno built up Indonesia's diplomatic and military power in order to resist Dutch recolonization efforts. He established a version of managed democracy that stabilized a fragile nation and introduced a national ideology, known as Pancasila, based on five principles: nationalism, internationalism, democracy, social justice, and belief in God.

Though the wearing of headscarves was neither common nor encouraged during the Old Order state, clothing did have a role in Sukarno's vision for Indonesia. He promoted the Western suit for Indonesian men as a way to "demonstrate we are as progressive as our former masters."[3] For women, however, he continued to favor *kain kebaya,* which he thought better represented the essence of traditional Indonesian women. "I like the unsophisticated type," wrote Sukarno. "Not the modern ladies with short skirts, tight blouses and much bright lipstick."[4] Sukarno wanted men's dress to display modernity, while women's dress would demonstrate local authenticity, defined during this time as rooted in Javanese culture.

Sexual politics was also at play in the first post-independence transition of power. By the 1960s, a number of social and economic factors had created political instability in Indonesia, culminating in an attempted coup by a group of mid-ranking leftist army officers on September 30, 1965. In the weeks after the failed coup, the military press blamed the Communist Party for masterminding the operation and accused Communist women of participating in the torture of six top-ranking generals who were killed that night. Eyewitnesses had supposedly seen Communist women dancing naked in front of the generals before slicing off their penises and gouging out their eyes. Official autopsies, however, showed no evidence of such mutilation.

The propaganda campaign against the Communists succeeded nonetheless. The army, under the leadership of Major General Suharto, began a violent anti-Communist purge. Suharto rose to power, eventually replacing Sukarno as president and ruling for thirty-one years (1967–1998). The sociologist Saskia Wieringa argues that the public smear campaign against Communist women was essential to Suharto's quick rise to power and was undertaken deliberately to manipulate the Indonesian population.[5] This campaign exploited traditional Javanese views of proper women as meek and sexually shy and roused anxieties among Muslims about women's sexuality creating social disorder (fitna).[6] The widespread chaos resulting from this campaign allowed Suharto to legitimize his radical regime change.[7]

Suharto's New Order brought enormous economic gains through its ambitious centralized development program. It also brought increased social control of women. Government organizations like Dharma Wanita (Women's Duty), a mandatory organization for civil servants' wives, emphasized feminine citizenship through domestic duties and encouraged women to adopt kain kebaya, the same Javanese style of dress favored for Indonesians by the Dutch and by Sukarno.[8] Suharto also instituted new regulations on women's dress. Because he believed a stable society would only be possible if Islam were eradicated from politics, he banned headscarves in government offices and schools from 1982 until 1991. Suharto's wife, who combined sarongs with lacy blouses, became the sartorial model for an official vision of public femininity.

Yet Suharto's policies affected aspects of Indonesian culture and society that ultimately laid the groundwork for increased popularity of *jilbab* during his term. For instance, when all citizens were required to declare themselves adherents of one of five official religions, millions of Indonesians came to understand their Muslim identity in a new way. And because Suharto suppressed Islamic political parties, he inadvertently pushed Muslims to assert their faith in cultural ways. This created an opportunity for the expression of Islamic values to flourish in the public sphere and led to the rise of what scholars have called a form of Islamic normativity. Suharto himself even began to present a more public Muslim identity, including completing a pilgrimage to Mecca in 1991. Within this context, *jilbab* became a desirable way to communicate cultural adherence to Islam.

During Suharto's New Order, the dominant style of *jilbab* was rather austere and could thus function as a public critique of Suharto's notorious corruption, in the same way that sartorial protests were directed against the shah of Iran. For Indonesians who believed that Suharto's embezzlement of vast sums had led to widespread immorality, Islamic piety, including modest dress, promised to serve as an antidote.

Jilbab styles were also affected by the government's attempt to increase tourism through traditional arts and crafts.[9] The promotion of batik cloth was part of this campaign, and wearing batik became a way to demonstrate support for the nation. During official events, Suharto, his ministers, and their wives often wore matching outfits made of the same batik patterned cloth. The association of batik with local aesthetic values endures today and is the basis for its incorporation into a number of pious fashion styles.

Overnight, the 1997 Asian economic crisis undid all the financial gains of the Suharto regime, leaving Indonesia bankrupt. Faced with large-scale protests and a three-day occupation of Parliament, Suharto resigned in May 1998. During the next five years, referred to as the era of Reformasi, Indonesia made the transition from authoritarianism to democracy, and a new phase began in cultural politics and public expressions of Islamic piety. *Jilbab* became even more popular. During this period, Indonesia elected its first female president, Megawati Sukarnoputri, who favored Western suits for official business but donned a headscarf on visits to more conservative regions of Indonesia, such as Aceh Province, located in the northern end of Sumatra.

Although Indonesia is a Muslim-majority state, it has never had an Islamic government. Parliament has never seriously discussed mandating *jilbab* by law. But recent years have witnessed regional efforts to regulate women's dress, and in 2001, legislators in Aceh passed a bill requiring women to wear headscarves in public. Other local governments have since introduced regulations on women's dress as part of morality bills, often as a way to assert a province's Islamic identity or to discourage the sex trade.[10] In Java, the island on which Yogyakarta is located, these efforts have not succeeded.

Women's bodies have been legally regulated in other ways, however. The most dramatic example is a recently passed pornography bill. Originally drafted in 1999, this piece of legislation gained traction in 2006 when the first Indonesian issue of *Playboy* hit local newsstands. After years of intense debate, pornography became illegal in Indonesia in 2008.[11] In addition to outlawing "man-made sexual matters," including everything from photographs to poetry, the bill mentions "conversations and gestures," opening the possibility of regulating a wide range of public acts. Displays of public nudity can be punished with ten years in prison and a fine of up to $500,000. Although a compulsory *jilbab* dress code was not created by this law, its sponsors were obviously concerned about women's sartorial practices. For example, the bill includes allowances for tourists to wear bikinis and other revealing clothes, implying that Indonesians who dress in these ways might be culpable.

Muslim women were used throughout the twentieth century by a variety of political leaders—from Dutch colonizers, to Sukarno, to

Suharto—all of whom promoted different images of the ideal Indonesian woman to create support for policies that limited the choices of actual Indonesian women. The irony is that in Indonesia, Islamic gender norms have been successfully mobilized most often by secular politicians, not Islamic revivalists. And women continue to be linked with public morality more broadly, as demonstrated in the recent legal regulation of pornography.

Style Snapshot

Indonesian women did not historically wear a head covering (*kerudung*) unless they had completed hajj. In fact, since uncovered hair and shoulders are part of the traditional Javanese aesthetic of beauty, until quite recently, *jilbab* in Indonesia "was synonymous with lack of taste, provinciality, or rejection of beauty."[12] But pious fashion is extremely popular now; it is considered to demonstrate cosmopolitanism, sophistication, Muslim femininity, and good taste. Anthropologist Nancy Smith-Hefner documented this shift on college campuses in Yogyakarta. In the 1970s, she judged that less than 3 percent of students at the prestigious Gadjah Mada University (GMU) wore a headscarf. By the 1990s, it was more than 60 percent.[13] When I visited the GMU campus in 2011, the proportion was up to 70 percent.

During the first wave of pious fashion, in the 1980s and 1990s, the dominant style was to pair loose, long tunics in pale pastel solids or dark colors with headscarves of thin material draped over the head and tied under the chin. Hair, neck, and shoulders were completely covered, and the look was stiff and formal. These styles came to be seen as antithetical to modern Muslim femininity, as well as aesthetic failures. "Indonesian women have learned how to veil so that we do it more beautifully now," Arti, a twenty-one-year-old student at GMU told me. "Those baggy pastel outfits were not attractive, no one wants to look at that. Today we know *jilbab* should be modest, modern, and beautiful." The second wave of pious fashion is often described using this kind of language of enlightenment. Like others,

Arti believed that Muslim women who wore those old styles did not properly understand how to present themselves in public. Their intention was good, but they lacked fashion know-how.

Spring 2011

Although Yogyakarta is the second case study presented in this book, it is the place where I first realized there was a compelling cross-cultural story to tell about Muslim women's modest dress, beyond the global narrative of Islamization. Initially, I was struck by the distinctive look of pious fashion in Indonesia: it often incorporated tight, form-fitting garments, like an undershirt called a *manset,* or belts to emphasize the waist. Modesty, it appeared, was achieved by covering oneself with cloth, not by disguising one's womanly shape, as is legally mandated in Iran.

In addition, I found that the task of enhancing one's beauty was explicitly tied to the cultivation of character in Indonesia, prompting me to think more carefully about how aesthetics and ethics interact in Muslim women's dress. Take Raissa's *bun ciput,* described in the opening vignette. *Ciput,* which means "snail" in Indonesian, is used to refer to any tight cap worn under a headscarf. This cap serves the dual purpose of covering the hair and providing a base to attach a slippery headscarf to. Sarah, a bubbly second-year student at GMU, called the *ciput* "a bra for the headscarf." But if it is a bra, a *bun ciput* is a padded push-up bra, creating a shape that meets cultural expectations of attractiveness. Padding under a headscarf was something I was accustomed to in Tehran. But in Tehran, padding occurred within the context of a required dress code and thus might be seen as a form of resistance to officially permitted expressions of femininity—an aesthetic loophole, if you like, that abides by the letter if not the spirit of the law. However, Raissa's *jilbab* was a voluntary expression of modesty, and her use of a *bun ciput* was not a form of resistance but rather the material expression of an ongoing negotiation between aesthetic and moral values. "Doing pious fashion right" in Indonesia, then, could mean adding volume where there is none, or otherwise sculpting and rebalancing features that are not deemed ideal.

It is difficult to identify a single form of pious fashion specific to Yogyakarta. No two women use the same items of clothing for their *jilbab*, and the variety of ways headscarves are draped, tucked, pleated, and pinned is constantly multiplying. In this section I take a close look at the styles that were popular in spring 2011, drawing from a month of fieldwork.[14] Much *jilbab* during that season was constructed out of "secular" clothing. Long-sleeved, tight *mansets* were often layered under off-the-rack clothes, like strappy dresses, making them instantly Islamic appropriate. The leggings that all my students were wearing to class in the United States were also worn that season in Indonesia as part of Islamic dress—sometimes under a skirt with a slit or above-ankle hemline, or, among younger girls, paired with only a long shirt and a headscarf. Clothing designed specifically for pious fashion was also increasingly available in 2011. That season, women could buy imported modest tunics in various lengths, from hip to ankle, to be paired with long flowing skirts, wide-legged palazzo pants, or straight-legged "carrot-style" pants (known as "cigarette-style" elsewhere, but renamed to avoid an immoral reference to smoking).

As *jilbab* became more acceptable and desirable, the opportunity arose to promote local designs and fabrics. Using these local elements was justified for ideological, as well as practical reasons. Some Indonesians were concerned that Islamic dress, especially stricter versions of covering, imposed an oppressive Arab culture on tolerant, multicultural Indonesia. If women were going to cover themselves with cloth, the type of cloth mattered. Batik became an important design element in Indonesian pious fashion because it infused an outfit with local aesthetic value. In 2011, "batik *jilbab*" was trending; batik was incorporated into everything from school uniforms to complete head-to-toe looks, as well as being used more sparingly on edgings and hems. Despite this widespread popularity, batik *jilbab* is symbolically a little jarring because of the Hindu and Buddhist motifs in its design—imagine a

Jewish prayer shawl covered in a Santa Claus pattern. It has also been suggested that batik had lost its significance as a marker of good taste after Suharto began promoting it as a tourist item.[15] Nevertheless, batik remains associated with an Indonesian genealogy of cloth production that predates colonialism.

There were practical reasons for local designs as well: many women complained to me that imported versions of *jilbab* were made for Arab women living in the dry desert climates of the Gulf region and were not suitable for a tropical climate. This was the rationale for favoring airy fabrics over the heavy crepes and twills found in Tehran and Istanbul. Women in Yogyakarta wore garments made of thin, flowing fabric, like chiffon, in light pastel colors that suggested breathability and coolness. When clothing was tailored, it did not tend to be stiffly structured. Islamic clothing boutiques in malls and pedestrian shopping areas in Yogyakarta were filled with various loose and flowing *jilbab* styles such as oversized cardigans, tops with dolman sleeves, and baggy harem pants with yards of fabric gathered at the knees or ankles. Many of these items played with volume to generate aesthetic interest, sometimes by creating volume in unexpected places.

Pastel chiffon sounds rather precious, but women in Yogyakarta were able to style these light colors and fabrics in ways that looked more cosmopolitan than prissy. One memorable outfit I saw that spring was worn by a woman who was shopping in Ambarukmo Plaza, a popular indoor mall. Over a tight black *manset* and ankle-length black leggings, she had layered a light-blue silk chiffon sleeveless dress. Her headscarf was a slightly lighter shade of blue and was pinned tightly around her neck and chin. The dress had a cream yoke, a small amount of pleating just below the left shoulder, and a tuck at the right hip that created the illusion of a dropped waist. But its most distinctive design element was an asymmetrical hemline, bordered by six inches of black silk, which drew the eye from just below her left knee to the tip of the toes on her right foot. Her carefully painted toenails and a refined neutral strappy sandal did not distract from the drama of the hemline. The dress by itself would not have been *jilbab* appropriate, but

This outfit highlights a knee-length batik jacket in a style considered suitable for semiformal events. The colorful batik pattern combines designs from the Javanese cities of Pekalongan and Solo. The headscarf color picks up the lime green in the jacket, and the slim black pants blend into the background. The studded white platform sandals add just a hint of hardness. Photograph by Benita Amalina, January 23, 2017.

The headscarf in this outfit is elegantly draped under the chin and fastened at the right ear. The harem pants are in a silky satin. A basic black *manset* top is covered with a floral-patterned scarf that pulls the entire outfit together. Photograph by Benita Amalina, October 23, 2016.

her styling allowed it to be both pious and fashionable. She had accessorized with a small taupe bag that resembled a Birkin bag and a gold pendant on a long chain. The overall effect was uncluttered and exceptionally elegant.

In 2011, most women in Yogyakarta covered their legs, shoulders, and arms. This was true even for women who did not wear *jilbab*, as Indonesians tend to cover their skin to protect themselves from the intense sun and pollution. It was not uncommon to see a young girl, or for that matter a young boy, with a hooded sweatshirt and gloves on a motorbike, despite the heat. However, two things distinguished *jilbab* covering from non-*jilbab* covering: first, *jilbab* was worn as an expression of piety rather than as protection from the environment, and, second, it incorporated a headscarf or other covering to conceal the hair. Headscarves, locally called *kerudung*, took many forms, including a square scarf referred to simply as a *scarf; pashmina*, a long scarf made of thin cotton, silk, or linen worn loosely around the head and shoulders; and a *bergo*, or "instant *jilbab*," a ready-to-wear headscarf designed to be worn without draping, twisting, or pinning. Some styles were quite glitzy: they had shiny crystals on the borders, were made of metallic fabrics, or were worn with multiple brooches. There were many stores devoted entirely to headscarf accessories, something my informants told me was not the case ten years earlier. Light pastels, primary colors, busy florals, modern tie-dyed fabrics, and lace edging were all popular in 2011. Lace, in particular, was much more common in Yogyakarta than in Tehran and Istanbul. It created an elegant transition from cloth to skin when edging headscarves, cuffs, or hemlines.[16] Layered in copious quantities, it signaled refinement and luxury.

Each season, designers create new versions of headscarves with distinct fabrics, patterns, and colors. The goal, according to Irna Mutiara, the Indonesian designer of the popular brand Irna La Perle, is "to encourage all the Muslim girls around the world to cover up with the edgy kind of style."[17] In 2011, one new style that many women I spoke with saw as an exciting fashion innovation was a reversible scarf

In this outfit, black lace covers a simply cut jacket worn with a salmon-pink, ankle-length satin skirt. The head covering includes two wardrobe basics: a beige *ciput* and a solid black headscarf. Photograph by Benita Amalina, January 17, 2017.

with a floral pattern on one side and stripes on the other. Other designs incorporated head coverings into jackets and sweaters. I purchased one of these and have worn it regularly for years in my everyday life in the United States. Made of an inky indigo material, it has an open front and long sleeves and is cut to have a lot of movement and swing at the bottom. What appears to be a wide lapel is a hood that can be worn instead of a scarf. With the hood down it looks like any other cardigan, but it quickly and easily converts into headgear, making virtually any outfit into pious fashion.

In addition to the use of different head coverings, variation was created through different wrapping and pinning styles: from pinning scarves tightly under the chin to allowing large, loose headscarves to billow; from showing no hair to letting hair cascade out the back; from completely covering the ears and neck to completely exposing them. Other styles created volume on the top of the head (by twisting or pleating the scarf or adding an accessory) or the back of the head (by adding a padded bonnet under the scarf or using a large and loosely wrapped scarf). To help a woman arrange her headscarf, boutiques stocked *ciputs* in every color. The nicest ones were made of buttery soft cotton or high-quality Lycra blends. Employees offered advice about color and style. For instance, one salesclerk insisted that, given my skin tone, I had to stay away from white *ciputs*. I had already figured out that this was not the style for me, since a white layer under a dark headscarf made me look like I was wearing a nun's habit. She steered me toward more colorful prints. New styles in May 2011 included one called the "ninja *ciput*," a tight base layer that covered the entire head and neck and was worn under voluminous pashmina shawls, and Raissa's *bun ciput*, which created the illusion of a coif of hair under the scarf.

The range in variations possible through styling is quite astonishing. This can be seen in a photograph of the five core members of the Yogyakarta Hijabers Community Committee, taken at the launching of their committee in March 2011 and posted on their website.[18] This group shares tips for how to wear *jilbab*, and in the photograph they are all wearing the same headscarf, styled in different ways. I would not have realized they were wearing the same scarf if I hadn't seen it myself in a boutique earlier that week. The scarf was designed by Indonesian designer Ria Miranda as part of her spring 2011 collection. It is made of fine, pale peach cotton jersey with a tie-dyed pattern in dove gray. The five members of the committee are lined up, smiling at the photographer. At first, my eye was drawn to a woman wearing a bright magenta dress. She has wrapped the scarf in a style I was unfamiliar with: one end hangs over her left shoulder, and the solid peach portion of the scarf is draped across her chest, grazing the top of her belt. The gray tie-dyed part of the design begins just below her right shoulder, and the scarf then travels up to the top of her head and back down over her left shoulder. The wrap of the scarf is very loose and freeform, but her black ninja *ciput* conceals her hair and neck. Another woman has coordinated her outfit with the gray color in the scarf: she wears a full, ankle-length skirt with a dropped waist and a matching gray twinset. The tie-dyed portion of the scarf is draped over her shoulders and chest and pinned very closely under her chin. The pale peach section covers the top of her head and is fastened with two sparkly silver headbands. A third woman sets off the softness of the scarf with a long-sleeved, floor-length gunmetal dress and a contrasting wide orange belt. She wears her scarf in a popular style. It lies smoothly on top of her head, falls loosely across her chest, fits tightly under her chin, and is secured at her right ear with a large brooch encrusted with black glittery stones. The woman next to her has paired the scarf with a maxi skirt with white and gray horizontal stripes that contrast with the tie-dye pattern. She has wrapped the headscarf in a similar way as the third woman, but because she has placed a different part of the pattern on the top of her head, layered it over a black *ciput* that is pulled down to cover most of her forehead, and not added a brooch, the effect is very different.

The fifth woman, who is standing in the center, stares confidently into the camera. She is easily the most design savvy of the group. Her charcoal dress skims the floor; its deep tone, darker than the grays chosen by the other women, highlights the light gray color in the scarf. In a similar way, the pinky peach of her patterned cardigan is a more saturated version of the peach color in the scarf. The cardigan comes to her mid-thigh and has long, tight sleeves. She wears it open, under a skinny belt of the same fabric as the dress. The scarf is folded in such a way that on the top of her head it looks striped, with a band of gray framing her face. Only at her neck is the tie-dye pattern clearly displayed. She has tied the scarf into a flower-like knot just below her right ear that creates an asymmetrical shape, much like a low side ponytail.

The diversity of *jilbab* styles does not mean that anything goes. My informants were quick to dispense severe judgments against women seen as aesthetically failing at *jilbab*. For instance, women criticized the practice of allowing long hair to hang out the back of a headscarf. Sometimes they attributed failure to wearing dated styles. These older styles were deemed not only plain and unsophisticated but also impious, because they demonstrated that a woman had not kept up with recent trends and thus was undisciplined. The anthropologist Carla Jones notes this phenomenon as well, in which unfashionable *jilbab* is judged as "ingenuine witnessing." One of Jones's informants declared that oversized *jilbabs* "make Islam look rigid, unfashionable, whereas in fact our God likes beauty."[19] Fashion itself is the maker of and the means to piety.

Finally, it is important to note that a full body and face veil, locally called *cadar*, is very uncommon in Indonesia and rarely seen in public.[20] During my month of study in 2011, I only saw face veils twice: once in a train depot in central Java and once on the street in Jakarta. Unlike in Iran, where the *chador* is sometimes worn over the mouth, there is no traditional form of Islamic dress that covers the face in Indonesia. As a result, to Indonesians, *cadari* (women wearing *cadar*) appear foreign. I met more than one young woman who thought face veiling was the predominant style throughout the Gulf and Iran.[21]

I want to end with a few words about men's pious fashion in this location. Presidential fashion is a good place to start. In 2011, Susilo

Bambang Yudhoyono was seven years into his ten-year stint as president. For official business he wore a dark Western suit, button-down shirt, and tie, most often with a *kopiah,* or *peci,* a small hat worn by men throughout Southeast Asia. The cap is brimless and resembles a Turkish fez. It is usually black and made of felt or velvet. Although *peci* caps are associated with Islamic cultural identity throughout much of Southeast Asia, in Indonesia they are also worn by secular nationalist leaders such as Sukarno and are thus linked with nationalism, as well. This kind of headgear is thus pious for both religious and political reasons.

During my fieldwork I noticed that ordinary Indonesian Muslim men had also adopted a form of everyday pious fashion: the batik shirt. Traditionally, Javanese men wore batik sarongs. But as men adopted a more Western version of clothing, such as tailored pants, they also began to wear button-down shirts made of batik cloth. In 2011, men wore long-sleeved batik shirts (often with a *peci* cap) for formal occasions, and short-sleeved batik shirts in informal and semiformal settings. Batik shirts were considered fashionable because they were relatively recent clothing innovations, and they were considered pious not for religious reasons but rather because they symbolized both modernity and local authenticity.

A Choice to Start

Muslim women who live in Yogyakarta are free to choose if and how they will wear modest clothing since it is not legally compulsory, and the *jilbab*-wearing women I spoke with fell into two broad categories. A minority of them were from conservative families. This group assumed they would veil once they reached a certain age because that was the norm in their family or community. Raissa is one such example. She told me that it was her father who determined when she would start wearing a headscarf.

However, for the majority of women I interviewed, their pious fashion began with a conscious choice to start covering themselves. These women saw *jilbab* as self-improvement and described covering as part of becoming more reflective about personal values and goals. They changed their style of dress after some coming-of-age event, such as going to college or moving outside the family home for the first time. Nurul is a university student at UGM who, on the day I interviewed her, was wearing a strappy off-the-rack sundress over a *manset* and a simple headscarf. "One year ago I decided to wear *jilbab*," she told me. "Why? . . . I don't know. I just wanted to use *jilbab*, follow the obligation to wear *jilbab*. But this occurred without any request from my parents. My mother started veiling when I was in high school. My grandmother only veils for weddings or to go to the mosque." Or take Shika, a bright UGM student with perfect English and an ambition to study abroad. She wasn't wearing *jilbab* in 2011, but she told me over lunch one day: "I'm thinking about wearing *jilbab*, because I know Muslim women should cover their hair. But don't tell my mother! If I am forced to do it I will stop. If it is my choice I will continue to do it." For Shika, *jilbab* only had meaning if it was freely chosen. And yet since she was at the age when most of her friends were veiling, her delay seemed puzzling. It turned out that her decision was in part pragmatic: she confided to me that she thought her chances of getting a scholarship to study abroad would be hurt if she wore *jilbab*.

In conversations with the women, I discovered that the choice to start covering involved substantial fashion research. Tari was a twenty-one-year-old student who participated in the same focus group as Raissa and Dika. Most of her college friends wore a head covering, but no one in her family did. Tari told me she had done research before putting on *jilbab*, consulting her peers and reading books in the widely available genre of Indonesian advice literature about how to wear a headscarf. Her first step was to purchase the recommended starter kit: a number of pins and a couple of *ciputs* to keep the scarf in place and cover the hair. Next, she focused on selecting a headscarf in a color and pattern that would flatter her skin and eye color and complement the rest of her outfit. She purchased a marigold chiffon scarf that "picks up the yellow in this pretty shirt I already had," she said. Her next decision proved the hardest: which technique to use for tying

In this self-portrait, photographer Benita Amalina wears harem pants and a bright red scarf. The otherwise basic blouse is embellished with silver snaps down the front placard. Photograph by Benita Amalina, January 22, 2017.

and pinning the scarf. "There are over a hundred variations," Tari complained, "and I have to figure out which style is the best for me." When I complimented her on her outfit that day, she beamed and said, "Yes, it's more colorful . . . and it looks good on me." Raissa, trying to explain Tari's enthusiasm, said, "she's getting excited about *jilbab*, excited to try a new trend, new fashion, new style." At that point Ayu, another member of the same focus group, chimed in: "Oh, me too. I love fashion, and that's how I choose a style. I know that I have a wide forehead and I've tried many styles. I think this style is the best for me," she said, gesturing to her visor *ciput*, a base layer with a built-in brim.

But the choice to wear *jilbab* is more than just a fun new type of dress-up. I asked the focus group, "How can wearing *jilbab* make you a better person?" Dika thought that after she started to wear pious fashion, she automatically "became more careful" with her attitude. Raissa elaborated: "Women who wear *jilbab* are expected to have a certain attitude such as a calm disposition; to be solemn, elegant, quiet, submissive, not too showy." When wearing *jilbab*, she continued, "you'll be reminded of the norms and rules of what you should do and what you shouldn't do." These women were expressing the idea that *jilbab* is a way to become more pious, and thus the decision to start veiling is sometimes motivated by a desire to cultivate a particular sort of Muslim subjectivity.

In Indonesia, the transition to wearing *jilbab* has recently started being described with the word *hijra*. This term is Arabic in origin. Its root—h-j-r—means "leaving one's tribe," and it is often translated as "migration." In the Islamic tradition, *hijra* is used to refer to the migration of the Prophet Muhammad and his followers from Mecca to Medina in 622 CE. It is also the term used in South Asia to refer to male-to-female transgender individuals, those who have "left" one gender to embody a new one. In Indonesia, however, *hijra* has increasingly been used to refer to the transition to wearing *jilbab*, popularized by celebrities like the actor and pop star Laudya Chintya Bella, whose choice to start wearing *jilbab* was very public.

Shika explained that the term got picked up by some *jilbab* supporters who argued, "If you're not wearing *hijab*, it means that you have some unfinished journey." In this usage, secular sartorial practices—uncovered heads and exposure of arms—are being left behind when *jilbab* is adopted. The metaphorical Mecca of this *hijra* is the pious Muslim female subject, an identity that is visually marked by *jilbab*. Used in this way, *hijra* is not neutral. It rests on the assumption that all good Muslim women will eventually wear *jilbab* and implies that if a woman does not, she has not finished her moral education or fully cultivated a good character. As Shika put it, "For women who are not wearing the *hijab*, like me, being asked why haven't I performed the *hijra* sounds a bit condescending." But the assumption that pious fashion reflects a pious character is called into question when we learn that there are some women who wear *jilbab* primarily as a fashion statement, uninterested, it would seem, in ever arriving at the sartorial Mecca.

Occasional Jilbab

There is an equivalent in Indonesia of *bad hijab* in Iran, which consists of not covering properly. I asked my focus group on the bamboo-surrounded patio to help me understand what "not covered enough" meant in Yogyakarta. Raissa, my fake-bun–wearing informant, said right away "showing your hair." Heads nodded in agreement: hair cascading below a headscarf seemed to be one indication of improper *jilbab*. I continued to press the group: "What about a tight *manset*?" A couple of them giggled at that. "Yes, it's okay." "A belt?" I probed. "Yes, no problem," Ayu asserted. "And short sleeves?" Tari had hit her limit: "In my opinion, girls who wear short sleeves are just following the trend. They're not covering their body out of their heart. Or, perhaps they're new at it . . . so they're not familiar with the proper *jilbab*. But for me, personally, it's not okay." There was no consensus among the group about what improper *jilbab* looked like, although all agreed it was possible. But the group wanted to talk about something they thought was far worse than bad *jilbab*: women who wear *jilbab*, and in particular, a headscarf, inconsistently. I call this practice "occasional *jilbab*."

A woman might decide to veil herself temporarily to attend a religious celebration (e.g., Eid) or to go to a particular place (e.g., work, school, or mosque). However, my informants also insisted that there is a common practice in Indonesia of wearing pious fashion for purely aesthetic reasons. Raissa was the first one who brought up the issue of women who occasionally wear *jilbab*. "She might think, okay," Raissa offered, "today I'm wearing a headscarf but tomorrow my outfit might not match the headscarf [so I just won't wear it]." This got a laugh from the group. Restu chimed in: "Some women wear *jilbab* in the office but they don't wear it at home." Ayu confirmed the practice but tried to downplay its prevalence: "In my opinion, the majority of women wear *jilbab* because of their own conscience and religious reasons. However, I also see some women who are just following the trend. They might wear *jilbab* today, but not tomorrow." Inconsistency was the only way to prove someone was engaged in the practice of occasional *jilbab*: once a headscarf is worn, not wearing it immediately raises questions about motivations. For instance, a woman who did not regularly wear modest dress might don a headscarf to go shopping with friends at the mall, or even on a date, because a particular outfit was "more fashionable" with a headscarf than without.

Restu explained the justification for occasional veiling as follows: "Before, wearing *jilbab* was considered out of fashion, or not fashionable. Now it's the opposite. There are many fashion designers who are focusing on modest dress right now." It was the "look" of a headscarf, its color and pattern, its drape or volume, which motivated this clothing decision. The aesthetic value of pious fashion had become so accepted that it was in danger of overwhelming the moral intent of this sartorial practice. Like the *bad hijab* of Iran, this is a controversial form of pious fashion. In the case of occasional *jilbab*, the danger is that a woman might wear what looks like an aesthetically successful version of *jilbab* without having any intention of improving her character.

Aesthetic Authorities

When Indonesian women are asked why they veil, they either offer a narrative of transforming themselves into a pious subject, or they merely say, "because the Quran tells us that Muslim women should cover." But once a woman in Yogyakarta decides to wear *jilbab,* there is a complicated network of aesthetic authorities that all have something to say about exactly what she should wear.

Dika was a twenty-one-year-old college student who participated in a focus group. She wore wire-rimmed glasses tucked into her snug *ciput* and offered only carefully thought-out answers to my questions. When I asked why she thought *jilbab* was so popular in Yogyakarta, she gave a precise three-part response. First, she told me, there was a religious reason: "Women should cover their *'awrah.*"[22] Second, she continued, there was a political and institutional reason: "Women were forbidden to wear *jilbab* during the New Order, but now wearing *jilbab* is obligatory in many schools." Third, she offered, "*Jilbab* is fashionable now, so more and more women wear *jilbab.*" Dika's three types of reasons for the popularity of *jilbab*—having to do with religion, politics, and fashion—give a fair overview of the Indonesian context. I will loosely adopt her three categories in the following discussion.

I begin with Dika's category of religious motivation. The women I spoke with did not mention the Quran or hadith as sources for learning how to wear *jilbab,* beyond a cursory reference to covering one's *'awrah* or a general reference to the veiling of the Prophet's wives. Instead, they pointed to the popular genre of advice literature, which builds on a presumed connection between outward appearance and the inner cultivation of character. In terms of the second category, political motivation, I consider aesthetic authorities related to the state, one ideological ("Consumption and Corruption") and one institutional ("Educational Institutions"). The connection of *jilbab* with fashion can be linked to a number of tastemakers. I discuss the fashion elite by describing the collaboration between an Indonesian fashion magazine and a prominent local clothing designer. A final category, not explicitly mentioned by the studious Dika, is social media. Through social media, which is very popular in Indonesia, ordinary women can become aesthetic authorities. I discuss a local blogger who was popular in 2011: a stay-at-home mother named Rania.

Advice Literature

Since Arabic literacy is much lower in Indonesia than it is in Muslim-majority countries of the Arab world, ordinary women rely on others to interpret the traditional sources that address Muslim women's dress (such as Quran 24:31).[23] But it was striking to me that when women described their own understandings of *jilbab*, they rarely mentioned religious interpretations provided by men (with the exception of Raissa, whose father was part of the local *ulama*). We might expect religious expertise on *jilbab* to be disseminated through the mandatory religious courses, starting in primary school, that focus not only on Islamic doctrines and rituals but also on how to live a moral Muslim life. These courses include discussion of gender roles, but none of the young women I spoke with recalled a lesson specifically devoted to *jilbab*.[24] Or we might expect that juridical or clerical elite would claim expertise on these issues in Indonesia, much as they do in Iran. But none of the women named this sort of traditional religious figure as guiding their decision about what to wear.

Most often, it was headscarf advice literature that women consulted when selecting a style of pious fashion. Advice literature has proliferated in the past ten years, and it now has its own section in Gramedia and other major Indonesian bookstores.[25] This literature might not appear to be religious in a traditional way, since it does not follow the genres of *tafsir* (Quranic interpretation) or *fiqh* (legal analysis). It does have some similarity to the genre of virtue ethics called *adab*, since it discusses a number of ways in which women can cultivate a good character.[26] But it most closely fits into a larger genre of Indonesian self-help publications, which offer practical advice for happiness that fuse Sufi notions of ethics with Western pop psychology.[27]

Jilbab advice literature describes the duty to wear modest clothing only indirectly, with statements such as "The most important thing is that [the headscarf] is big enough to cover the hair and hang down to cover the neck."[28] Some books give a cursory summary of the modesty sura (Quran 24:31), and others mention the sura about obedience (Quran 24:52).[29] However, the majority of the discussion concerns what to wear: practical advice for the "active Muslim woman" who "longs for a simple but stylish headscarf."[30] The authors of *Creating a Beautiful Veil* (*Aneka Kreasi Kerudung Cantik*) ask their readers:

> Are you planning to wear the headscarf but you are hesitant and do not know how to start? *Alhamaduillah,* you have planned to do it. However, how do you wear a headscarf in practice and still look beautiful and elegant? How do you take care of those headscarves? How do you keep them? How do you overcome the problem of hair covered by the headscarf?[31]

These authors, who are both women, can commiserate with their readers: "We were exactly like you, starting the process of wearing the headscarf step by step, guessing, reading, asking friends or family that have worn a headscarf before."[32] Having veiled successfully (understood as fashionably), they can now offer their opinions as authoritative: "We composed this book to help other Muslim women who want to start wearing the headscarf so that they can implement this Islam sharia comfortably and more easily, still looking beautiful and being in accordance with the sharia."[33]

These advice books give step-by-step instructions for wrapping, twisting, and pinning headscarves to create different forms; suggestions about "starter kits" that women should buy, such as the number and color of pins, brooches, *ciputs,* and scarves; recommendations for how to match the pattern and color of a headscarf to the rest of the outfit; and guidelines for how to choose a style, emphasizing the importance of wearing *jilbab* in a flattering way. Some of this literature discusses the comfort of various styles, warning that a *ciput* of the wrong style or size can hurt the ears or even make a woman dizzy.[34] Try out a *ciput* before purchasing it, one author recommends, and in case of discomfort, choose a *ciput* that does not cover the ears.[35] Other authors discuss which fabrics are the most comfortable. The author of *The Charm of Headscarf Style (Pesona Gaya Kerudung)* asserts that "the most comfortable and healthy [fabric for a headscarf] is cotton, and especially Paris cotton. Not only is it soft but it also absorbs sweat, and even though it is thin it has a tight weave."[36]

Rather than comfort, however, most of the advice in these publications centers on how to choose a tasteful and appropriate style. One topic is how to coordinate patterns and colors. For example, "If the outfit is already patterned, the safest thing is to choose a scarf without a pattern and in the dominant color of the rest of the outfit."[37] In some cases, the appropriate style is dictated by where the woman is going. Embellished scarves with crystals or sequins are discouraged for use in the office or when conducting official business.[38] But for casual or festive events, accessories are encouraged, such as those that mimic an earring on the side of the head or create a sparkle. Batik is also recommended for formal or semiformal events, a practical suggestion, since almost every Indonesian owns some clothing made of batik.

The look of *jilbab* is so important that eighteen of the mistakes listed in the book *60 Common Veiling Mistakes* are classified as "aesthetic mistakes of wearing *jilbab*," which the authors distinguish from mistakes according to "sharia ethics" (e.g., not covering the chest) and mistakes of "perceptions" and "motivations" (e.g., wearing *jilbab* to get praise). The entire list of aesthetic failures follows:

10. wearing colors that are too bright
11. headscarf does not match the dress that is being worn
12. fabric of headscarf makes you overheated
13. fabric of headscarf is rough

14. not wearing a *ciput*
15. headscarf style does not complement the shape of the face
16. *'awrah* / hair exposed
17. not wearing *jilbab* neatly
18. wearing *jilbab* with wet hair
19. wearing *jilbab* for too long
20. for those with long hair, not tying the hair up before wearing *jilbab*
21. wearing a dark-colored headscarf in the heat of the sun
22. not changing the headscarf
23. wearing too many accessories
24. not appropriate for the moment / event
25. the color of the base layers does not match the color of the headscarf
26. not ironing the *jilbab*
27. not wearing safety pins[39]

We can see that many of these faux pas have little to do with sexual modesty. Most are grounded in cultural assumptions that a woman's public appearance should be neat and refined (mistakes 16–20 and 26), varied (mistakes 22 and 24), and appealing (mistakes 10–11, 13, 15, 23, 25).[40] Authors of these advice books present themselves as authorities who, by articulating current conceptions of proper public femininity, can help women avoid these mistakes.

Aesthetic value is accorded to styles of head covering that flatter a woman's face. The first step is to know what you are working with. What is your skin tone? Best to choose colors that complement it. What about the shape of your face? An oval face is ideal, and is defined as a face approximately 1.5 times as long as it is wide, so that the distance from the forehead to the jaw and from one temple to the other looks proportional. Women with oval faces can wear many styles of head-scarves.[41] However, women who have square faces, for instance, characterized by a length-to-width ratio close to 1 and "strong jaw lines," are given the following warning:

> Avoid wearing headscarves or base layers that cover the forehead, because they will give the impression that the face is shorter. Avoid wearing a headscarf in the style that is pinned on the back of your neck, because it will emphasize the chin and the jaw. It is better to wear a visor *ciput* with a wide visor that covers the ears so that it will give the impression that the face is longer and more oval.[42]

In this case, pious fashion corrects what are regarded as unfortunate flaws of a woman's face by creating the illusion that a square face is oval. Women who have just started to wear *jilbab* devour this sort of practical advice and debate with their peers the merits of various styles for their own bone structure.

Consumption and Corruption

The role of the government in the surveillance of clothing choices in Indonesia differs from what we have seen in Chapter 1, in Iran, and will see in Chapter 3, in Turkey. Legislation plays a part in regulating public dress in some regions, like Aceh, but for the island of Java, only the recent antipornography law has come close to codifying gender roles related to public presentation through dress. Although there have been some reports of vigilante groups harassing women for wearing what they perceived as improper *jilbab*, Indonesia does not have an equivalent to the morality police that play a significant role in regulating women's dress in Iran. There is a large armed paramilitary group in Indonesia, the Pancasila Youth, that boasts more than 3 million members and has been linked to the massacres of presumed Communists in 1965, but this group has not focused on enforcing Islamic piety and dress.

Nevertheless, current dress norms are intimately connected with the suppression of headscarves during the New Order. Twenty-year-old

Restu recounted a widely circulated narrative that connects the "trendiness" of *jilbab* to this political history: "Under Suharto, women were forbidden to wear *jilbab,* including students. After political reforms, let's say since 2000, women have been more free to wear *jilbab,* and it's getting more and more fashionable." Rather than embodying a political form of Islam, the way it does in Iran and Turkey, pious fashion in Indonesia symbolizes a stand against the collusion of religion and politics and serves as an expression of cultural Islam independent of state apparatus or policy. This is why the Golkar Party's attempt to highlight the candidates' *jilbab*-wearing wives appears to have backfired in the 2009 presidential campaign. Expressions of Muslim identity and piety have a place in Indonesia but not in official party politics.

A second New Order legacy for pious fashion is an enduring concern over the connection between consumption and corruption. The economy grew at an unprecedented rate under Suharto's rule. People had jobs, consumer confidence was high, and consumption increased. The financial crisis of 1997 revealed that all those gains had come at a price: the country was faced with weak institutions, public debt, depletion of national resources, and, perhaps most striking, extraordinary corruption in both governmental and private sectors. The currency plummeted, asset values dropped, and retail prices rose.

State corruption and overconsumption have been blamed for this economic crisis, and women have been made the scapegoat of these concerns. Some say that it was women's demand for consumer goods that drove men's financial ambitions, whether in the guise of personal greed or high-risk governmental development programs. In this context, *jilbab* that is intentionally fashionable raises anxieties about moral corruption.

In theory, the practice of *jilbab* should erase socioeconomic differences and thus disincentivize consumption. But even the intentionally plain and demure styles characteristic of the first wave of post-Suharto veiling were indicators of upper-middle-class status. More recent versions of pious fashion, styled to convey chic and modern worldliness, explicitly signal socioeconomic differences, since they tend to mark not only middle-class status but also aspirations for upward mobility through the public display of respectability and piety. When Indonesian women claim to achieve virtue through the consumption of stylish clothing, some believe that this is merely a new form of overconsumption disguised as public piety.

More is at stake here than just the waste of resources. Consumption is understood to corrupt the individual's character, achieving the opposite of the intended result of cultivation of virtues. Vice is both material and aesthetic. As Carla Jones explains,

> So serious is the existential bond between consumption and corruption that many middle-class Javanese I know take care to avoid consuming goods that might contaminate them, for consumption in some ways entails corporal absorption. An object that was bought with tainted resources, especially goods that touch the skin, such as clothing or food, can enter the body in ways that are disturbing and polluting.[43]

Today, wearers of pious fashion can be accused of being motivated by the vice of vanity rather than the virtue of modesty.[44] The danger is that the *jilbab*-fashionista might be improperly using sacred items; in doing so, she would pollute her body and corrupt her character.

The Indonesian clothing brand Zoya recently tried to get around this dilemma by simply certifying that the *jilbab* clothing items they produced were halal. *Halal* is the word used in the Islamic legal tradition to refer to something that is permitted or lawful. In the case of meat, halal certification designates that the animal has been ethically slaughtered, for instance, by having had its throat cut while it was still alive. In 2016, Zoya launched a new marketing campaign claiming that their *jilbab* products were the first to have been certified as halal by the Indonesian Ulama Council (MUI). They advertised all over Java with large billboards that had slogans like, "Are you sure the *hijab* you're wearing is halal?" The campaign was a failure. Many women posted negative comments on social media, pointing out that the concept of

Using a common Indonesian color palette, this outfit of a blouse and crepe slacks is accessorized with a patent leather handbag in a Chanel style and a headscarf draped so the darkest color frames the face. Photograph by Benita Amalina, October 27, 2016.

"halal hijab" was offensive because it implied that non-Zoya-brand items sold for *jilbab* in Indonesia were not halal. In addition, it was ridiculous: How could a headscarf be *haram* (forbidden)?

Educational Institutions

The young women I interviewed most often named colleges and universities as the institutions that had shaped their ideas of proper Islamic dress.[45] The influence of educational institutions actually begins in primary school, where religious education is part of the curriculum, often as a one-hour religion class on Friday. This instruction focuses on how to be a good Muslim, with an emphasis on how one should behave in public. In this educational setting, religion is both normalized and universalized. Wearing *jilbab* during Friday's required religion classes is mandatory. This means that in secular schools, girls have two school uniforms: a regular uniform for Monday through Thursday (typically a white shirt and navy-blue knee-length skirt), and a *jilbab* uniform for Friday. Yet there can be pressure to dress in *jilbab* during the week, as well. One young woman told me she would have been graded down if her religion teacher had seen her without a head covering outside of class.

Yogyakarta is referred to as the "City of Learning" (*Kota Pelajar*) because of its concentration of colleges and universities. In this way it reminds me of my hometown, Boston: college students make up a large proportion of the population, and street life is dominated by youth culture. The college years can be an important time in any young woman's life: a time when she begins to separate from her parents, form her own identity, and seek independence. It is also a time when many Indonesian women begin to wear pious fashion. On coed campuses, unwelcome advances from young men might be a concern. But the women I spoke with explained their decision to wear *jilbab* less in terms of these potential interpersonal interactions than in terms of their own moral development. Attending college was for them the life event that initiated a process of moral enlightenment marked by increased self-control and greater self-confidence.

In the 1980s, the Suharto government banned *jilbab* in universities. The ban was lifted in 1991, and within a decade most campuses began to develop their own dress codes with the goal of cultivating and projecting a particular form of public Islamic piety. National Islamic University in Yogyakarta (UIN) has had an explicit dress code since 2001, and today, six-foot-tall posters with images of people in proper dress are displayed around campus in order to show young women and men what to wear (and what not to wear). The ideal dress is not only modest but also neat and formal. Ripped jeans are not allowed, and male students are encouraged to wear shirts with collars. One first-year student, who did not know that the posters existed (despite one being displayed about forty feet from where she sat with her friends), told me she thought pants were not allowed for women but said that the university was "not overly strict" about such matters. During my fieldwork in 2011, I observed that most female students at UIN were wearing long skirts or floor-length overcoats. I spent three days on campus while class was in session and did not see a single student wearing a tight *manset*. The informal social groups, such as those sitting around campus between classes, tended to segregate by gender.

Dress practices at UIN were decisively less fashion-forward than on other campuses I visited. Sukma, a first-year UIN student who had always attended Islamic school and had worn a headscarf since primary school, justified the "neglect of fashion," as she put it, on her Islamic campus: "Many people wear *jilbab* because of fashion, in order to follow the trends. But that is not proper *jilbab* and its does not follow the rules. We are supposed to wear simple things and not stand out." She went on to explain that although she found fashionable *jilbab* beautiful, she did not think it was "following the Islamic rules. . . . A scarf should cover your chest, and the beautiful headscarves do not always cover their torsos." Sukma acknowledged the aesthetic value of pious fashion, even if she suspected that in some cases the pursuit of fashion undermined the moral objectives of *jilbab*.

Another university with a strict dress code is the Universitas Islam Indonesia (UII), the oldest private university in Indonesia. In 2001, "Muslim clothing" became required. The dress code was updated in March 2005 to specify four types of clothing that all female students had to wear, and these types were displayed, with pictures and detailed descriptions, on posters around the campus. According to Eve Warburton, an Australian scholar who studied dress practices at this university, mentoring programs for new female students emphasized *jilbab*, and the student newspaper published cartoons making fun of students who wore improper clothing. Only international students were exempt. From interviews, Warburton learned of cases where female students were not allowed to enter class or participate in exams because they had not followed the university dress codes, wearing clothing judged to be too tight. Students reported threats that improper dress would result in grades being docked.[46]

Compare this to the campus attire at Gadjah Mada University (UGM), Indonesia's oldest and largest state institution of higher learning. There is no requirement to wear *jilbab* on campus, and in 2011 the only official statement I saw about a dress code was a prohibition on miniskirts and tank tops. Shika, the student who told me she was waiting to begin wearing *jilbab* until after she secured a scholarship to study overseas, explained that different academic divisions had their own sartorial norms. Within the Faculty of Cultural Sciences, approximately half the students wore *jilbab*, but there was an enormous range of styles, including short sleeves. In the sciences, most students wore *jilbab*. I was told that this was because science is considered to be a more "conservative" major. This variation in dress could result from several different factors. It could be that students with more conservative religious views are attracted to the sciences as a reliable avenue to employment. Or perhaps gender dynamics are responsible. The majority of faculty and students in Engineering at UGM are male, so female students in this field might choose to compensate by wearing more modest dress.

Layers of gray fabric in different hues worn over skinny jeans give this outfit a casual look. The pattern of the striped outer cardigan is loosely based on a traditional Javanese weaving pattern called *lurik*. The black *ciput* is pulled down across the forehead, and the scarf is attached at the top of the head with a dangling brooch. Photograph by Benita Amalina, January 19, 2017.

Fashion Elite

Consumers, designers, and the print media work together to promote a vision of "Muslim lifestyle" that includes fashionable *jilbab* as one of the primary markers of public femininity. This vision emphasizes being covered, elegant, and modern and demonstrates a distinctive Indonesian perspective on tasteful *jilbab*. I discuss an example of such a collaboration in this section—specifically, how consumers played an important role in the launching of the Muslim fashion magazine *NooR*, and how this magazine then launched the career of one of Indonesia's most prominent designers, Irna Mutiara.

Femina has been Indonesia's leading women's magazine since it was established in 1972. *Femina* is not and never has been an Islamic publication, but in the 1990s, when public forms of Islamic dress were becoming more common, readers of the magazine wrote letters requesting that it include photographs of women wearing Islamic dress. According to Carla Jones, these readers asserted that "the exclusion of pious dress . . . denied them the pleasure and edification of being treated as consumers. . . . [and] echoed the more general disdain women who chose to wear Muslim dress felt on the street."[47] Requests for images of Muslim fashion reflected a desire to be acknowledged not only as part of an important demographic of *Femina* readership but also as one with its own buying power and role in consumer culture through what was coming to be seen as a cool and desirable "Muslim lifestyle."

Femina responded by including women in Islamic dress with head coverings in fashion spreads alongside non-*jilbab* styles. (In the next chapter, we will see a similar marketing tactic in Turkey, where print campaigns included both covered and uncovered women, in order to encourage the covered female consumer to see her dress option as just as desirable, modern, and normal as that of a woman who does not cover.) However, even after *Femina* began to include images of women in *jilbab*, it did so only occasionally, and it drew inspiration from global trends in pious fashion rather than from local styles.

Thus, a gap remained in the market: there was no Indonesian Islamic fashion magazine that featured the pious fashion of local women.

In 2006, *NooR* was launched to fill that gap. According to its mission statement,

> *NooR* is the first cosmopolitan Muslim women's magazine in Indonesia. Its mission is to answer all the needs, challenges, and lifestyle questions of modern Muslim women and their families, as well as to improve the quality of life and empowerment in Indonesia, while still abiding by Islamic moral teachings and law. Confident, intelligent, and stylish, *NooR* invites Indonesian women to be closer, more loving, and more pious for Allah.[48]

The word "cosmopolitan" here means globally informed, as well as urban and upwardly mobile. "Confident" pushes back against the view that Muslim women should be shy or demure. The implication of "intelligent" is that the magazine's readers are not only educated but also capable of independent thinking. And by describing itself as "stylish," the magazine emphasizes that Indonesian women can be both fashion-forward and pious. *NooR* claims that through confidence, intelligence, and style, it can assist women in their spiritual journey to be closer and more obedient to God.[49]

The magazine displays a distinctly Indonesian pious aesthetic. As *NooR*'s editor in chief put it, "Many countries have rules about how a woman has to wear *hijab,* but here in Indonesia we are so free. We are so colorful. We have a wealth of design and style. Thank God for that."[50] By supporting the idea that Indonesia has its own particular aesthetic perspective, *NooR* has been important for the growth of the local pious fashion market. It features advertisements from Islamic fashion houses, sponsors fashion shows, and publishes layouts of collections. Activities like this are how *NooR* came to launch the career of Irna Mutiara, one of the most prominent Indonesian designers of Islamic women's fashion.

A graduate of the Indonesian University of Education (UPI) in Bandung, Irna won first prize in *NooR's* 2005 design competition and subsequently had her clothing featured in the magazine, gaining her exposure and an instant customer base. She has become well known for her intricate wedding dresses and formal gowns, with elaborate beading and layers of satin, lace, and organza, and for her high-end brand, Irna La Perle, which features clothing that incorporates soft textures and colors in layered chiffons, as well as more nubby woven fabrics. Customers and retail buyers in France, Egypt, Dubai, Abu Dhabi, Hong Kong, and Malaysia have sought out her designs after seeing them in international exhibitions and fashion shows.

Irna's clothing lines are extremely modest but never boring; she creates aesthetic interest with details such as layering, pockets, straps, seams, and buckles. Her formal headscarves resemble bonnets topped with twisted fabrics, embroidery, broché, lace, and crystals. Replayshion, the name of her 2011 collection, spotlighted airy whites and creams, some pastels, and multiple layers of gauzy fabrics. More recent collections, such as the 2014 collection aptly named Luminescence, create visual interest through asymmetrical elements, such as coats with different hemlines in the front and back or right and left.

Irna also designs a ready-to-wear line, Up2Date, which has the tagline "Chic, Comfort and Covered Up." She launched this more affordable line in 2006 with two other designers. "We started with the styles that we ourselves would like to wear," Irna said in an interview with the *Jakarta Globe*. The line was to be "fresh, casual and easy to mix and match."[51] Up2Date's first collection featured tunics, blouses, pants, and long skirts, all cut wide and long and constructed of a lightweight spandex fabric. Use of this fabric was "a breakthrough," according to Irna: "At that time, no one used spandex for Muslim clothing."[52] The 2011 Up2Date collection incorporated bodices styled like those of overalls on long flowing dresses with horizontal seams or large square pockets. The 2014 collection of this line was titled Ingenious. It avoided patterns and bright colors, focusing instead on clothing cut wide through the torso, with layered fabrics and symmetrical hems.

The catwalk models for this collection wore custom-designed head coverings with a flap hanging down over each ear to the mid-chest area. Aesthetic interest was created with geometric lines that sometimes featured exaggerated elements, such as cap sleeves that hinted at the visor of the popular visor *ciput* style.

Irna, who is often quoted in the press, is an eloquent advocate for Indonesia's fashion industry. "I believe Indonesia can soon be the Paris of the International Muslim vogue," she told a *Jakarta Globe* reporter in 2012. "Our beautiful fashion styles have always invited other pilgrims to start a conversation."[53] Local Islamic clothing is seen as one way in which Indonesia can gain prestige globally. Designers are both the architects and ambassadors of a specifically Muslim form of economic development.

Mom Blogger

During informal interviews and in my focus group, young Indonesian women told me that they learned about Muslim fashion online through Internet searches, YouTube videos, Facebook, Instagram, and fashion blogs. Fashion-forward women take pictures of themselves wearing stylish *jilbab*, alone or with friends, and upload them to social media sites. These photos become a collective resource for how local pious fashion looks, or should look, and a resource for women when searching for their own style or constructing a specific outfit. Some sites help women prevent aesthetic failures, such as the controversial Facebook page Jilbab Boob, which posts images of women wearing tight tops that emphasize the size of their breasts. But the majority of blogs and websites provide models of creative and elegant *jilbab*.

In 2011, one of the most popular *jilbab* bloggers in Yogyakarta was Virginia Iswarani, a stay-at-home mother, whose site is called Style Whimsical (formerly FashFaith.com). Virginia, who blogs under the name Rania, describes her English-language site as "a fashion and covered-style blog with a glint of vintage."[54] She posted 125 times in 2011, including 18 times alone in the month of May, while I was conducting fieldwork. She affectionately refers to her readers as "lovelies," and as of April 2015 she reported having an average of 15,000 page views per month, 1,740 Facebook fans, and 1,416 Pinterest followers.[55]

Bloggers have a reputation for being slightly narcissistic, but this could not be further from the truth for Rania. When we met over coffee in 2011 at Ambarukmo Plaza, a glitzy mall in Yogyakarta, she was shy and quiet. During our conversation, she confided that she had only started wearing *jilbab* three years previously, "in order to become a better person."[56] It was this decision that motivated her interest in fashion. "Before I covered," she admitted, "I thought that people who were into fashion were materialistic." She gave me a small smile. "But when I started to wear *jilbab* I realized that I didn't have anything to wear except T-shirts and jeans." Out of necessity, she began to pay attention to fashion for the first time. "For me, *jilbab* was a fashion opportunity."[57] Note that for Rania, pious fashion was about both character formation ("to become a better person") and style ("a fashion opportunity"). In fact rather than seeing it as restrictive, Rania understands *jilbab* as a new form of consumption that requires a specific aesthetic education, because, in her words, "we need to be clever about how to mix and match clothes, how to mix and match materials."

Rania's process of learning "fashion skills" began with searching the Internet for styles she found appealing. This collection of images eventually became the foundation for her blog, now a repository of practical knowledge related to Islamic dress. "The things I post on my blog are the things I found interesting or helpful, and I want to share them with other *hijabis*."[58] This method allowed Rania, who had no formal fashion training, to establish herself as an unlikely aesthetic authority. She curates images of styles she admires, applies what she has learned when choosing her own outfits, and advises others on how best to wear *jilbab*. For Rania, a successful *jilbab* outfit has two features: modesty and chicness.

Rania's blog identifies international celebrities wearing outfits that have unintentional *jilbab* style—such as the model Olivia Palermo—as well as pious fashion style icons, especially those from Malaysia and

Europe. At least weekly, the blog features headscarf-wrapping tutorials. It also documents Rania's personal style, which favors girly vintage pieces—like circle skirts, jumpers, Peter Pan collars, and oxfords with ankle socks—and home-sewn items. In her commentaries, she describes how she chose certain items and color combinations, as well as the context within which she wore the featured outfit. On November 11, 2011, she posted a picture of herself under the theme "Going Out with Friends" in a dress with a pattern of large blue and white flowers, worn over a white *manset* and blue pants, and topped with a cropped denim jacket and a gray-blue headscarf. The outfit was fresh and casual. In the picture, she is standing in a shop looking at funky hand-crafted purses and streamlined home furnishings.[59] A week earlier, the theme was "Hobby / Recreation"; for a day of hiking, Rania had put together an outfit of a belted khaki jacket, loose blouse, white pants, and an earth-toned floral headscarf.[60] I admired how polished and fresh this girly safari outfit was, even as I wondered about the practicality of white pants for hiking. Also featured that month was an outfit intended for a teacher-parent conference, designed to convey her pride in motherhood: a gold-buttoned burgundy blazer over a pastel floral dress, pink satin headscarf, and lilac kitten-heel strappy sandals. The accompanying text reads, "A mother is a graceful leader for the leaders of tomorrow."[61] The clothing conveyed authority (blazer), femininity (floral dress), and elegance (satin headscarf), with just a little bit of modern sass (kitten heels). In recent years, Rania has emphasized her role as a mother by including her toddler daughter, often perched on her hip, in shots of her everyday outfits.

Through a feature she calls Style Notes, Rania offers practical ways to translate runway trends and red-carpet looks into Indonesian-appropriate *jilbab*. On May 24, 2011, for instance, she responded to a reader's question about how to wear a one-sleeved long dress to a prom. Rania's post both acknowledges the aesthetics of the dress and tries to offer options for wearing it in a modest way. She begins by pointing out the crucial visual elements of the style: "Basically, this kind of dress was designed to highlight its asymmetrical design." She then identifies the challenge for converting it into pious fashion. "For a *hijabi,* this dress is rather difficult to be styled . . . because you can't add the usual bolero, cardigan, or jacket on [top of] the dress to cover the bare arm." Finally, Rania makes practical suggestions that preserve the visual impact of the dress but allow it to be *jilbab* appropriate. She suggests wearing a *manset* under the dress, a long-sleeved cropped T-shirt over the dress, or, the option she finds most elegant, draping a shawl over the bare arm. "If your shawl is in a different color with the dress, the asymmetrical sense of the dress can still be achieved."[62]

During 2011, Rania endorsed long-sleeved maxi dresses as good options for women who were "tired of layering," because they can be "grab-and-go" dresses. For off-the-rack maxi dresses with low-cut necklines, she suggested using two scarves: one covering the head and pinned at the chin, and one wrapped about the neck to cover the décolletage.[63] With a few additions, an immodest secular fashion trend can be repurposed for Islamic ends. But she is equally concerned with the aesthetics of the outfit, giving advice on how to tastefully pair a headscarf with a maxi dress: "Opt [for] a vivid hijab / headscarf if you are wearing a solid natural-shade dress; and go the opposite route if your dress is a printed dress."[64]

Finally, there is a subtle theme of national pride in her blog. In her May 17, 2011, post, for instance, under the tag "sneak peak," she posted images of Ina's Scarf, a collection of headscarves designed by Irna Mutiara, which had just hit the market. Rania gushed about the aesthetics of these scarves' design but also emphasized the ethics of their local production and the importance of their use of Indonesian cloth, with its tradition of "rich and bold colors, unique fabrics and prints."[65] According to Rania, Indonesia *jilbab* fashion provides an explicit critique of Western conceptions of beauty. She told me, "*jilbab* attracts a younger generation who want to protest the image of Anglo beauty of media and TV. Wearing hijab we are free."[66] Rania clearly believes that this freedom is available to anyone, not just Indonesians: she posts in English, she says, "to help *hijabis* all over the world."

Becoming the Modern Muslim Woman

Yogyakarta stands out among the three locations in this book as a place where pious fashion is a very recent phenomena. Because the combination of a headscarf and a modest outfit was not common practice in Indonesia a century ago, or even forty years ago, this style avoids the risk of appearing "old-fashioned." Pious fashion in Yogyakarta, in a way not possible in Tehran and Istanbul, can be invented as a thoroughly modern form of dress, an innovation even, to deal with the challenges of being a modern Muslim women.

Jilbab's recent rise in popularity has resulted in differences in sartorial practice among generations, with pious fashion more likely to be adopted by young women, while their mothers and grandmothers in the family do not wear it. Thus, women must often make a conscious decision to start wearing *jilbab*. When asked to explain why they wear *jilbab,* most women in Yogyakarta tell a predictable narrative of piety: I decided to wear pious fashion to make me a better Muslim. Yet as we have seen, there is also a complex network of aesthetic authorities that encourage *jilbab*. Learning to negotiate this network is part of a woman's moral education.

Moral authority in Indonesia has traditionally been wielded by the local male elite, by sacred texts, and, in the twentieth century, by the global Muslim community (*umma*). As a result, women's sartorial practices occur within a web of norms not always of their making. But women are also the necessary synthesizers of these norms when they decide whether and how to wear pious fashion. Choosing an outfit involves a process of discerning what moral values are associated with particular items or styles, as well as determining what presents an appropriate and yet attractive image. And some women shape the very values they are constantly negotiating by means of a variety of platforms, such as social media, design houses, and magazines. Wearing and giving advice about *jilbab* is one way women contribute to debates about how Islamic belief should be expressed in public spaces.

Just as in Iran, the political meaning of pious fashion in Indonesia has changed over time. The first wave of pious fashion arose as an aesthetic critique of a regime that was repressing Islamic belief and practice. More recent versions are visual expressions of Islamic identity and character in which clothing is used as moral capital.[67] Pressure continues within Indonesia for women to adopt conventional gender roles, but many young Indonesian women see *jilbab* as a sign of Islamic womanhood that is more modern than state-advocated approaches, which they associate with failed development initiatives, or Javanese cultural traditions, which they regard as provincial. Islam, not secularism, is the marker of modernity and cosmopolitanism for the *jilbab* fashionista. Modesty is still integral to pious fashion, but modesty is not only about discouraging sexual attention from men; it is also about what is tasteful and attractive.

My own commitment to a kind of feminism that downplays the importance of beauty was unsettled by my informants' quest to find a flattering head-covering style. I had considered attempts to flatter the shape of the face to be exercises in vanity, as well as counterproductive for women trying to make public statements of empowerment through their clothing. But my discomfort became an opportunity to rethink my assumptions about the limitations of beauty. For one thing, the quest to find a flattering style of Islamic clothing presumes that this form of dress can enhance a woman's beauty, and that there is no tension between being attractive and being modest. Women described how physical beauty was connected to character through the concept of "inner beauty." It is clear that physical beauty alone is not the goal for a virtuous Muslim woman; rather, what is important is cultivating this deeper, inner beauty. As one Indonesian advice publication declares, "When that inner beauty is surrounded by beautiful designs, it can radiate even more."[68] In other words, outer beauty can intensify virtue, at least for the observer.

This link between inner and outer virtue means that pious fashion has a potentially dangerous side as well, such as the contamination of a woman's inner character through materialism or superficiality. This concern is resolved not through asceticism but rather through pious

A sleeveless orange batik dress is layered over a black *manset* to make this outfit *jilbab*-appropriate. An orange and gold batik belt and coordinating orange headscarf complete the look. This style of batik, with a black background and colored floral pattern, is common in Yogyakarta. Photograph by Benita Amalina, October 23, 2016.

consumption. And even in social contexts that do not immediately seem "religious," such as a trip to the mall with friends or a date, this form of consumption becomes important. At the mall, it is what justifies consumption: secular materialism is repurposed for religious goals. On a date, it is what might lead to a second date and, eventually, a marriage proposal—because a wife who presents herself properly in public adds to a man's prestige and the family's honor.

It is within this context that *jilbab* has become associated with women who are educated, upwardly mobile, and stylish, a stunning shift when we remember that until very recently *jilbab* was a symbol of provinciality. The common explanation I heard was that a headscarf complements some outfits better than a bare head does. But of course this is not as simple as it seems. Why is it better? How does it enhance an outfit? *Jilbab* has been so completely rebranded as the marker of good taste and modern style that today some women wear a headscarf only occasionally, and primarily for its aesthetics.

Does purely trendy *jilbab* really exist? Yes and no. It is a little like the Iranian phenomenon of *bad hijab*. The women who are judged as wearing *bad hijab* in Tehran do not wake up one morning with the intention of dressing in a way that will be regarded as an aesthetic failure. And yet because some outfits are viewed as extreme failures by various observers, *bad hijab* exists as a phenomenon. Likewise, I doubt that Indonesian women in large numbers are intentionally wearing headscarves merely as fashion statements, a doubt that is reinforced by the fact that I did not meet anyone who admitted to doing this themselves (just women who insisted they knew others who did it). But even the perception that trendy *jilbab* exists is significant. As a style of pious fashion, trendy *jilbab* in Yogyakarta, like *bad hijab* in Tehran, uncouples Islamic dress from other ideals of femininity. This means that women can submit to a gendered religious directive while also expressing values that might be in conflict with some interpretations of that directive. This form of social critique, however, comes with substantial risk: once a woman in Yogyakarta is judged to be veiling occasionally, she is implicated in deeply ingrained ideologies that link material consumption with moral corruption.

⤷ **THREE** ⤶

Tesettür in Istanbul

APRIL 13, 2013 (ISTANBUL, TURKEY)

We were at the Messt Restaurant, high up on the hill of Üsküdar above the Bosporus. I had taken a ferry from Beşiktaş and then a taxi up a winding road. I felt queasy from the ride and was disappointed to see that the rain and clouds had almost completely obscured the view. The restaurant had placed heaters on the patio, trying to lure patrons outside despite the cold and wind. There were a few families, along with a couple of men in business suits who were talking in loud voices over piles of fried food. Midafternoon is not a time when Turks tend to linger in more formal restaurants. I made a mental note to return some time in the evening, when the space would be filled.

I found the five members of my focus group quite easily, since they were the only group in their mid-twenties in the establishment. Nur was the oldest and the most self-confident. She was also the only one who was married. She had selected a table for us inside, so that the wind would not interfere with our conversation. All the young women were wearing headscarves and had been invited to participate because they described themselves as interested in *tesettür*. They were current university students or recent graduates, with majors ranging from philosophy to finance.

I ordered a round of coffee and sweet drinks, and three different versions of fried snacks that women of this age tend to enjoy. I then pulled some materials out of my bag, including the latest issue out of *Âlâ*, a Turkish Islamic fashion magazine. Eyes rolled immediately. Someone groaned. Nur snatched the magazine out of my hand, and the group passed it around. Only Asiye, the youngest of the group, who was studying financial math at Bilgi University, had never seen the magazine before. This was not where I had intended to start our conversation, but I decided to go with the flow. "So, what do you think of *Âlâ*?" I asked tentatively. Three of them shook their heads. Suzan, an international relations major declared, "I have no interest in it and care nothing about it," but she leaned over Nur's shoulder to take a closer look. Nur, who had studied media and communications at Istanbul Commerce University, was the most agitated. "This magazine is awful. It's not suitable to Islam to put a headscarf on the cover of a magazine. Their target audience is upper-class elite ladies, but they showcase the worst style." "What do you mean, the worst style?" I probed. Another exasperated sigh came from Nur. She turned to a two-page layout that featured the cover outfit: a yellow Gucci tunic embellished at the collarbone with elaborate brooches in yellow, jade, and gold; a green silk headscarf layered over a bright yellow bonnet; white tailored pants with a slight flare at the ankle; and six-inch crocodile turquoise high heels. Using sweeping dramatic hand gestures, Nur said:

> This outfit is too, too bad. It makes me want to cry. Yellow shirt and a yellow bonnet? Impossible that one out of a hundred stylists would like that. They even used yellow eyeliner. Pairing the green scarf with the tunic just because there is some green on it is silly. A white scarf would be better. And the scarf covers the brooches. Those brooches are on there to be seen. Those stiletto heels are supposed to be the essence of a modern woman, but they are all wrong with this outfit. When they made this outfit they thought everyone would like it. But most women will criticize these clothes. Now the Gucci tunic is very nice. But the styling is all wrong.

ALTHOUGH NUR BEGAN BY CATEGORICALLY declaring that she thought it was inappropriate to show a person in a headscarf on the cover of a magazine, the critique that followed focused on the outfit, based on her diagnosis that it was an aesthetic failure. The color matching was overdone: a clear sign, she thought, of an incompetent stylist who lacked a sophisticated understanding of design. The style of headscarf wrapping was a problem, too: the loose style covered the embellishment on the expensive Gucci tunic. And the shoes, while not themselves a problem, did not go with the boot-cut pants.

I found this phenomenon, in which one woman wearing *tesettür* ("pious fashion" in Turkish) harshly critiques another, to be very common in Turkey. Banu Gökarıksel and Anna Secor noted a similar phenomenon during their 2010 study of veiling fashion: when shown images of women in *tesettür* in Turkish apparel catalogs, women for the most part did not like them. "In all of the groups, women responded to the catalog images by overwhelmingly stating that none could be considered *tesettür* by their standards." Even in groups that disagreed on what appropriate modest clothing should look like, there was general agreement that the catalog did not get it right.[1] Similar harsh critiques emerged in my focus groups, especially in the reaction to *Âlâ* magazine.

I had not expected this reaction, seduced as I was by the glossy pages and highly stylized fashion layouts of *Âlâ,* which reminded me of the American magazine *In Style.* It is illustrative that *In Style,* not *Vogue,* immediately came to mind. Part of Nur's accusation was that *Âlâ* was not setting fashion trends but was merely highlighting existing trends. Similarly, *In Style* features what is already trending, in contrast with *Vogue,* which has a reputation for shaping future trends. In the case of *Âlâ,* the focus group resisted the magazine's attempt to influence their taste even as they pored over the *tesettür* fashion spreads.

There is another reason for Nur's strong reaction: what Muslim women wear in Turkey is a politically fraught subject. For most of the previous century, the choice to wear a headscarf has been interpreted as a challenge to the country's secular tradition. Because *tesettür* has been so controversial, women express extraordinary concern about the style. Wearing an on-trend modest outfit and a visually pleasing headscarf allows a woman to express Islamic piety while avoiding accusations from the secular elite—journalists, politicians, and bloggers—that veiled women are ugly and unfashionable.

Turkish Politics of Modest Dress

In February 2013, photos of new Turkish Airlines flight attendant uniforms that had been designed by the prominent Turkish fashion designer Dilek Hanif were leaked on social media. They were often contrasted online with the uniforms from 1980, which included bright red miniskirts and fitted jackets. The proposed new uniforms featured skirts with hemlines well below the knee, thick black socks and stockings, full-length sleeves, high collars, and thin scarves tied at the neck. Ottoman-style fez caps were perched on two of the models' heads. Three uniforms featured dark-red brocade-like fabric, invoking Turkey's Ottoman past. The fourth, solid-red uniform looked similar to the overcoats that Muslim women wear as part of pious fashion. It was thus difficult for the average Turk not to read Hanif's designs as a radical Islamization of the uniforms. The most vocal critics of the proposed uniforms were concerned that the designs were a sign of a new era of Islamist politics in Turkey, resulting from the recent electoral successes of the AKP (Adalet ve Kelkınma Partisi, the Justice and Development Party). "Turkish Airlines is leaning toward a more conservative line," Serdar Tasci, a sociologist and consultant to the main Turkish secular political party, was quoted as saying to the Turkish press. "On the one hand it is trying to be a global brand, and on the other it is allying with the neoconservative policies of the political power."[2] Tasci voiced the fear that the formerly strict separation between

Islam and the country's secular culture was breaking down, a fear that intensified later that year when Turkish Airlines banned red lipstick and nail polish for flight attendants and stopped serving alcohol on some routes. In the end, the airline went in a different direction with the uniforms. Today, female flight attendants wear a tailored navy suit with a knee-length skirt, gold-buttoned vest, and short-sleeved oxford button-down shirt. The only reference to Ottoman aesthetics is the scroll motif on the scarf that is worn tied at the throat.

The controversy surrounding flight attendants' uniforms is just one example of the politicization of Turkish women's dress. For the past century, the headscarf has been the terrain on which various leaders and political parties have fought over what it means to be Turkish, Muslim, and democratic. When the Young Turks successfully forced the last Ottoman sultan into exile in 1908, one of their first reforms, as part of their vision for a modern form of political Islam, was to campaign against the Islamic headscarf. To their disappointment, this campaign did not result in a mass "unveiling" of women. It did, however, encourage a change in elite urban women's fashion, which became a mixture of Muslim, Russian, and European clothing styles, more decorative than concealing.[3]

After World War I, the Allied Powers dissolved the former Ottoman parliament, and Mustafa Kemal Atatürk became the first president of the Republic of Turkey. Atatürk's secular state associated itself with the West and worked to contrast itself with the dying, decadent Ottoman Empire. His ideology, known as Kemalism, promoted not only Western political institutions but also Western aesthetics: the West was modern, and modern was beautiful, so anything not Western was considered both backward and ugly. European trends—such as tweed sports jackets and brimmed hats for men and tailored skirts and blouses for women—were equated with good taste. The headscarf became by definition an aesthetic failure. Although Atatürk never officially banned the headscarf, the fez was outlawed for men in the Headgear Act of 1925.[4]

As a result, during the first few decades of the republic, most Turkish women in urban areas went about their daily routines with their heads uncovered. They tended to dress modestly, wearing high collars and long sleeves and skirts, but their modesty was a symbol of professionalism, not Islamic piety. Headscarves, consisting of a scarf loosely knotted under the chin, were more common in the rural areas of Anatolia, where they were referred to as *başörtüsü*. The government, however, regarded these head coverings as expressing the "wrong" type of Islamic identity, whether in terms of ethnicity, culture, or class.

With the death of the charismatic Atatürk in 1938 and the beginning of World War II, the country's process of secularization slowed. At the end of the war, Turkey attempted to return to its path toward secular democracy by establishing a multiparty system. During the 1960s and 1970s, however, corruption and treachery were rampant and resulted in a series of political coups.

During these tumultuous times, one feature of the state remained constant: a powerful military, which saw itself as the defender of Turkish secularism (*laiklik*). For the secular military, a Muslim woman's headscarf was an inappropriate symbol of religious affiliation and created an obstacle to progress. When General Kenan Evren led a successful military coup in September 1980, Muslim women's modest clothing re-emerged as a central social and legal concern. It was under Evren's leadership that a headscarf ban at universities was instituted.

At the time of this coup, a new style of headscarf had become popular: it was larger, completely covered the hair and neck, and was secured with pins. Turkish authorities saw this style as a dangerous sign of the encroachment of Islamism into Turkey. In 1981, the National Security Council and the Council of Higher Education (YÖK) issued a ban on headscarves for staff and students at colleges and universities on the grounds that headscarves challenged the neutrality of institutions of higher education.[5] YÖK relaxed the rule slightly in 1984, when it passed a provision allowing what was called turban style, a headscarf that covered the head and hair but not the ears and neck. But in 1987, this style, too, was banned. In 1988, a separate law passed allowing students to wear a headscarf out of "religious conviction," but the Turkish Constitutional Court quickly annulled it. In the mid-2000s, when universities were no longer strictly enforcing the ban, the parliament passed amendments to the constitution that would have ended the ban altogether. This was a gross misjudgment of the political climate, however. The Turkish secular elite saw the amendments as violating Turkish secularism, and in October 2008, the Turkish Constitutional Court annulled them. It wasn't until 2010, when the secular Republican People's Party (CHP) spearheaded a campaign against the ban as a way to gain the favor of religious voters, that the ban was finally lifted.

While it was in place, the ban did not eradicate pious fashion in Turkey; in fact, the 1980s saw a new interest in the headscarf, an interest that was connected with the emergence of an Islamic bourgeoisie that had different desires and consumption patterns from those of the secular Turkish ruling class.[6] Women from this emerging Islamic economic class were interested in obtaining higher education and working outside the home, and they wore headscarves and other items of modest clothing as they did so. This trend coincided with the appearance of a new style of pious fashion in Istanbul that became known as *tesettür*. Since *tesettür* was favored by urban and educated women, it could no longer be seen as a sign of provinciality, like the older-style *başörtüsü* was.

In 2002, the AKP did spectacularly well in elections, winning 363 of the 550 seats in the Turkish Grand National Assembly. While not exactly an Islamic party, the AKP does support public expressions of Islamic identity, including headscarves and modest dress. This became a source of tension between the AKP and the executive branch, which remained committed to a secular vision for Turkey. In a highly publicized snub, for example, President Ahmet Necdet Sezer refused to invite AKP ministers' wives who wore *tesettür* to the 2003 National Day ceremonies.

A headscarf was even implicated in the 2007 failed military coup. At that time, Abdullah Gül emerged as the likely successor to President Sezer. An experienced politician, Gül nonetheless had two liabilities: a background in Islamic politics and a headscarf-wearing wife. Attempts to block his election ranged from a boycott of elections to a legal challenge in the constitutional court. The military staff headquarters also released an extraordinary memorandum that threatened a military coup if Gül were elected, for the purpose of defending Turkish secularism. This threat did not work, and when Gül became president in 2007, his wife, Hayrünnisa Gül, became the first headscarf-wearing first lady since the Turkish Republic was formed.

Under the leadership of the current Turkish president, Recep Tayyip Erdoğan, who was elected in 2014, a new political ideology has emerged that is referred to as neo-Ottomanism by observers outside Turkey. If Kemalism looked to the West for models of development, neo-Ottomanism looks to the Turkish Ottoman past. Some elements of this political shift include a renewed engagement in regions that were formerly part of the Ottoman Empire and a strong presidency, which critics have equated to the Ottoman sultanate. In the cultural realm, neo-Ottomanism has led to the revival of Ottoman aesthetic and moral values. Although court life, the iconic fez hat, and the luxurious brocade fabrics of the Ottoman court might be associated by outsiders with Turkish culture and identity, for most of the past century they had been stigmatized within Turkey as signs of backwardness. It is only recently, by promoting specifically Turkish elements of Ottomanism, that these elements have been successfully reclaimed as symbols of status and beauty. This process has helped make headscarves, even in official uniforms, more acceptable. In 2016, for instance, Turkey for the first time allowed policewomen to wear headscarves under their caps while on duty. And unlike the proposed Turkish Airline uniforms that had caused such controversy three years earlier, this rule passed without much backlash from Turks.

Style Snapshot

Turkish *tesettür* in the 1980s might have been stylistically different from past versions of Muslim women's dress, but it was not particularly fashion-forward. It included a boxy overcoat (*pardesü*) and a tightly pinned headscarf that covered ears, neck, head, and chest.[7] The colors of the boxy overcoats were muted, the fabrics of the headscarves inexpensive. As the market for *tesettür* became better established, however, the rather plain versions of the 1980s gave way in the 1990s to intentionally fashionable *tesettür.*

Today, *tesettür* styles change dramatically from season to season. Buttons, ruffles, and shoulder pads embellish overcoats, dresses, and pants. Colors and patterns vary, especially in headscarves. *Tesettür* outfits are no longer handmade or produced by local tailors but are purchased at specialized shops. Once stigmatized, the headscarf is now normal—and even iconic of modern urban life.

Spring 2013

The Fatih neighborhood is one of the best places in Istanbul to observe a wide range of *tesettür* outfits. When I was not visiting college campuses or conducting focus groups, I spent most of my time in this area, observing and photographing women and visiting shops.[8] Traditionally a conservative Muslim neighborhood, Fatih has become a popular pedestrian shopping destination for middle- and upper-class Muslims. The main thoroughfare, Fevzi Paşa Street, is lined on both sides with shops. Women walk in groups, window-shopping. In 2013, their colorful headscarves were patterned with everything from polka dots to paisleys, often folded so that the brand name could be seen from behind. Vibrant primary colors were everywhere. Overcoats were embellished with raised shoulders, ruffles, and fur. Sunglasses were perched on top of enormous round headscarves, handbags were slung on forearms, and pointy pumps peeked out from under long pants and skirts. Status symbols of global fashion were prevalent, from the distinctive Louis Vuitton monogram pattern to off-brand versions of Burberry plaid.

My first day in Fatih, I spotted an exquisite navy and brown *tesettür* ensemble on a woman who was window-shopping for gold jewelry. Her long, structured navy overcoat had brown piping at the cuffs, pockets, and shoulders. The sleeves were full length and the neckline

Displaying two popular colors—camel and light gray—this outfit layers a flowing mid-length tunic over skinny black jeans. The combination of the fur collar with sneakers gives it an easy sophistication for a day of shopping in Üsküdar. Photograph by Monique Jaques, February 4, 2017.

high. The woman's trim waist was emphasized with a wide leather belt, and she clutched a quilted leather handbag and sported leather booties in the same warm brown tone. Her headscarf was perfection. It was covered in an abstract animal print and included the same warm brown color as her accessories, along with some cream and black for visual interest. No hair was visible. Every item she wore looked expensive and carefully chosen. Her *tesettür* conveyed high socioeconomic status and aesthetic flare, as well as modesty. I was mesmerized.

Across the Bosporus, on the "Asian" side of Istanbul, is Üsküdar, a very different kind of Muslim neighborhood. Although only a twenty-minute ferry ride from the hustle and bustle of the old city center of Istanbul, Üsküdar feels like an entirely different city. Lacking the tourist sites of the old city, it attracts few visitors, although it is home to over 180 mosques, many dating back to the Ottoman period. Housing prices are much cheaper in Üsküdar than in Fatih. It is an area favored by the Muslim middle class and also has a large student population.

The first time I got off the ferry and strolled along Üsküdar's promenade, I was stunned by the views west across the Bosporus toward the minarets of the Blue Mosque and Hagia Sophia. But I found myself distracted from the view by a loud group of *tesettür*-wearing teenage girls, who were also walking along the promenade. They were wearing older styles of overcoats, but their bright, printed satin scarves shimmered in the sunlight and fluttered in the wind. Their chaperone, a woman who appeared to be in her forties, was the only one wearing a plain headscarf. Her loose overcoat was beige, with large buttons from the neck down to the ankles. She wore her navy headscarf in a style that was typical of the 1980s: knotted under the chin and falling loosely over the neck and back so that it covered not only her hair but her entire neck.

The girls wore a style that was similar to their chaperone's from the neck down. Their ankle-length overcoats were simple, embellished only with buttons and belts and in demure colors such as beige, black, gray, and mauve. None of them wore the trendy short overcoats I had seen in Fatih. And none of them had accessorized with status symbols such as name-brand handbags. I did not see any sunglasses. But as I looked back at the group after continuing a little farther on the promenade, I was again struck by the girls' colorful headscarves, in bubblegum pink, shocking fuchsia, blood red, electric purple, deep green, and cool turquoise. Every scarf had a different pattern, whether floral or graphic. Many displayed their brand name in a text box that could clearly be read from behind. Even if these young girls did not exhibit cutting-edge pious fashion, those styles had influenced their selection of headscarves in terms of color, pattern, and brand.

On the hillside above the promenade in Üsküdar, just north of the ferry landing, is Fethi Paşa Korusu, a meticulously landscaped park with charming rock formations, winding paths, and flowering trees and bushes. Groups often stop halfway up the hill to take photos. They pose in front of the grand sweeping circular staircase of a two-story neoclassical building known as Beyaz Köşk, or White Mansion, facing out toward the Bosporus, with a view down the hillside.

When I climbed up to the White Mansion, a woman snapping a photo of the view stood out to me even within this upscale crowd—an obvious aesthetic success. But why? From a distance, her scarf and overcoat were nothing special. Her scarf, which appeared to be olive green, was a silk shawl wrapped in a style that created volume around her face without the apparent use of pins. On closer inspection I realized it was not olive green but rather a two-tone weave that only appeared greenish from a distance. Her overcoat was solid black; it hugged her upper body, was nipped in at the waist, and then flared out to a fuller skirt. The cut was a mid-length fit and flare, similar to the midi dresses that had been popular in the United States and Europe in the 1950s and 1960s and had recently made a comeback. It was a cool day, but she had not paired her overcoat with pants or a long skirt. Twelve inches of calf were exposed. Instead of buttons down the front, the coat had an asymmetrical leather placket from the left shoulder to the center of the bottom hem. Similar trimmings were at the shoulders, with buttons and strips of leather like a military jacket.

The three-quarter sleeves ended in six-inch cuffs of the same leather fabric, split up the back of the forearm. These trimmings added visual interest to the otherwise plain crepe overcoat. It was a sophisticated mashup of trends: the cut was soft, feminine, and retro, but the trimmings were edgy, modern, masculine, and fashion-forward.

A Louis Vuitton–style handbag carried over her left forearm was an obvious nod to European aesthetic value. I noted that it was the Speedy design, perhaps vintage, but probably a fake, since it had three grommets instead of one attached to the handles and the main body was constructed of pieced leather. But it was a decent fake, and it gave her ensemble a look of luxury.

Everything she wore was fashionable, but her shoes made the outfit. They combined aspects of formal men's shoes, such as a wingtip toe, with a three-inch heel. The tip of the toe was cool purple-gray, then there was a shocking tomato-red stripe, and finally, tan leather pierced with dainty grommets and laced up the front to just below her ankles. These shoes were thoroughly European, covered in decorative perforations as in brogue shoes.

Men's street fashion in Istanbul during 2013 was similar to street fashion in other European cities, with lots of jeans, T-shirts, and sneakers. One local design element was Ottoman-inspired band-collar shirts combined with jackets tailored without lapels. Dilek Hanif's controversial designs for Turkish Airlines featured extreme versions of these trends that looked costumey, but on the street, worn more casually, these design elements had a fresh look. Styles did not differ between men who identified strongly as Muslim and those who did not. If women in Istanbul were either covered or not, either wore a headscarf or did not, no such clear distinctions existed for Turkish men.

This was even more obvious among elected officials. At the time of my stylesnap (2013), Abdullah Gül was president of Turkey, having successfully run as the AKP candidate in the 2007 presidential election. Because of his Islamist background, his presidency was described as marking a new era in Turkish politics. One might have expected Gül to use his clothing to make a statement about the new era. But his clothing was unexceptional. He wore the same thing that presidents before him had worn: a suit and tie. He favored dark navy and charcoal suits with blue striped ties. For formal events, he wore a tuxedo with a bowtie. His only style signature was his bushy mustache and a full head of salt-and-pepper hair that he wore somewhat long, with a "swoop" in the front. Gül's clothing, like that of previous presidents, reflected secular clothing trends and presented a vision of Turkey that was at least sartorially allied more with the West than the East. Reference to Islamic politics was apparent not in his own clothing but in that of his wife, as discussed in more detail later in this chapter.

◆ ◆ ◆

Even from this small sampling of Istanbul's pious fashion in spring 2013, it is clear that there is little agreement among *tesettürlü* women about what modest dress should look like. Some wear off-the-rack secular styles in modest cuts, with a headscarf, seeking to look elegant and youthful. Others prefer specially designed overcoats, sometimes lavishly embellished. Their *tesettür* is a sign not only of religious identity but also of elite socioeconomic and cultural status. Different aesthetic values are at play in each of these cases and are occasionally in contradiction, such as the masculine wing-tip decorations on a feminine high-heeled ankle boot. Despite this tremendous variability, five features of *tesettür* stood out that made it distinct from the Iranian and Indonesian versions of pious fashion.

The first feature that distinguished *tesettür* in Istanbul from *hijab* in Tehran was the extent to which women were covered. It would be fair to say that pious women took seriously the importance of nonexposure. Overcoats were long. Sleeves full. Necklines high. Hemlines low. Headscarves were tight and often worn with an inner bonnet to keep the scarf in place and the hair covered.

Although nonexposure is still characteristic of Turkish pious fashion, this norm seems to be shifting. For instance, some young women I spoke with claimed that pinning was overkill. "It's true, my

This *tesettür* outfit is a play on hard and soft: a long leather dress, tailored through the torso and opening into a fuller skirt, is paired with a soft lace headscarf and a colorful girly handbag. Photograph by Monique Jaques, October 14, 2014.

head can be seen if the wind blows my scarf off," twenty-two-year-old Merve confessed, "but I'm not worried. I like to wear a bonnet so my hair doesn't show. Since I know the scarf can open at any time I prefer to wear a high collar. But pinning is just too much." For Merve, pinning takes the directive to cover too far; she's not going to take the added step to ensure that her bonnet remains hidden. But Asiye's reason for not pinning is different: it is just not the current style. "Some years ago we were using pins," she told me, "but now, we prefer not to use them anymore. So now our scarves open." The pin, it seems, has gone through a number of evolutions: first as a political statement in the 1980s, when it was interpreted as a sign of Islamism, then as a fashionable and pious style, and more recently on its way out of fashion, as well as no longer considered necessary for piety.

A second feature characteristic of *tesettür* in Istanbul was the "verticality" of pious fashion; it was as if the clothing had been designed to form a woman into a pillar or column.[9] Women achieved this vertical look by wearing long overcoats and dresses or pairing a shorter tunic with long pants or skirts, often in the same color. Clothing was tailored close to a woman's body, often nipped in at the waist. A popular style was to tuck the scarf into a high collar, resulting in a continuous line of cloth for the eye to follow, from head to toe. This characteristic of pious fashion did not exist to the same extent in Tehran or Yogyakarta.

The third distinctive feature of *tesetür* that season was the manner in which local politics influenced its aesthetics. Just as European brand and style accessories had been used by the government in the past to promote Kemalism, more recently, women's choice of European brands has begun to signal a political aspiration: the European aesthetics of the *tesetürlü* woman is not linked to secularism but instead to the type of modernity that full European Union membership promises. In fact, Turkish women often identified themselves to me as Europeans when distinguishing themselves from the women in the two other locations I studied. Ready-to-wear *tesetür* that season also incorporated Ottoman motifs and traditional embroidery, especially on overcoats, and many clothing catalogs featured Ottoman court–like backdrops. This period invokes luxury and opulence; but in addition, when women purchased or wore Ottoman-inspired clothing, they were emphasizing a Turkish identity that contrasts with the dominant Arab identity of the Middle East, thus undercutting Gulf societies' claims to be the guardians of Islamic orthodoxy.[10]

Finally, headscarves in Istanbul had a distinctive style. This is not to say they were uniform—in fact, they were far from it. *Tesettürlü* women readily admitted that they owned large collections of scarves in many different styles. Suzan said her household owned approximately fifty scarves, shared among herself, her sisters, and her mother. Nur said she owned fifty herself. "Only fifty?" her sister Hande teased. "Okay, more like eighty," Nur confessed. "Everyone owns at least thirty," Hande said. "The number depends on how long you have been wearing and collecting them." "It's such an easy gift," Mine offered. "There is no size, and since you can't go about without a scarf, you will eventually use it." Many scarves worn in Istanbul were brightly colored, and they came in a wide variety of prints, colors, and fabrics. In April 2013, women favored silks, satins, and other fabrics with sheen. Large floral prints, geometric patterns incorporating paisley, stripes or polka dots, and animal prints were common. Many scarves were designed so that different kinds of folding revealed different patterns or colors.

There were two popular headscarf shapes in 2013, a rectangular shawl (*foulard* or *sal*) and a square scarf (*esarf*), which lent themselves to two distinct categories of head wrapping. The shawl was simply thrown over the head and shoulders, without pinning or knotting, as in the case of the chic woman I noticed in front of the White Mansion. In 2013, this seemed to be the favored style among young women, with the scarf most often wrapped two times around the neck, occasionally tied or fastened with a brooch. Square scarves were worn tucked into the collar of the shirt, as in the case of the navy and brown ensemble that had caught my eye in Fatih. Larger scarves were pinned or knotted asymmetrically, with the corner of the scarf hanging down

These friends share a similar style: clunky boots, light-gray wool jackets, and colorful headscarves that feature neo-Ottoman designs. Photograph by Monique Jaques, February 4, 2017.

the back, almost like hair. Most women intentionally display the brand name of the scarf by folding it so that the name was visible.

One distinct characteristic of head covering in Turkey is the preferred smooth, rounded, and symmetrical shape of the scarf, called *düzgün*.[11] This shape takes a great deal of skill and time to construct and is often achieved by wearing a bonnet under the scarf that is padded in the back, to create the illusion of an elongated head.

Brand Display

Vakko is the most prominent luxury brand in Turkey, with a presence in the global fashion scene and strong ties to Western fashion. It is not an Islamic company, however; it was founded by Vitali Hakko, a Turkish Jew. Supermodel Gisele Bündchen became the face of the brand in 2006, the same year the company collaborated with American designer Zac Posen for the Zac Posen Vakko label. The company now produces everything from chocolates to household linens, but within Turkey it is best known for intricately patterned scarves of fine silk and cashmere, worn by wealthy *tesettürlü* women.

In 2012, Vakko was the first major fashion house to open a boutique in the famous Grand Bazaar of Istanbul. I was interested in visiting the boutique because of the controversy created by rumors that Vakko was actually an Israeli company, presumably because of the founder's Jewish background. I had intended to simply take a peek, but I ended up spending forty-five minutes inside the store, seduced by the finery. The shop was small but luxurious, filled with glass, mirrors, and white and black accents. The tile floor was a modern geometric pattern of triangles, but ornamental elements in the ceiling and the storefront window had organic shapes that nodded to Ottoman designs. Glass cases displayed some scarves and a few men's ties. Shelves on the back wall above the register held handbags. A few scarves were draped on busts inside mirrored cases. But most scarves were folded in drawers behind these cases, inaccessible without a salesclerk's help.

The sales staff was three that day: a young man and two bareheaded young women dressed in dark pantsuits. Their clothing was luxurious

Two women chat, with the Bosporus as a backdrop, during Istanbul Modest Fashion Week. From this angle the roundness of the headscarf styling can be seen. Both women hold statement handbags, the one on the right from American sportswear designer Michael Kors. Photograph by Monique Jaques, June 15, 2015.

but not particularly Islamic. The shorter female clerk, a pretty young woman with long hair, approached me immediately. Addressing me in English, she encouraged me to try on some scarves. She steered me to bright, boldly patterned prints in the finest cashmere I had ever touched. Soon enough, innocent browsing became a full-on shopping experience. Knowing that I would not necessarily be wearing the scarf as a head covering, the clerk draped different options over my shoulders and chest. I liked a scarf with orange, green, and blue leaves, but she insisted that an indigo and brown tie-dyed one was more flattering. The scarf she suggested was twice as expensive and seemed impractical; I was sure its ultrafine cashmere would catch on things and snag.

But I walked out of the boutique that day with the salesclerk's choice, the most expensive item of clothing I have ever purchased. Even wrapped up in tissue paper, folded into a flat box, and placed in a shopping bag, it elevated my outfit: leaving the Grand Bazaar with my Vakko parcel, I felt as if I was wielding the ultimate sign of *tesettür* success. Almost immediately, though, I regretted my purchase and realized that I was too embarrassed to let anyone see it during the afternoon's focus group. I stuffed everything—scarf, tissue, box, and bag—into the bottom of my sensible purse. When I finally did wear it, it was only after I had carefully removed the Vakko tag hand-sewn into the hem. It spends most of its life now in the back of a drawer because I worry that by wearing it I will ruin it.

My embarrassment over the Vakko tag was not shared by most Turkish women. Part of what defined pious fashion in Istanbul in 2013 was the deliberate display of brand names on scarves. Turkish brands— Armine, Aker, Arnisa, Karaca, Gizia—as well as European brands like Gucci, Dior, Hermès, and Burberry, were common, often appearing in a box that set the name off from the rest of the design. Sometimes the brand insignia was itself the design element, as in a Louis Vuitton scarf.

Some *tesettürlü* women, however, criticized this practice. Twenty-five-year-old Mine got very animated when I brought up the topic. "We

go to many shops and check out which scarves are usable and affordable, not just what is the best brand. We make our own fashion. We
don't buy brand names. It's not because we can't but because we would
rather buy something that suits us." Mine was confident that she had
enough fashion know-how to construct an outfit without relying on
brand names.[12] Furthermore, she considered the display of brand
names to be an ostentatious symbol of overconsumption. But at the
same time, she was sure to mention that she had the means to purchase a name-brand item if she wanted to, thus situating herself within
the Islamic bourgeoisie.

Other women defended the display of brands, especially from a
practical standpoint. After Mine's harsh criticism, the soft-spoken
Hande pointed out one benefit: "Well, sometimes seeing the brand is
helpful. If you see a scarf on someone and you admire it, then you
can buy it." Almost all the women confessed to spending an enormous
amount of time shopping for headscarves, and many argued that
branding saved time. One of the women interviewed by Banu
Gökarıksel and Anna Secor in their 2010 study stated that she became
annoyed when she couldn't see a headscarf's brand: "Sometimes what
they do is they tuck the brand name underneath, instead of displaying
it at the back, which I hate. The other day, I saw a scarf on someone,
I looked from behind and couldn't see the brand name. If I could've
seen it, I'd go and get it."[13] The implication is that it is a *tesettürlü*
woman's duty to display this crucial information so as to share her aesthetic knowledge with others.

Full-Body Covering

In Turkey, the most common full-body style of modest dress for
Muslim women is called *çarşaf* (literally, "bed sheet"), and the women
who wear it are known as *çarşaflı*. This fully covered style is less
common than in Iran but more common than in Indonesia. The *çarşaf*
resembles the Iranian *chador* in terms of its visual effect, draping a
woman from head to toe in black cloth, but unlike the *chador*, it consists
of two garments: a long, wide, floor-length skirt, and a combination

A fur collar peeks out from under a nautical-themed headscarf by the high-end Turkish designer Armine. Note how the placement of the text box on the scarf encourages display of the brand name. Photograph by Monique Jaques, January 31, 2017.

headscarf and top that hangs below the waist. The top can be pinned at the neck, thus exposing the face, or at the temple, creating a face veil with only the eyes exposed. The *çarşaf* was popularized in Turkey in the late nineteenth century by Sultan Abdul Hamid II, but a 2006 survey found that only 1 percent of Turkish women wore the style.[14] In the Muslim shopping district of Fatih, however, that number is much higher. In 2013, I would estimate that about 5 percent of the women I observed in Fatih wore a *çarşaf*, often walking with women in *tesettür*. This style of dress is not necessarily an indication of affiliation with a specific religious group or political party; rather, some Turkish Muslim women prefer it as a way to express religious piety. Its increased popularity can be explained as part of the more general trend toward modest clothing.

The *çarşaf* does not have as wide a range of meanings as the *chador*, which is worn by various types of Iranian women, such as professionals, students, and traditionalists, to signal formality, status, and other kinds of identity. Because the *çarşaf* was never used as a symbol of protest or reform in Turkey, it is not imbued with political symbolism to the same extent as the *chador*. *Çarşaf* is important to our discussion of pious fashion in the Turkish context for a different reason: it occupies one end of the spectrum of modest dress.

Tesettürlü women can be harsh critics of *çarşaf*. Some of them claim that *çarşaf* is not in fact a "free" choice at all. "There is no distinct fashion in Turkey," Zeynep, a twenty-year-old finance major told me, "but if you wear Arab style [*çarşaf*] people will stare at you and you will seem different. In Turkey everyone should wear what they like. Otherwise we are all like the Arabs—in *abaya*." Freedom to choose a style is important to Zeynep. Any style, that is, except the *çarşaf*, which she considers an alien import from the Gulf region. Zeynep's argument against *çarşaf* is similar to the argument secularists deploy against covering in general: it is a sign of a woman's submission to external pressure.

Tesettür-wearing women also describe *çarşaf* as failing to fulfill the directive to be modest: its aesthetic is so extreme that it actually becomes an ostentatious public display. One of Gökarıksel and Secor's informants clearly describes this effect: "Even in Fatih when a woman wearing the *çarşaf* or a face veil walks by, everyone, even covered women, turn and look."[15] In Turkey, as in Tehran and Yogyakarta, modesty is assessed by how much an outfit blends into local style cultures, not only by its level of "coveredness."

Finally, some *tesettürlü* women warn that *çarşaf* can be a form of false veiling. The concern is that full-body covering might not be an accurate outer reflection of inner piety. Instead, it could be a mask allowing even the most impious woman to pass as a good Muslim. Thus, *çarşaf* is a potentially deceptive form of dress "where the real intent and the deepest feelings and desires of a woman can be hidden from view."[16]

Tesettürlü women's condemnation of *çarşaf* reinforces the idea that women's clothing is a public issue. If proponents of Kemalism viewed the headscarf as an obstacle to modernizing, today, *tesettürlü* women use that same logic to criticize *çarşaf*: *çarşaf* becomes the sign of an unruly body that needs to be modernized. Their critique of *çarşaf* also helps justify their own sartorial choices by designating full-body covering as a clothing failure. This allows women who wear *tesettür* to claim their role as the proper representatives of public femininity and to deflect any criticism that fashionable Muslim dress is morally ambivalent at best, and immoral at worst. In addition, by harshly judging *çarşaf*, *tesettürlü* women are also changing the conversation about what counts as successful Islamic dress. Specifically, they uncouple outer appearance from inner character, so that women who cover in more "conservative" ways do not get to claim moral superiority.

Aesthetic Authorities

A wide range of stakeholders and ideologies are involved in regulating and influencing women's dress in Turkey. Taken together, these factors—which include the concept of secularism, public scrutiny, the apparel industry, and fashion magazines—generate the pressures that women in Istanbul face when deciding what to wear in public.

Turkish Secularism

The principle of secularism in Turkey (*laiklik*), like its counterpart in France (*laïcité*), is based on maintaining a strict separation between politics and religion, with religious display and practice restricted to the private realm. What distinguishes the Turkish from the French version is the involvement of the state in regulating and administering religious institutions as a way to keep certain forms of political Islam suppressed. Even as President Atatürk dismantled the caliphate and sharia courts, he established new mechanisms for regulating Islam: the government controlled mosques, trained imams, and even suggested content for sermons. As a result of this process, the government has become an aesthetic authority with a powerful role in shaping expectations about proper Muslim behavior and practice, including how Muslim women should dress.

During Turkey's nationalist awakening under Atatürk, there were attempts to form a new emancipatory public sphere. Covered women were considered a risk; they could destabilize that project by creating visual differences among citizens according to gender and religion. In the late 1970s, when university students started to wear headscarves, governing authorities viewed this shift as a sign that the secular republic was in crisis. Muslim women were supposed to go to college, work outside the home, and participate in politics. But they were not supposed to cover their heads—this was the wrong sort of visibility. And it was occurring in one of the most sacred spaces of the secular republic: the university, regarded as both the incubator and the defender of modernity.

In 1981, the National Security Council and the Council of Higher Education took action, issuing an administrative provision requiring that university staff and students in both public and private institutions wear clothing "compatible with Atatürk's reforms and principles." For women, this was further specified as an uncovered head.[17] Headscarf-wearing students staged public protests. Some students dropped out rather than attend classes bareheaded. Others transferred to departments or universities that were lax in enforcing the headscarf ban. A few wore wigs, either on their bare heads or on top of their headscarves. Universities responded by banning wigs. In the 1990s, "persuasion rooms" were introduced on campuses, where female students were urged to remove their headscarves, through what some have called psychological torture.[18]

Even though the headscarf ban was lifted in 2010, it had a number of residual effects on how women dress. First of all, it forced some Turkish women to make the choice between pursuing higher education and wearing pious fashion. Approximately two thousand female students who refused to remove their headscarves were denied access to education in Turkey during the time of the ban.[19] Those who could afford it pursued higher education in foreign countries, including President Erdoğan's daughters, who both studied in the United States in part because they wore headscarves. It is ironic that a ban implemented to make Turkey more secular and Western sent many young Turkish women to Western universities where no such ban was in place.

Second, the ban turned the wearing of headscarves into a political act. This unintentionally politicized young Muslim women, many of whom joined protests, becoming politically active for the first time. In terms of Islamic politics, the ban actually had the opposite effect from what was intended.

Third, the ban heightened generational tensions in some families by creating a conflict between two Islamic values: education and public modesty. College attendance is an important marker of status for Muslim families in Turkey. It brings honor to the family and provides upward mobility for the next generation. Even in traditional families, Islam is invoked to support women's access to education. So when young women jeopardized their access to education by insisting on wearing a head covering, it was a moral crisis for some families.[20]

Finally, the Turkish headscarf ban led the European Court of Human Rights to set a legal precedent about the right of a government to regulate women's pious fashion. The case was brought to the court on behalf of Leyla Şahin, a medical student. Şahin enrolled in medical school at the University of Istanbul in 1997 and attended without incident until February 1998, when the vice chancellor of the university released a memo prohibiting students who had beards or wore an Islamic headscarf from attending lectures or registering for courses.[21] Şahin refused to remove her scarf; as a result, the university initiated disciplinary action against her and did not allow her to take exams or attend lectures. In 1999, Şahin left Turkey and continued her studies in Austria.[22]

Şahin pursued a legal remedy through the European Court of Human Rights, to which Turkey is bound as a member of the Council of Europe. In her testimony, Şahin said that she wore a headscarf because of the ideals it represented and because she believed that it was required by her religion.[23] On the opposing side, lawyers for Turkey argued that a headscarf imposed religion in what should be a religion-free zone and thus impeded secular students' access to education.[24] Both sides agreed that two basic rights were at stake—the right to religious freedom and the right to an education—but they disagreed about how the headscarf affected these rights. Leyla Şahin's case was assessed under Article 9 of the Convention for the Protection of Human Rights and Fundamental Freedoms, which protects the right to possess and practice religious beliefs freely as long as they are in accordance with the interests of a democratic and safe society.[25] The European Court of Human Rights ruled that the university did interfere with Şahin's ability to practice her religion freely, but that Article 9 was not violated because it does not protect all behavior associated with one's religious beliefs.[26] Thus, a powerful legal precedent was set: violations of religious freedom can be justified for other political goals—specifically, for the purpose of defending the secular traditions of the state.

This court decision allowed the headscarf ban to remain legally in place for the next decade. In fact, as discussed earlier, the ban was lifted in 2010 only because it became politically advantageous for the secular Republican People's Party (CHP) to do so. The precedent set by the European Court of Human Rights in the case of *Leyla Şahin v. Turkey* means it is legally possible that a ban on headscarves or other forms of pious fashion could be activated again.

The lifting of the ban made it easier to wear pious fashion in Turkey, especially for students and employees on university campuses, but it did not erase entirely the negative attitude toward Muslim women's dress. Secularism remains a powerful ideology in Turkey, and it is associated with a particular aesthetic that encourages Turkish women to present themselves bareheaded in public. Even as *tesettür* is becoming more fashionable, there is still a strong preference for clothing that reflects secular values. Women feel that they must take great care when selecting a modest outfit because if they fail to do so fashionably, they provide evidence that *tesettür* is indeed doomed to be ugly. It is as if *tesettür* only loses its threat of being politically destabilizing when it becomes attractive.

Public Scrutiny

Another form of surveillance and regulation of women's dress in Turkey is intense public scrutiny and commentary. The mainstream media, for example, denigrates pious fashion by publishing "scientific" evidence that criticizes *tesettür*, including claims that it endangers a woman's physical health. Women have been informed that *tesettür* causes osteoporosis because lack of exposure to the sun causes vitamin D deficiency, and they have been warned that the pins used on headscarves can be inadvertently inhaled, damaging the lungs.[27] At best, these reports attempt to disconnect pious fashion from a healthy lifestyle; at worst, they are scare tactics involving the intentional circulation of disinformation.

Female public figures have also faced harsh public censure and ridicule for their versions of Muslim clothing. In 1999, a thirty-one-year-old engineer named Merve Kavakçı was elected to the Turkish parliament. The day of her swearing-in ceremony, before she could even take the oath, she was booed out of the parliamentary chambers. Her offense: wearing a headscarf into the chambers, which was seen as a violation of Turkish secularism. The leader of the Democratic Left Party declared that while Kavakçı was free to wear what she liked in her personal time, "Parliament is not the place to challenge the state."[28] The president of Turkey at that time, Süleyman Demirel, went even further, accusing Kavakçı of being an agitator, working for foreign powers like Hamas. Her own party accused her of jeopardizing the party's reputation.[29] Kavakçı was stripped of her Turkish citizenship and banned from holding political office for five years. Her political career had been irrevocably damaged, and her political party, the Virtue Party, was shut down.

Perhaps the most visible female public figures in Turkey are its first ladies, and in the past decade these women have been on the receiving end of intense criticism for their pious fashion. Hayrünnisa Gül was the target of much of this criticism. The wife of Abdullah Gül, who became president in 2007, Hayrünnisa Gül was the first Turkish first lady to wear a headscarf. For the first three years, she kept a low profile, greeting state visitors within the privacy of the presidential palace. Separate official receptions were organized so that secular government officials and military personnel would not have to shake hands or mingle with her. But beginning in 2010, when the headscarf ban in universities was lifted, Hayrünnisa Gül began to appear at official diplomatic events in *tesettür*. Her appearance that year at a welcome ceremony for German president Christian Wulff and then at the official Republic Day banquet caused quite a scandal. It would not be an exaggeration to say that the first lady was publicly humiliated by all sectors of the Turkish secular elite, from the press to university presidents, at almost every official public appearance she made. She received criticism from Muslim women, too. The women who participated in my focus groups often described her clothing as in bad taste: "too matching," "too pink," and "too shiny."

Hayrünnisa Gül's personal style was a form-fitting business casual version of *tesettür*. She favored monochromatic ensembles, with scarf, overcoat, and pants or skirt in the same color or variations of a single shade. While she often wore beige or light gray, she was not afraid of brighter colors, and was photographed during her husband's presidency in turquoise, mauve, hunter green, and royal blue. Most of her overcoats were closely tailored to her ample figure. When she did add visual interest in cut and design it was often as embellishments on the chest area or the collar. She favored pumps, usually with a chunky stacked heel. In a high-profile fashion faux pas, Gül teetered on a pair of six-inch stiletto booties, perfectly coordinated with her dove-gray outfit, when she met the queen of England in 2011. Photographers snapped photos of what was clearly disapproval on the face of the queen, as she stared down at Gül's shoes. It was a public relations scandal. The press in the United Kingdom ran stories with headlines like "Queen Welcomes Turkish President Gül (but All Eyes Are on His Wife's Heels)," and a popular YouTube video (with almost 800,000 views) is titled "The Queen's look of horror at Turkish first lady's footwear."[30]

From the moment her husband took office as president in 2014, Emine Erdoğan wore a head covering in public. Erdoğan is an attractive woman who fits predominant Turkish norms of beauty with her high cheekbones, almond-shaped eyes, and trim figure. And unlike Hayrünnisa Gül, Emine Erdoğan is also, by most standards, a very fashionable woman. She favors turban styles, expertly wrapped, often worn over an inner bonnet. Her headscarves vary from bold giraffe prints, to shiny satin floral designs, to soft silky solids. Her personal style is glamorous, feminine, formal, and elegant. But she is as scrutinized as the less fashionable Gül was. As one commentator put it, "Tastelessness [is] manifested in almost every outfit Erdoğan wears."[31] Online postings have compared her outfits to upholstered furniture, her wrapped head to an alien's, and the overall effect of her *tesettür* to a "ninja turtle." Even the *tesettürlü* women in my focus groups made fun of her style, calling it "ridiculous" and "tacky," and accusing her of "trying too hard."

Emine Erdoğan's dress is not only criticized for being unfashionable and unattractive—or an aesthetic failure—but also for being an ethical failure, particularly as a sign of overconsumption. The Erdoğans in general have been accused of maintaining a lavish lifestyle. Recently, for instance, it was reported that the first lady drinks white tea that costs \$2,000 per kilo.[32] Turkish women I spoke with thought she spent too much on her clothing and that her *tesettür* style was another sign of waste.

These three cases of women who are in the public eye reveal several aspects of the politics of dress in Turkey. One obvious conclusion is that people are concerned with how these women are representing Turkey to the rest of the world. No one seemed to care if Kavakçı, Gül, or Erdoğan wore headscarves on their personal time, but when they were on the parliament floor, receiving diplomats, or making official state visits, people regarded their dress as representing Turkey to the world in a certain way.

We have also seen two other cases in which *tesettürlü* women adopted and redirected aesthetic judgments against other covered women. One was the criticism by members of my focus group of the outfit featured on the cover of *Âlâ* magazine, and the other was women's harsh judgments of *çarşaf,* the full-body covering. In both of these cases, *tesettürlü* women justify their own styles of pious fashion by judging others, thus staking out a position for themselves as the proper representatives of Islamic femininity. Some might see this attitude as a positive expression of Muslim women's agency and authority. But it should be recognized that these women are involved in an Orientalist project when they do so, contributing to the idea that Muslim women's clothing is ugly. In contrast to the fashion failures described in Tehran and Yogyakarta, which are considered failures because they violate local aesthetic and moral values, in Istanbul, we see a case where failures are identified from the point of view of the outsider—that of the secular European who sees pious fashion as a sign of political extremism and cultural backwardness. Merve Kavakçı, who became a U.S.-based academic after leaving politics in Turkey, calls this sort of scrutiny the signature discourse of the "Orientalized Oriental," an internalization of the Orientalist's judgment that all things Eastern (and Islamic) are uncivilized and backward.[33] The public ridicule of the clothing of Muslim women is thus a form of inadvertent Orientalism deployed by Turks against Turks.

Apparel Industry

When *tesettür* first came on the scene in the 1980s, the Turkish apparel industry was already a major player in the global textile market, well known for producing European styles at reasonable prices. The first version of *tesettür* manufactured in Turkey emphasized affordability and utility over design innovation, and the early catalogs were austere. To avoid putting Muslim women on display, the catalogs used drawings of women with faces left blank instead of photographs.

This situation changed quickly, fueled by domestic demand from a growing Muslim middle class and a foreign market that clamored for Islamic modest clothing that reflected global fashion trends. The design, production, and marketing of *tesettür* became big business for the Turkish apparel industry. In 2014, Turkey was the seventh largest exporter of clothing in the world, according to the World Trade Organization. By some estimates, *tesettür* accounted for 40 percent of Turkish clothing exports.[34] In Iran, Turkish overcoats dominate the hijab market. Indonesians see Turkey as their main competition in the global market, as they ramp up *jilbab* production and exportation.

The first decade of *tesettür* marketing focused on convincing women to buy ready-to-wear overcoats instead of having them tailored or hand sewn. By the 1990s, that consumer base was solid, and *tessetür* apparel companies turned their attention to distinguishing and promoting their own brands. Marketing of *tesettür* began to incorporate aspirational lifestyle elements, showing fashion models posed at luxurious locations, such as a tropical vacation destination or an opulently decorated home with a view of the Bosporus.[35] These models held handbags, cell phones, and other "modern" accessories, thus connecting the brands to broader consumption patterns. Companies began designing scarves so that the brand name could be displayed, placing the logo at the corner most likely to be exposed. Billboards advertising *tesettür* popped up everywhere.

There are currently about two hundred Turkish apparel companies producing *tesettür*. Tekbir (literally, "God is great") is the largest one.

Established in 1982, the company started out selling special-order over-coats and long skirts. It launched a new line of ready-to-wear *tesettür* separates during a highly publicized fashion show in 1992. Today, 90 percent of Tekbir's production consists of pious fashion items. It employs 1,450 people and earns over 20 million Turkish lira yearly.[36]

Tekbir is one of only a few Turkish apparel companies that present themselves as Islamic companies, using Islamic banks for investment and seating men and women separately at fashion shows.[37] Its well-designed website states (in Turkish) that "The company aspires to be a model Islamic *hijab*-wear garment industry, by applying sacred Islamic values to a contemporary, multinational company."[38] Positioning itself as an Islamic company provides Tekbir with a few strategic benefits. First, it allows the company to claim expertise in determining what an ethically appropriate version of *tesettür* looks like and to pitch its marketing campaign as a medium for the moral education of Turkish women. Tekbir can also use its Islamic identity to deflect potential criticism that it is merely exploiting *tesettür* for its own benefit. "We have no intention of using *tesettür* for the purpose of fashion," Tekbir's CEO Mustafa Karaduman has declared. "Just the opposite, in fact, we intend to use fashion for the agenda of *tesettür*."[39] Presenting itself as an Islamic brand allows Tekbir to justify its growth and financial success as an Islamic project—one that encourages modesty by making it fashionable.[40] "There are women who decided to cover after seeing the varieties in our exhibition," Karaduman claimed in a 1994 interview. He went on to credit Tekbir with changing the reputation of *tesettür* in Turkey. "Women thought that they would be forced to enter a sack if they practiced Islam," Karaduman explained. "We broke this conception. All organs of the media had to admit that covering is beautiful. What preachers could not accomplish through their sermons, we were able to communicate through our shops and fashion shows."[41]

The shopping experience created by Turkish brands also influences what women consider pious fashion in Istanbul. In the early days of *tesettür*, shops carrying items for fashionable Muslim dress were relegated to side streets. Today they are located in prominent pedestrian shopping streets and other prime locations. *Tesettür* in Istanbul is most prominent in the Fatih neighborhood, and Tekbir's shops anchor the main commercial street of Fevzi Paşa. In 2013, I admired the display windows of a Tekbir store that announced the end-of-season sale with large decals and color-coordinated *tesettür* outfits featuring red, coral, and white items. All the female mannequins wore patterned headscarves and were fully accessorized. Prices were clearly listed. One window displayed two male mannequins and one female. One of the male mannequins was dressed in an unassuming beige suit, and the other wore a casual outfit with a tan shirt, dark pants, and a sporty jacket. The female mannequin was dressed in a bright coral floor-length dress, with a large crystal neckpiece. Women were obviously the marketing focus; the male mannequins and male clothing merely provided a background. Inside the shop, Tekbir employees wore *tesettür* uniforms with matching headscarves.

Armine, also established in 1982, is a much smaller apparel company but is well known for its slogan "Dressing is beautiful." Armine has a prominent three-story store on Fevzi Paşa in Fatih, with a huge two-story billboard that is often photographed. Armine began by producing headscarves in sophisticated patterns, but by 2012, when I first visited its Fatih store, it was also selling a small selection of other *tesettür* items like overcoats and mid-calf skirts and dresses. Armine's shop felt exclusive. This was caused in part by the store's architecture: there were no windows on the upper levels, since the billboard wrapped the entire building on two sides, which created a very private shopping experience. Compared with Tekbir, Armine had fewer items for sale and fewer customers perusing the selection. The first time I went there, shop clerks outnumbered customers by about three to one.

Stores in Istanbul that sell pious fashion items, unlike those in Tehran, employ an almost exclusively female sales force. The position of salesclerk is considered a temporary job, not a career, and the young women employed range in age from eighteen to twenty-five and work for minimum wage. No matter what their sartorial practices are in their free time, while at work they wear full *tesettür*—a headscarf, as well as some sort of modest outfit.[42]

A salesclerk can have enormous influence on what a customer considers stylish and what she ends up purchasing. As was the case at Vakko, many scarves are not on display, even in more moderately priced boutiques. Thus, it is up to the clerk to determine what style might be appropriate for a specific woman and to select some scarves for her to try. Clerks provide guidance on the color and pattern of a scarf, how to tie or pin it, and how best to combine it with the rest of the *tesettür* outfit in order to be tasteful, elegant, and modern. Harmony and coordination of color and patterns are imperative. Dark colors are often recommended for light skin tones, lighter colors for those with darker complexions. Headscarf shape is also important. An Armine salesclerk, for instance, told me that a rectangular shawl would be more flattering than a square scarf because I have a rather round face, and the drape of the fabric would make it look longer and thinner.

Islamic Fashion Magazines

Islamic forms of media proliferated in Turkey in the 1980s, including women's magazines. Some of the first ones were *Kadın ve Aile* (Women and Family), *Mektup* (Letter), *Bizim Aile* (Our Family), and *Kadın Kimliği* (Woman's Identity). Although these magazines were targeted toward Muslim women, as a whole they were critical of pious fashion. It is not that these magazines were entirely against consumption, since they promoted certain forms of austere consumption as important to the Muslim community. But they portrayed attention to global fashion trends as a secular preoccupation that would lead to exhibitionism, waste, and even promiscuity.

In the past twenty years, however, pious fashion has not only become more acceptable in Istanbul but is now seen as integral to the modern Muslim lifestyle. This has made it possible for a new form of media to appear in Turkey: the Islamic fashion magazine. *Âlâ*, the first magazine of this kind, began publication in June 2011. Printed on heavy paper, with professional photographs and expensive ads, the magazine seeks to depict a Muslim luxury lifestyle. Although not readily available at news kiosks, it is available by subscription and can be purchased in a variety of locations, including a few supermarkets like Migros and D&R bookstores.

While the staff has always insisted that their customer base is not restricted to Muslim women, the magazine has a decidedly Islamic orientation. The name, *Âlâ,* comes from the Arabic word *ali,* meaning "the best of it," as well as "the sublime," or the process of reaching an apex, which invokes Sufi images of a spiritual journey toward God. The magazine is framed as Islamic in other ways as well: editorials quote hadiths, wish readers well during holy weeks, and use the acronym s.a.v., meaning "peace be upon him," in reference to the Prophet Muhammad.

When I first interviewed *Âlâ* staff in 2012, the magazine's offices were in a two-story building in Çamilica, a residential neighborhood in the Üsküdar district of Istanbul. I met with Mehmet Volkan Atay and Ibrahim Burak Birer, the dynamic duo behind *Âlâ,* as well as Hülya Aslan, *Âlâ*'s editor. The male cofounders moved around the office, talking on cell phones, signing contracts, giving out assignments to staff. The two men were clean-shaven and dressed in expensive jeans, button-down shirts, and jackets. Their style was hip, but their vibe was more "entrepreneur" than "fashionista," which made sense once I learned that their background was in marketing, not apparel or design. But in 2012, *Âlâ* did employ a fashion maven: Hülya Aslan, the editor in chief, was a prominent *tesettür* icon who was popular on social media. On that day she was wearing a structured leather jacket and leopard scarf. Exuding the confidence of Anna Wintour, she was by far the most glamorous woman I had ever met in person.

In an interview published in the *New York Times* in 2012, Birer said that he had decided to start the magazine after seeing a photograph of a transsexual person in a see-through dress on the cover of an international fashion magazine, an image that Birer regarded as representative of the "diktat of nudity" common in women's magazines.

"Not all women dress like those girls from 'Sex and the City,'" Birer said. He decided to create *Âlâ* as a way to showcase female fashion that was not seductive.[43]

This makes for a dramatic story, but the other cofounder of the magazine, Mehmet Atay, told a different version during interviews with the international press on the heels of *Âlâ*'s successful first year. "We had no experience with magazines," Atay told a reporter for *Der Spiegel*. "We're marketing people. . . . We specialized in recognizing market niches."[44] The pair had identified an untapped market: the emerging Muslim bourgeoisie, who had been spending their money on vacation resorts, day spas, and luxury gated communities. They gambled that these same women would be willing to pay for a fashion magazine that featured headscarved women in modest attire wearing luxury brands from Turkey—such as Armine, Vakko, Tekbir, and Tugbo—and Europe—like Gucci, Hermès, and Louis Vuitton. Birer came up with the motto "Nothing incompatible between living a good life and being a good Muslim," and they planned a monthly publication that would be glossy, expensive, and highly designed. The gamble appeared to pay off, at least during the first eighteen months, when *Âlâ*'s circulation rose to forty thousand.

When I contacted *Âlâ* in 2013, a year after my first meeting with management, a lot had changed. The magazine had relocated to the suburb of Ümraniye, a working-class area of Istanbul that had experienced a recent flurry of housing and commercial development. Public transportation is limited, but the area is linked to the European side of Istanbul by a well-maintained highway and bridge. *Âlâ*'s offices were located in a twenty-eight-story building set within a small pedestrian shopping throughway. Beyond the shops was a ring of affordable apartment buildings and condos. I glimpsed a children's playground. Not exactly an exclusive address, although the building itself was impressive, with an enormous open atrium that filled the center of the building.

Hülya Aslan had recently left to take up a position at a competing fashion magazine called *Aysha*. Zeynep Hasoğlu, an elegant but soft-spoken woman who was a nutritionist by training, had taken her place as editor. Hasoğlu, whose gold bangles clinked quietly during our conversation, was forthcoming about the realities of magazine publishing. She confided to me, "We are struggling, but doing okay." Circulation had gone down to twenty thousand. I suspected that the office change might have been motivated by financial reasons, not the view. Hasoğlu did not want to discuss why Hülya Aslan had left other than to say, very diplomatically, "We at *Âlâ* wish her well." She did take a dig at Aslan's new employer, *Aysha,* remarking, "We are flattered when our competition tries to imitate us."[45]

In answer to a question about *Âlâ*'s mission, Hasoğlu explained that the magazine provides a service to Muslim women, even when displaying non-*tesettür* items. "I have to make something clear," she said. "When we show details and accessories, belts, for instance, we are not saying this is what *tesettür* is, we are not saying this is what the Quran or sharia defines it as." After a small pause, she continued. "If a woman finds one of our outfits not appropriate for her, she might wear it with a *manteau* over it. What we are trying to do is to bring global trends and famous brands into line with *tesetür.*" Her premise is that all aspects of fashion are of interest to Muslim women, and even items that a reader might not choose to wear could be modified or at least serve as inspiration. *Âlâ* features bareheaded models and celebrities on the red carpet alongside headscarved models, showing that *tesettür* has a place in the fashion world.[46] This strategy can be visually jarring, however, when the same model appears in the same layout both with and without a headscarf.

When I asked Hasoğlu if she thought there was a conflict between being pious and being fashionable, she was clever enough to let other authorities justify *tesettür* for her. She pointed me to an interview with a Muslim theologian and popular television host, Nihat Hatipoğlu, in the most recent issue of *Âlâ* (April 2013). Hatipoğlu wrote, "I am not at all disturbed by the fact that these types of magazines [Islamic fashion magazines] are being published. I see these magazines as fulfilling the need to ease people into *tesettür,* as well as the needs of those wearing *tesettür*." He went on to argue for the compatibility of modesty and attractiveness. "In my opinion, it is possible to be aesthetically pleasing while also living one's religion. It is not against religion if a young woman wears nice clothing while trying to make her dress *tesettür* appropriate."[47] Hatipoğlu conveniently justifies *Âlâ*'s mission from an Islamic theological point of view, as a vehicle "to ease people into *tesettür*" by presenting an "aesthetically pleasing" option.

In addition to making connections with religious experts like Hatipoğlu, the same issue of *Âlâ* linked itself with secular fashion tastemakers. In an editorial, Hasoğlu wrote: "In the 1930s, Atatürk had Coco Chanel design the uniforms for the Turkish armed forces. Until the 1980s, the Turkish military wore uniforms that carried the Chanel logo on them."[48] With these two sentences, the mother of modern European fashion is connected to the Turkish military, the self-proclaimed protector of secularism. By writing about and displaying European brands like Chanel as part of *tesettür*, *Âlâ* tries to bridge secular and Islamic traditions.

Later in our interview, Hasoğlu again picked up the most recent issue of *Âlâ* from her desk. The table of contents listed stories ranging from the red-carpet styles worn recently at the Oscars, to colorful shoes, to fashion week in Paris. But what she wanted to discuss turned out to be the very same cover image that had been trashed by my focus group earlier in the week, featuring the yellow Gucci tunic. "I love this cover, especially the Gucci tunic," she said. She turned back to the spread in which it was featured, "Monochromatic Style: It's Not New but It's Striking." "This is a dress that ends at the knee. You," she said, gesturing at me, "could wear it by itself. What I do to make it fit into *tesettür* is use it with pants and a shawl. We do this because designers have not yet produced clothing in line with *tesettür*." By designers, Hasoğlu obviously meant high-end European design houses, like Gucci.

Gazing at the two-page spread of the yellow tunic, Hasoğlu let out an audible sigh and confessed, "I wanted this tunic for myself, but it's really expensive!" The price listed in the magazine was 7,104 Turkish lira (approximately $2,400). Even for the editor of Turkey's premier fashion magazine, whose job it is to identify, curate, and display pious fashion, many of the actual items deemed fashionable are aspirational, not attainable.

Thinking of my focus group's disgust at how the tunic was styled, I asked Hasoğlu to tell me how this particular outfit was put together. "Well, lemon yellow is a very trendy color right now. We paired it with turquoise, a recent Pantone color of the year, to soften it." It was only then that I noticed what looked like a paint chip just to the left of the model, identified as Pantone color 15-5519, the 2010 color of the year. I then realized that a number of other outfits were tagged with Pantone colors, too. According to Pantone's website, the company "is the world-renowned authority on color . . . known worldwide as the standard language for color communication from designer to manufacturer to retailer to customer."[49] By creating outfits around official colors of the year, Âlâ was associating itself with this international design authority.

A regular feature of most issues of the magazine is "Âlâ Cadde" ("The Best of the Street"). This feature highlights photographs of women on the streets of Istanbul. The accompanying text tells us something about the woman (e.g., her age, job, favorite book) and lists the brand of each item of clothing and every accessory she is wearing. My focus group much preferred the style of these women to those in the Âlâ fashion shoots, commenting favorably on the color combinations, accessories, and personal style of the street fashion. It could be that they were predisposed to accept the aesthetic authority of their peers, ordinary Muslim women, over the stylists at Âlâ. But it's also true that the street styles had an ease that was missing from the Âlâ photo shoots. The women were wearing affordable brands such as Mango, H&M, and Zara. And certainly there was a difference in the way colors were combined. Fashion spreads in Âlâ were usually impeccably color coordinated: if a tunic or headscarf featured green, that was picked up in accessories or other clothing items. I have to admit that after my interaction with Nur, I too found the color coordination in Âlâ overdone and its overall visual effect juvenile rather than sophisticated. In the street style spreads, however, colors and patterns were combined in ways that were complementary, not necessarily exact matches. Of course, ordinary women do not have the same access to clothing items or accessories that Âlâ's staff does, but perhaps these limitations forced them to be more creative. At least according to the focus group I met at Messt, the result of this creativity was more visually pleasing.

In addition to clothing and accessories, fashion magazines also emphasize paying attention to body shape as an element of good *tesettür* style. *Âlâ* and *Aysha* both ran articles in 2013 about dressing for various body types. In *Aysha*, an article titled "Is Your Waist Getting Thicker?" advised women how to choose the right exercise for their body type: pear, apple, celery, or hourglass.[50] This article could have been in any Western secular women's magazine (except that the celery body type is usually called straight or banana in the West). An hourglass body type, with "a thin waist, and shoulders and hips of similar width" was described as the preferred body type, and these women were told to exercise all muscle groups. The prescription for an apple body type emphasized health concerns, especially reducing "fats [that] accumulate around the internal organs" through at least thirty minutes per day of cardio. But the exercise routine prescribed for pear and celery types focused on reshaping a woman's body. Pears were told that yoga or lifting arm weights can correct narrow or saggy shoulders and create balance in body proportions. Celeries "should try to get the body to gain some curves and to reach some balanced proportion" by doing exercises that focus on the arm and lower-body muscles.

The issue of body type becomes more complicated when discussed in conjunction with proper Islamic fashion, as in an article in *Âlâ* titled "Create Your Style According to Your Body Type."[51] After a primer on how to diagnose one's body type—pear, banana (instead of celery), apple, or hourglass—the article provided advice about what style of modest dress a woman with each body type should wear. Hourglass types could wear almost anything, but the author suggested that something nipped in at the waist shows off this figure to its best advantage.

Women with pear shapes were told, "You should not emphasize the hip area but instead you should draw attention to your waist area, which is slimmer." Specific suggestions included wearing flared mermaid or bell-shaped skirts. A belt at the thinnest part of the waist was encouraged, but women were warned not to use a belt at the hips "because this will give the impression that your legs are shorter than they actually are and it will draw attention to your hip area and will make it look wider." Apple types were told to "stay away from shoulder pads and voluminous dresses"; they should choose items that emphasize volume in the hip area and are tailored on top. Banana / celery types should "reveal the figure as much as possible" by wearing, for example, pendulum tops and jackets with loose skirts or wide, cuffed pants that "expose the waist curve."

In these articles, putting together a *tesettür* outfit involved creating an attractive figure. What defined this figure as attractive was not being "sexy," but neither was it simply being healthy. The attractive body was the slim yet curvy body. Waists defined. Volume added to slim hips. Large hips disguised. Legs elongated. *Tesettür* items were employed to make every woman look as if she had an hourglass shape. This is why Turkish *tesettür* in 2013 (the season featured in this chapter's style snapshot) had no flowy, loose versions, like the Iranian Arab *chador* described in Chapter 1. Nor was volume created where none is expected, as with the harem pants and giant pashminas found in Indonesia, described in Chapter 2. When volume was played with in Turkey, it was in the "expected" places: adding volume to hips with a full skirt, to shoulders with ruffles or shoulder pads.

During my meeting with the focus group at Messt Restaurant, once the rant over the Gucci tunic had run its course and the April 2013 issue of *Âlâ* magazine was returned to me, I flipped to the article about body type and asked, "What do you all think of this?" Nur looked at the article and shrugged. "Oh that, that is no problem. It's just common sense. You don't wear huge pants if you have a big butt." Later, when defining proper *tesettür,* Nur told me, "When the outfit is tight and shows the outline of your body, that is what is against the spirit of

This outfit, worn by a woman attending a style event put on by the Turkish Muslim clothing retailer Modanisa, demonstrates the vertical look created by a *tesettür* style that uses the same color from head to toe. The matching pink handbag has a print reminiscent of Louis Vuitton's monogram collection. Photograph by Monique Jaques, June 15, 2015.

tessetür." Nur believed that the illusion of curves created by fashionable *tesettür* was not a problem, because it fell under the category of good aesthetic sense. But any clothing that displayed a woman's actual curves was in danger of being an ethical failure. It's a fine line to walk.

Muslim Lifestyle within a Secular Republic

Pious fashion rarely flies under the radar in Turkey, and a number of stakeholders are engaged in efforts to convince Muslim women to dress in a certain way. We have seen how proponents of Turkish secularism have criticized *tesettür,* thus raising the stakes for this style of dress and intensifying women's self-regulation in matters of fashion. The apparel industry markets *tesettür* items in ways that influence what women think is fashionable. And Islamic fashion magazines present visions of stylized *tesettür* that, even if not entirely successful aesthetically or ethically, introduce readers to aspirational clothing and accessories.

Although determining the causes behind clothing trends is difficult, it is evident that the aesthetic visions of various authorities do affect women's clothing choices. For instance, the practice of displaying the brand names of headscarves is made possible by an apparel industry that designs and manufactures scarves with conspicuously placed brand names. This trend also demonstrates that *tesettür*-producing companies have successfully created cachet around their particular take on pious fashion, thereby fostering consumer desire not only to wear *tesettür* but also to buy specific brands of *tesettür* items.

The popularity of "vertical" styles, which enable women to dress modestly while at the same time creating a long lean line, shows the influence of the ideal of thinness that is presented in venues like fashion magazines. Despite the fact that many women rejected specific outfits in *Âlâ*, the magazine's ideals of body image were easily accepted and internalized by *tesettürlü* women. Even Nur, despite her criticism of some style choices in *Âlâ,* thought the advice to wear clothing that created an illusion of a thinner body was "just common sense."

The disdain among *tesettürlü* women for full-body covering is an interesting twist on the aesthetics associated with Turkish secularism and provides a way for Muslim women to redirect the public scrutiny of their dress. For most of the last hundred years, a bare head was the sign of a secular Turkish woman, and a headscarf the sign of a religious extremist. This shifted when increasing numbers of urban, educated, and career-minded women began to wear *tesettür* in the 1990s. Today, even the Turkish first lady wears pious fashion. But in order for people to be able to accept Muslim modest clothing as compatible with Turkish secularism, they had to find something else to take its place as an inappropriate expression of Muslim identity and piety. *Tesettürlü* women made *çarşaf* the new enemy of secularism by claiming that women who wear it are not exercising free choice and are overemphasizing modesty and religious identity.

But even among supporters of *tesettür*, there is a struggle over aesthetic and moral expertise. The disputed cover of *Âlâ* magazine is an outstanding illustration of this struggle. Under an editor's guidance, stylists designed an outfit that would highlight international color trends and European luxury brands. They assumed they had created an outfit that Turkish women would want. But Nur was not impressed. Although she did appreciate the Gucci tunic, she refused to acknowledge the expertise of the fashion professionals, who in her opinion put together an outfit that was all wrong and did not show off the statement piece to its best advantage. Instead, she exerted her own taste with confidence as she critiqued the outfit, head to toe.

This struggle for aesthetic authority is also behind the harsh criticisms deployed against high-profile women who wear *tesettür*. Once a woman in *tesettür* attains a very visible public position, for secularists she becomes the embodiment of a stigmatized category and thus an obvious target of critiques. But less obvious, perhaps, is why these women are also the target of verbal attacks by other *tesettürlü* women. It helps to remember that any fashion faux pas by a public figure creates a media frenzy, and thus it can appear as if these women are contributing to the negative view of pious fashion either

Three stylish women attend the 2013 Fashion Week Istanbul. From the black, belted fur vest and turban-style headgear on the left, to the perforated pleather jacket with gold studs in the middle, to the white shift and black caplet punctuated with a gold cord necklace on the right, these three outfits are perfectly on trend. Photograph by Monique Jaques, March 13, 2013.

as ugly or as overly materialistic. *Tesettürlü* women may thus prefer to distance themselves from these women. In addition, as in the case of the rejection of the expertise of fashion experts, *tesettürlü* women may be refusing to accept that women in powerful positions necessarily have good taste. After all, these high-profile public officials are not elected to serve as fashion ambassadors by *tesettür* constituents.

An interesting concept used in Turkish debates over pious fashion is that of *nefis*. In the context of Muslim women's clothing, *nefis* refers to the materialistic desire for aesthetically pleasing but ethically problematic versions of *tesettür*. Women talk about it as an urge that they cannot control.[52] A Gucci tunic, a Vakko headscarf, a padded bonnet, a tight overcoat—an improperly controlled *nefis* could be blamed for all of these. These items then provoke the *nefis* of other women, tempting them to give in to their desire to have pretty things. An Istanbul-based salesclerk interviewed by Gökarıksel and Secor blamed her naughty *nefis* for her failures to wear *tesettür* in the most morally ideal forms. She said she knew she should spread her scarf wide over her shoulders. "Though I want to, my *nefis* tells me to make a cute bow."[53]

This concept can help us understand how character formation is viewed in Turkey. Pious fashion is worn to govern *nefis*, and thus any fashion failure is the sign of an incompletely or improperly formed character. A woman's everyday activities, such as purchasing clothing, both reflect and serve to form her character. In addition, *nefis* reveals the intimate relationship between ethics and aesthetics, between being good and looking good. *Nefis*'s relationship to aesthetics is like conscience's relationship to morality: it is the inner voice that can discern and make judgments about aesthetic value. In their recent work on *tesettür*, Gökarıksel and Secor argue that anxiety over *nefis* shows that fashion and piety, or aesthetics and ethics, are not so easily reconciled in Turkey.[54] But there is a different way of interpreting *nefis*: it can be seen as evidence of the deep connection between aesthetics and ethics, fashion and piety, desire and virtue.

We can see this connection expressed in critiques of *tesettür*: there is often a slide between an accusation of aesthetic failure (an ugly outfit) and an assumed moral failure (a deception). It goes the other direction as well but not in as straightforward a way as one might think. In response to my question, "Can you trust that someone wearing good *tesettür* is a good Muslim?" Hande replied, "Well, we can trust that good *hijab* means she is a good Muslim because she is living her religion nicely, so we can trust her. But this is only a first impression. We aren't going to ask her to watch our pocketbook while we go to the bathroom." So while modest dress might be some indication of piety, it's not foolproof enough to let you trust someone with your purse.

ᥫᩗ FOUR ᥫᩗ

Pious Fashion across Cultures

PIOUS FASHION SHOULD NOT BE VIEWED as a problem to be solved; but neither is it a trivial matter, as the preceding chapters have made clear. Indeed, "clothing matters," as the anthropologist Emma Tarlo puts it in her book about dress in India.[1] But Muslim women's clothing does not matter only to non-Muslims trying to make sense of it. Within Muslim communities, there are multiple, competing opinions about what pious fashion should look like. The story of pious fashion is not a simple one of patriarchy or orthodoxy; rather, it is one of religious politics grounded in local debates about taste, nationalism, authenticity, and public norms.

However, if pious fashion is not a problem in itself, the decision of what to wear is. The duty to dress modestly does not resolve this question: even if certain institutional structures and public norms related to taste, virtue, and femininity set limits and provide guidance, Muslim women have a great deal of choice when they get dressed every day.

In looking at Muslim women's dress in Tehran, Yogyakarta, and Istanbul, we have seen that there is tremendous variation among locations, reflecting different aesthetic and moral values and different political histories and trajectories. Exploring pious fashion in these three places has revealed how important local context is for understanding the profound political and religious implications that pious fashion has for Muslim communities, not the least of which is making visible the web of pressures that affect how women present themselves in public.

The diversity and unpredictability of pious fashion complicates the task of drawing conclusions that hold across multiple locations. But considering the commonalities in how pious fashion communicates and makes meaning can be illuminating. In this chapter, I identify six categories—designing citizens, displaying values, fashion failure, conveying expertise, consuming faith, and cultivating beauty—that are helpful for understanding how and why pious fashion matters, as well as what it can tell us, more generally, about the role of everyday ethics in religious belief and practice.

Designing Citizens

Each location has its own history of regulating Muslim women's clothing through official dress codes. Such regulations reflect the idea that women's modest clothing is a sign of something else—whether a "bad" sign that Muslim women need saving or a "good" sign of the honor and moral health of an entire nation. For much of the last one hundred years, battles over these signs have been instigated by male elites to further political agendas related to colonialism, nationalism, and reform; they have had little to do with improving the lives of actual women. But there is an unintended consequence of making Muslim women and their clothing important symbols of the nation: women are given a prominent role as citizens and their dress a prominent role in constructing what modern citizenship means. Thus, even if modest dress resulted from attempts to politically control women, it has become a practice in which women can exercise political influence.

Styles of pious fashion in Tehran show us that the modern Iranian woman might be willing to live by rules not of her own making but she also demands the right to interpret those rules. As a consequence, *hijab* turns out to be not a single form of dress: rather, it includes a range of styles from the full-body covering of traditional *chador* to tailored short overcoats and headscarves. In some sense, any woman wearing pious fashion participates in the physical and visual segregation of men and women in public, thus reinforcing a gender ideology that supports patriarchy. Some styles are interpreted as expressing allegiance to the current regime, whereas others are viewed as politically subversive, pushing back against state attempts to regulate public morality and presentation through a dress code. Over three decades after the Iranian revolution, *hijab* still needs to be enforced, evidence that attempts to refashion the female citizen from above have not been entirely successful. In fact if anything, pious fashion has served to display diversity among Iranian women—whether that diversity is based on identity, class, or political aspirations.

In Indonesia, the government's vision of the modern woman has always involved ideas about her presentation and comportment in public. But for most of the last hundred years, sarong-style skirts and blouses were the clothes officially promoted by the government. That changed dramatically three decades ago when the popularity of *jilbab* skyrocketed after Suharto resigned. As young, college-educated women increasingly adopted pious fashion, it became a sign of a cosmopolitan woman. In addition, since a headscarf and modest outfit were not historically part of Islamic practice in this country, women were free to wear these items to express a thoroughly modern identity that is entirely compatible with national development and progress.

Muslim women's clothing in Turkey has been connected with the complex conversation about national identity. The ideal modern Turkish woman does not aspire to strict secularism anymore, even if she does understand herself to be European. She can have a strong Muslim identity, reflected in a specific style of dress: *tesettür*. The prominence of pious fashion in Istanbul is a sign of the waning of the European forms of secularism that dominated much of Turkish politics in the twentieth century. In many ways, wearing pious fashion is a more politically radical act here than in the other two locations, because it involves a turning away from Turkey's Kemalist legacy.

In all three locations, secularism has been championed not only for the purpose of preventing the influence of religion on politics but also for exerting state control over religion. However, efforts to repress political Islam in the name of promoting secularism often backfired. Even if traditional Islamic parties and institutions were undermined for a time, cultural and social expressions of Muslim identity and values thrived, which in turn led to the creation of new mechanisms for gaining political power. In addition, this process meant that secular authorities became involved in shaping practices that were both religious and political, while at the same time they were negotiating the boundary between them.

If pious fashion reflects the state of Islamic politics in these three locations, does it also indicate the existence of a political movement, whether local or global? The answer depends on what we mean by a political movement. If solidarity, coordination, and collective action are essential elements, then probably not. But the existence of similar clothing trends gives the appearance of collective action, even if they are not intentionally coordinated. For instance, in all three locations, traditional forms of patterned cloth have become incorporated into local pious fashion. Wearing these "ethnic" styles is not just a way to reclaim local aesthetic traditions—it can also be a way to express social or political critique by valorizing alternative sources of national pride.

Displaying Values

Whether a woman's clothing is intended to protect or attract, it is part of her presentation of herself to others—and this presentation reflects the values of her society.[2] Thus, pious fashion can reveal not only how values differ between locations and over time but also how the display of these values through material culture puts ideal notions of womanhood and modernity into concrete form.

We can begin by identifying modesty as the core value of pious fashion. However, the meaning of modesty is quite different in Tehran, Yogyakarta, and Istanbul. Ways of dressing modestly are always influenced by culture, but why is this the case?[3] For one thing, modesty is an abstract idea about conforming to standards of what is considered appropriate. It is expressed through different sartorial practices because it is understood in relation to local perspectives on dress, gender, aesthetics, and so on. These perspectives are themselves constantly in flux, since they are based on informal, loose, and changing ideas rather than on fixed knowledge. This is why pious fashion constantly changes, as we saw with the appearance of several new styles between 2004 and 2011 in Tehran.

Second, modesty is best understood as a cluster of values rather than a discrete value. In terms of women's dress, modesty bundles together values related to protection, femininity, sexuality, and social order. These values are both aesthetic (e.g., nonexposure or simplicity) and moral (e.g., propriety or decency). Thus, not only local religious norms but also local visual culture influence the meaning of modesty, as we see by looking more closely at modesty in each of the three locations.

On the surface, modesty in Tehran requires concealing the shape of a woman's body, especially her waist, hips, and chest, as well as her hair. But pious fashion in this city expresses a number of related values, as well. For instance, because women's dress is legally regulated, pious fashion exemplifies the wider cultural value put on stability and conformity. This is part of what moderation means in Iran: not rebelling against local regimes of governance. Other values displayed in *hijab,* however, serve to unsettle this stability and conformity. The bohemian look of some styles, for example, reveals a more carefree and informal aesthetic value, which is reflected in the flowing design of the Arab *chador* as well as in gauzy, ethnic fabrics. But more than just a breezy look, these styles convey a vision of public femininity that, despite the strict rules of the Islamic Republic, valorizes a free spirit and sense of ease in the face of authoritarian rule.

The interaction between the official vision of public femininity and rebellion against it results in the valorization of competing aesthetic and moral norms in Iran. Even as authorities try to enforce covering, women push back by valuing a certain amount of exposure, as in the body-hugging tailoring of some overcoats and the display of hair from under a headscarf. Western influence (*gharbzadegi*) is also valued differently by different groups. Some religious experts and the morality police see Western clothing as having a negative cultural influence, but many women who dress modestly value denim and European brand names as status symbols. In fact, this is why I initially judged street styles as cooler in Tehran than in Istanbul and Yogyakarta. My early preference for some Tehrani styles does not mean that they were objectively better but rather that their aesthetics were more in line with the aesthetics of my own style culture.

Modesty looks quite different in Yogyakarta, as it does not involve hiding a woman's shape and hair but rather covering these features with cloth. Long-sleeved, tight *mansets* can be part of a modest ensemble. Belts and even leggings are not only common but are considered pious. In Yogyakarta, softness and lightness are the prominent visual values expressed in pious fashion. Chiffon and pastel colors are more popular than in Tehran and Istanbul. The movement of fabrics and the paleness of colors invoke a feeling of etherealness. This fabric and color combination also creates a distinctive aesthetic of primness, wholesomeness, and whimsy. Although crystal and sequin embellishments are found in Tehran and Istanbul too, they are highly valued in Yogyakarta, from dazzling wedding ensembles to shiny, jewel-covered brooches used as accessories for headscarves. Feminine beauty is highlighted by these embellishments, which visually link women to jewels. In all three locations, pious fashion is a hybrid of European and Asian clothing trends, but in Indonesia the influence of Asian clothing, especially from Malaysia and China, is even more prominent, as seen, for instance, in the ninja *ciput* and mandarin high collars. This valuing of Eastern aesthetics is connected to a view of femininity that takes its lead from Asian and not Western visions of proper womanhood.

In Istanbul, modest dress is characterized by high necklines, low hemlines, and complete coverage of the hair. Popular fabric choices and tailoring create a more structured look than is found in Yogyakarta or Tehran. Although women in Istanbul do not wear skintight undergarments like the Indonesian *manset,* they do favor clothing tailored close to the body. Tightness and neatness are the aesthetic values associated with this form, which also conveys a moral value of confining and controlling women's bodies. The visual value of verticality in Istanbul results from the image of the ideal feminine body as lean. This characteristic of being physically upright also implies having the inner characteristic of being morally upright. The value placed on proportion is evident in the look of a large head created by a padded headscarf. Modesty in Istanbul is about creating harmony through clothing: balancing color, proportion, and cut.[4]

For most of the twentieth century, the modern Turkish woman was supposed to be secular and bareheaded. Today, the acceptance of Islamic dress is possible because pious fashion allows Muslim identity to be expressed in fashionable forms, resulting in both visual and social balance. Because of Turkey's physical proximity to the rest of Europe and its aspirations to join the European Union, pious fashion in Istanbul incorporates a number of European aesthetics—from wingtip shoes to European brand-name scarves and bags. Thus, in contrast to Yogyakarta, visions of femininity in Istanbul take their lead chiefly from the West, not the East.

Fashion Failure

If some forms of pious fashion successfully display local values, others fall short. In all three locations, women in interviews and focus groups identified improper forms of pious fashion. Looking at the styles that are considered failures provides insight into anxieties around the public presentation of Muslim women. But these fashion faux pas can also shift the boundaries of successful pious fashion, sometimes expanding those boundaries, sometimes narrowing them. For instance, a style characterized as being in bad taste can become a critique of the aesthetic or moral authority of established tastemakers.

In Tehran, the ultimate sartorial failure is *bad hijab,* which is defined by a variety of norm violations such as exposure of skin, display of body contours, use of certain fabrics, and application of heavy makeup. *Bad hijab* is regarded as both an ethical failure (e.g., too sexy) and an aesthetic failure (e.g., not tasteful). Not only is it viewed as evidence of a bad character—marked by vanity and materialism—but it is also one means through which that bad character is formed. And since pious fashion is a social practice, *bad hijab* also has negative effects on social order. By displaying their bodies and flaunting their disregard for the legal requirement to wear sharia-appropriate dress, women wearing *bad hijab* disrupt the public Islamic space that the Iranian theocracy is trying to create.

As I have already mentioned, I am suspicious of the view that *bad hijab* is an intentional performance. Does a woman really say to herself, "Today I plan to wear an ensemble that is untasteful, unattractive, or possibly illegal"? That said, sometimes a woman might wear an outfit judged as *bad hijab* to set herself apart from her peers. In this case, what is deemed an egregious fashion failure by some is a form of self-expression for others.

The existence of this form of fashion failure has several consequences in Iran. For one thing, *bad hijab* influences what is considered proper *hijab*. As we saw with Homa and her cousins, extreme forms of *bad hijab* make less extreme violations of norms—such as wearing denim or exposing the ankles—more acceptable. In addition, this form of dress has shifted the way *hijab* is legally enforced. It would simply not be possible to arrest every woman wearing *bad hijab* in Tehran. Out of necessity, the authorities have had to loosen the enforcement of the legal dress code.

In Yogyakarta, failure of pious fashion is identified not as an improper style but as an inconsistent one: occasional *jilbab*. This is pious fashion worn on some days and not others, primarily to follow a fashion trend. It may not be an aesthetic failure, but its inconsistency demonstrates a woman's incomplete moral education and improperly cultivated character. When a woman is truly pious, she wears *jilbab* consistently.

The idea of occasional *jilbab* plays a similar role as *bad hijab* insofar as it is designated an unruly look by the women wearing correct pious fashion. With *bad hijab*, the failure can be aesthetic, even if it points to an ethical failure. With occasional *jilbab*, however, the failure is always ethical, regardless of whether it meets expectations for what pious fashion should look like. That is, in Tehran, *bad hijab* is not "false" dress: the aesthetic failure is seen as an accurate reflection of the bad character inside. In Yogyakarta, the falsity of occasional *jilbab* is part of what makes it dangerous: the woman appears to be wearing pious fashion even though she is only doing so for one day.

In Istanbul, there are two types of failures. The first is ugly *tesettür*, which former first lady Hayrünnisa Gül was accused of. Ugly *tesettür* displays a lack of fashion skills and taste. Gül's clothing failure was attributed to her overly color-coordinated style, her lack of finesse with creating interesting lines, and her general inability to wear modest dress that looked attractive and up-to-date. She was covered but not in a pleasing way.

The second failure is quite different: the full-body covering called *çarşaf*. Unlike in Tehran, full-body covering is not acceptable as a form of pious fashion to most women in Istanbul. Instead, many regard it as a failure for aesthetic reasons—for being old-fashioned, ugly, foreign—as well as an important moral one—for deceptively conveying piety with its yards of black fabric. At its core, this judgment of *çarşaf* condemns it as insufficiently fashionable and overly pious. By asserting that *çarşaf* is a failure not only of style but also of piety, *tesettürlü* women are critiquing a traditional ideology that regards women who are more covered as being more pious. This critique in turn enables other forms of pious fashion to be seen as exemplary of Muslim womanhood.

When women identify another woman's clothing as a fashion failure, they are also expressing ambivalence about their own personal sartorial practice and others' monitoring of it. Pious fashion creates aesthetic and moral anxiety. Am I doing it right? Do I look modest?

Professional? Stylish? Feminine? Women try to resolve this anxiety by identifying who is doing it wrong. Judging certain styles as failures of pious fashion can thus be interpreted as the expression of internalized anxieties regarding law-breaking (in Tehran), ugliness (in Tehran and Istanbul), vulgarity (in Yogyakarta and Istanbul), and deception (in Yogyakarta and Istanbul). At the same time, in all three cases the identification of improper pious fashion is what allows proper pious fashion to redefine itself away from stigma to style: wearing Islamic modest dress is not what stigmatizes women as unmodern but rather wearing it in the wrong way.

Conveying Expertise

The role of the expert in pious fashion is to help close the gap between ideas of what Muslim femininity should be and how women express these ideas in their daily lives.[5] In the case of fashionable modest dress, exploring the kinds of authorities women listen to, why these individuals and institutions are regarded as having expertise, and what this expertise looks like results in a different model than the one so often found in scholarly literature on the topic: the model of the legal scholar as sole expert in Islamic ethics.

Who holds authority in the realm of pious fashion? In all three locations, the government authorizes some forms of relevant expertise. In Iran, official expertise is communicated by means of religious experts, morality police, and government propaganda posters. In Indonesia, a form of political expertise was wielded during the period of nationalist awakening and is currently linked to combating corruption on a national level. In Turkey, the government has asserted its expertise through a series of regulations on headscarves.

Another category of experts includes the tastemakers: fashion designers, magazine editors, authors, apparel companies, and salesclerks. In general, their expertise depends on their role in the creation or selection of items used in pious fashion. Some claim additional expertise as a result of their status, whether religious, cultural, political, or economic, and they are able to influence definitions of pious fashion in a way that benefits them.[6] Other tastemakers owe their expertise to particular jobs. A clothing designer's expertise depends on skill, taste, and creativity. The salesclerk's expertise is a particularly intriguing case, since it is based neither on a social distinction nor on special training in the principles of design or religion. And yet customers seek the advice of salesclerks because of their proximity and access to the items used for pious fashion.

Designers and Muslim women claim a type of expertise when they use motifs drawn from local histories and identities such as Persian, Javanese, and Ottoman. One way we saw this was through the promotion of indigenous cloth and embroidery. This move not only claims local authenticity for certain styles of pious fashion but also pushes back against the idea that what counts as proper Islamic clothing is dictated by the Arab world and then merely adopted in other locations. This type of expertise resists the idea of a homogenized Islam.

Another form of expertise is that claimed by Muslim women simply as women, a claim that rests on the idea that women have special innate or experiential knowledge about how best to present femininity in public.[7] This claim to expertise is what allows an ordinary woman to become a popular blogger: if she is comfortable with her level of modesty and confident of her style, she conveys authority based on her own personal know-how. This type of expertise can be described as a form of corporeal charisma, since the attractiveness of the style inspires a form of devotion from others. The technical, religious meaning of charisma, "a special talent conferred by God," is appropriate as well: Muslim women who successfully wear pious fashion are seen as implementing God's plan by convincing other women to dress modestly.

Expertise is conveyed through a number of mechanisms—such as sharing practical tips, presenting images of fashion exemplars, setting rules, and providing stylistic options—which depend in part on who is exercising the expertise. The Iranian morality police deploy tactics of intimidation, while an Indonesian fashion blogger posts a selfie of an outfit styled for a specific occasion, but both help shape expectations of what pious fashion should look like.

One mechanism of conveying expertise that was prominent in all three locations involves gatekeeping practices such as watching, noting, and commenting on the actual sartorial practices of women. We saw police, legislators, and institutions all participating in forms of surveillance of Muslim women's clothing. Women themselves participate in this process, too, by constantly monitoring their own public presentations, as well as judging those of others. Homa's accusation of slutty *hijab*, Raissa's criticism of occasional *jilbab*, Nur's disdain for the style of *tesettür* featured on the cover of *Âlâ*—these are all examples of how women observe and critique each other. Opinions about correct pious fashion are diverse, so one woman's failure might be another woman's success. But everyone has an opinion, and the expression of these opinions helps to shape local expectations for pious fashion.

Women judge each other in all cultures, so this practice is not a "Muslim problem." It does, however, help explain why traditional gender ideology endures. Public incrimination and shaming of Muslim women's dress relies on a specific ideology of how women should appear in public, and women themselves are not exempt from promoting this aspect of patriarchy. Sometimes they even intentionally accommodate existing gender ideologies in order to improve their own status, at least temporarily. Thus, it is not just men but also women, who are responsible for maintaining conditions of gender injustice.

Consuming Faith

The role of consumption in a moral life has been a point of debate within Muslim communities for centuries. Early Islamic mystics, or Sufis, promoted asceticism because they believed that humans are corrupted by our desire for earthly goods. But strict asceticism did not endure as a central tenet of Sufism because it was problematic from an Islamic theological point of view. First, it devalued God's material creation, and second, it implied human dualism because the body was considered less important than the soul. By the late eighth century, an important shift had begun in Islamic mystical thought and practice that redefined asceticism to mean living in harmony with the environment, instead of rejecting the world. The ascetic mystic, who was motivated by the goal of overcoming evil, gave way to the ecstatic mystic, who was motivated by the goal of union with God and could use the material world for spiritual development.[8]

Another notable transition can be found in contemporary Muslim politics, which set the scene for a larger role of consumption in Islamic life. In the 1970s, Islamists were promoting an anticonsumerist lifestyle as a way to combat what they saw as the moral corruption caused by materialism and desires generated by capitalism. But by the 1990s, partly as the result of a growing Islamic bourgeoisie, they began supporting the idea of an Islamic lifestyle expressed through consumption.[9] In this model, religion is not corrupted by consumption; rather, consumption becomes the mechanism through which religious ideals are transformed into aesthetic style.[10] In Istanbul, it was only after the apparel industry successfully commodified modest dress as *tesettür* that pious fashion gained enough cultural capital to become widely viewed as acceptable.

In all three locations, we have observed flourishing economies of pious fashion—design, production, marketing, and sales—in which women participate at every level. These economies support a promise of self-actualization through shopping, a process that sanctifies the material world because purchased items are used within religious practice and for religious goals.[11] We saw this, for example, in the case of the Istanbul-based company Tekbir, which claims to be converting women to *tesettür* through its production and marketing of modest clothing. Fashionably dressed Muslim women act as role models and inspirations for others who are considering modest dress, as well as rehabilitating Islam's public image by showing Muslims buying things just like non-Muslims do. In these economies, Muslim women are not just the target of marketing campaigns; they are consumers in their own right, who demand designer handbags, flattering styles, and colorful headscarves.[12]

However, anxieties about consumption remain. For instance, Islamic economic theory favors sustenance over capitalist production, which is why waste (*israf*) is considered a problem: it represents the mismanagement of resources that could be put toward other ends. So if consumption related to pious fashion exceeds what is necessary for physical or spiritual sustenance, it becomes immoral. Another fear concerning consumption is that clothing and accessories will replace women's bodies as the desired object, although this concern seems to be more about stimulating women's material desires than about arousing men's sexual desires. And indeed, women in all three locations admitted to spending a great deal of time, energy, and money on pious fashion, for example, amassing large collections of headscarves that must be carefully washed, ironed, and folded. There were also political concerns about overconsumption in all three locations as a result of state financial difficulties. A common concern is that women lure the men in their lives into corruption to support their shopping habits. This accusation was leveled at Turkish first ladies, as well as the wives of Indonesian civil servants. But perhaps the most far-reaching anxiety is that overconsumption cultivates a bad character. In Indonesia and Iran we saw this belief expressed in concerns that some clothing items could literally contaminate the body.

Interestingly, some failures of modest dress are ascribed not to overconsumption but to underconsumption. In Istanbul, women wearing *çarşaf* are criticized for not engaging with the global fashion trends that are part of being a modern woman. Their lack of consumption is a sign that they are not worldly and thus not as morally and spiritually developed as their pious fashion–wearing sisters. According to this logic, consumption is one of the conditions of being properly pious. A woman who is knowledgeable enough, the thinking goes, can wear fashionable clothing without being vain or materialistic.

The acceptability and promotion of Muslim women's fashion is based on the assumption that purchasing clothing is a necessary part of being a moral person in the contemporary world. A similar assumption exists among Hasidic women in Brooklyn, as described by anthropologist Ayala Fader. Fader tells us that "the aim for Hasidic women and girls is to be able to discipline their bodies and desires, to use their moral autonomy to participate in and transform the material world. Vanity, adornment, consumption and secular knowledge are not denied but . . . must be 'channeled,' like the rest of the material world, and made to serve Hasidic goals of community building and redemption."[13] In a similar way, wearing pious fashion becomes a way to experience Islamic culture, morality, and identity that is both practical and accessible.

Purchasing habits can also raise awareness of group affiliations. The distinction between "class" and "status" made by sociologist Max Weber is helpful here. Weber described class as being about the control of resources, whereas status is about bestowing prestige and honor.[14] The two are usually conflated in the term "socioeconomic status," but separating them allows for more precise understanding of the mechanisms by which clothing creates hierarchies and inequities. While class certainly comes up in these case studies, class-consciousness often seems absent. This is not surprising, as we know that even when class is structurally pertinent, it is not always recognized as such by the people themselves.[15] In addition, many of my informants explicitly resisted class as an analytical category relevant to pious fashion because they assumed that the equality of Muslims before God negated the importance of class.

But pious fashion is clearly associated with the ideologies of honor and prestige that are important to status. And this has historically been true as well. The first known reference to a woman's headscarf is in an Assyrian legal text of the thirteenth century BCE, where it is a sign of nobility. And in the Quran (33:59), Muslim women are told to cover with a cloak when they leave the house so that their status as free Muslim women will be known to all who see them and their honor will be protected.[16] Women in our three locations are acutely aware of what others are wearing, as well as how their own appearance might be judged by others. Their choices about what to wear involve marking boundaries and creating rankings.

Cultivating Beauty

Beauty work is a term scholars use to describe the range of practices that individuals perform to make themselves more attractive. This concept is a useful one when considering clothing. Of course not all clothing is designed or worn to create beauty—some styles are intended to challenge existing aesthetic preferences. However, most fashion, including pious fashion, is meant to please the viewer and thus at times functions as a form of beauty work.

For instance, there is beauty work associated with headscarves. A woman typically chooses colors and patterns that complement her skin tone. She styles her headscarf to accentuate her good features and disguise her imperfections by adjusting how it is tied, draped, and pinned around her face. She also takes her head shape into consideration. In all three locations, accessories were used to create the illusion of a thick pile of hair: fake-hair scrunchies in Tehran, padded bonnets in Istanbul, and bun *ciputs* in Yogyakarta. So much time is spent on the headscarf—selecting, caring for, styling, and padding it—that it has become the new hair.

Women also pay attention to enhancing the attractiveness of their bodies when selecting a style of pious fashion. We saw this especially in the case of Turkish fashion magazines, where women were divided into body types and told how to dress so as to look thin and well-proportioned. Part of this beauty work involves creating the illusion of symmetry, balance, volume, or curves. Pleats and ruffles are used to create volume, body-conscious tailoring highlights narrow waists and long lean lines. These practices might seem to result in insincerity, or even deception. However, the importance of aesthetic success outweighs any possible ethical failure.

Some reasons for cultivating attractiveness through pious fashion cut across locations. On the most general level, women work to make pious fashion attractive because attractiveness has positive outcomes for them just as for people everywhere: making a good impression on others, fostering higher self-esteem, or gaining employment advantages. Sociologists have shown that people generally connect physical attractiveness with other attributes, such as competency in the workplace.[17]

There are also other, more theological, reasons for pious fashion to be beautiful. For one thing, the beauty work connected with pious fashion is similar to other forms of self-grooming and ritual purification so central to Islamic practice, such as the ritual of washing before prayer and the use of perfume by men. The aesthetics of beauty work can thus be reframed in Islamic ethical terms as fulfilling God's command to be clean, well-groomed, and pleasant looking. This makes attractive dress part of presenting a pleasant image not only to the public but also to God.

Women spend an extraordinary amount of time trying to counter the stereotype that modest dress is ugly by using the very skills of beauty work that secularists assume they do not have the capacity to learn. Beauty work thus helps to remove the stigma from modest dress by making this style of clothing more attractive to other Muslim women. Beautiful Islamic clothing can also make Islam more inviting to non-Muslims. One Indonesian advice pamphlet refers to pleasing styles of dress as the "friendly" public presentation of Islam to non-Muslims.[18] The Arabic word da'wah is used to describe forms of proselytizing of Islam to Muslims and non-Muslims. Thus, attractive pious fashion is a form of da'wah in the service of normalizing and even spreading Islam.

In each location, understandings of beauty are influenced by foreign ideals. Although local aesthetic values are based on local narratives and ethnic identities, they also sometimes involve implicit critiques of prevalent Western conceptions of beauty. In the case of the Indonesian blogger Rania, this critique was explicit: she regarded pious fashion as a "protest" against dominant images of Western beauty. But cultural representations of beauty in the West continue to influence ideals of femininity in Tehran, Yogyakarta, and Istanbul. When Turkish fashion magazines discuss an ideal body type, it is the same curvy body (small waist, wide hips, and ample bosom) emphasized in the West. In fact, in a 2013 article titled "Create Your Style According to Your Body Type," *Âlâ* named Beyoncé as having the body type all Turkish women should aspire to. Western features are sometimes assumed to be the goal when using headscarves in Indonesia to highlight certain facial features. Iran is famous for its high rate of nose jobs to make the nose smaller, rounder, and turned up.

One can understand the relationship between women's agency and their beauty work in several ways. On one hand, it is possible to view women as being manipulated by patriarchal beauty norms; in that case, beauty work involves complicity with those norms in a way that can lead to dangerous consequences. If a Muslim woman fails to create a pleasing appearance, she is condemned as ugly and unfashionable; but if she is successful, she has reinforced a system that defines her worth in part by her appearance.[19] On the other hand, this system is not entirely of men's making, nor is it organized solely around men's desires and interests. Clearly, some women who wear pious fashion are aware of the rewards that come with beauty.

Finally, there is something to be learned from pious fashion about the role beauty can play in an ethical theory. Fashionable dress is religiously tolerated and even encouraged in these three locations because beauty means something more than "superficial" appearance. As discussed in the Introduction, beauty is an accepted religious ideal in Islam. But at this point it might be helpful to look in more depth at why this is the case. From a theological point of view, beauty exists in the world because of God, and the more something approaches perfection, the more beautiful it is. In terms of ethics, this means that we would expect moral development to be reflected in the beauty of the believer. A moral person will be a beautiful person.

But in this theological conversation, beauty does not mean physical attractiveness; rather, it refers to the very nature and essence of the object in question. In his *Treatise on Love* (*Risala fi al'ishq*), the tenth-century philosopher Ibn Sina (also known as Avicenna) makes a distinction between "sensible beauty" and "intelligible beauty" that is helpful here. Sensible beauty is beauty that is physical, and thus observable. We appreciate sensible beauty because we get pleasure from looking at it. Intelligible beauty is a more hidden form of beauty that is knowable only through rational reflection. This beauty is appealing to us because it is a sign of God's design. For Ibn Sina, appreciation of sensible beauty is acceptable as long as it is subordinated to appreciation of intelligible beauty.

The interesting thing about pious fashion is that if we accept the premise that modest dress is required for Muslim women, then pious fashion done well embodies both sensible and intelligible beauty: sensible because it is pleasing to look at, intelligible because it is part of God's plan. Because pious fashion is linked to Islam, it allows women to avoid the possible traps of secular fashion, such as overconsumption, vanity, or inappropriate sexual arousal of men.

Piety as a Modality of Change

In thinking about piety, it is useful to consider its status within the Islamic tradition. The historian Marilyn Robinson Waldman argues that it is a mistake to see tradition as merely a repository of old ideas that impede change; she proposes that, instead, we regard tradition as a way for a society to cope with change by allowing it to become accepted and normalized.[20] In pious fashion, we have a concrete example of how tradition facilitates this sort of adjustment. "Piety" is a received notion that helps a Muslim-majority community deal with a variety of modern pressures, including globalization, national development, consumption, and sexual politics. And as the comparison of three locations makes clear, when piety is deployed to assist with these processes of adjustment within various cultures, it results in a diversity of practice and belief.

In the Introduction, I identified assumptions about fashion and piety that might initially make a study of pious fashion seem a fool's errand:

fashion as a superficial expression of materialistic desires and piety the mechanism through which these unruly desires are suppressed. Both of these assumptions, however, are challenged by the actual sartorial practices of Muslim women. Piety turns out to be not just about obedience to orthodox interpretations of sacred texts: it also incorporates good taste, personal style, and physical attractiveness. And fashion becomes a key location through which piety can be realized and contested. Piety is not only about being good—it is about appearing to be good as well.

What does piety look like in the case of pious fashion? It is the Indonesian stay-at-home mom who decides to wear *jilbab* and share her experiential learning through her blog. It is the Tehrani youth who stands up to the morality police who harass her for wearing jeans as part of her *hijab*. It is the recent college graduate in Istanbul who critiques the styling on the cover of an Islamic fashion magazine. These women are all pious, even though they do not agree about what modesty entails. Nor does their clothing look the same. Nor do they subscribe to the same school of interpretation of Islamic sacred sources. They are pious because they are engaged in public debates about the proper expression of their Islamic faith. They are pious because they are using tradition in their process of dealing with a variety of modern pressures. They are pious because they are using clothing and adornment to cultivate their own characters, to build community, and to make social critiques.

Epilogue

PIOUS FASHION has been vigorously discussed and promoted on social media and in women's lifestyle magazines within Muslim-majority countries for some time. But for the decade I have worked on this topic, Western journalists have all but ignored it. Then suddenly, in 2016, as I was finishing the final draft of this book, it seemed as if pious fashion was being talked about everywhere; it had finally been authorized as "newsworthy" for non-Muslim audiences.

In January 2016, Italian design house Dolce & Gabbana released its first-ever collection of headscarves and coordinated abayas, incorporating its signature logo into modest full-body robe-like garments similar to those worn in the Gulf region. The addition of pious fashion to the collection of a prominent fashion house resulted in much media fanfare. Mainstream venues such as the *Guardian, Daily Mail, New York Post,* and *Forbes* covered this release with enthusiasm. Though reporters noted that this was not the first time a major design house had paid attention to modest clothing, the extent and celebratory nature of the media coverage made the collection seem like a turning point for global fashion culture. Almost all media reports observed that the collection was an astute business move: Muslims currently spend about $230 billion a year on Muslim clothing, and some estimates predict that this will reach $327 billion by 2019.[1] Yet the Dolce & Gabbana abayas started at well over $2,000, excluding most of this potential market.

Among onlookers familiar with pious fashion, the collection provoked little more than a collective shrug. To me, Dolce & Gabbana's designs seemed very traditional in terms of cut, tailoring, and silhouette. I was not the only one who was underwhelmed. In a post titled "Designer Abayas, What's New?" popular British Muslim blogger Dina Torkia told her followers that the "line of lacy, embroidered traditional abayas and matching scarves" was uncreative, "something I've grown up with and a look that every Muslim woman is all too familiar with. Something that the local 'abayas r us' in Brummy [Birmingham] might have." Torkia went on to explain why she found the media celebration of the collection insulting. Pious fashion had been designed, styled, and promoted by Muslim women for years "with barely a nod of applaud or recognition, until D&G fancies putting their stamp all over a very traditional Middle Eastern style & claim its originality."[2]

Uniqlo released a more innovative collection of pious fashion later in the year. Designed by Hana Tajima, a UK-based Muslim fashion designer, the collection's separates were priced from $10 to $60 and could be worn by both Muslims and non-Muslims. The collection included jackets, tapered trousers, high-waisted and wide-legged jeans, flowy blouses, and tunics in a palette of wine, mustard, taupe, navy, and avocado colors. An ingenious innovation was a one-piece head covering that Tajima herself modeled in promotional materials. Fabric wings folded out from a center seam running from the top of the forehead down the back, creating a face-framing wave that reminded me of 1980s feathered bangs.

Although Tajima had designed for Uniqlo in the past, her former collection was only available in Southeast Asia. In contrast, her 2016 collection was available to customers worldwide, through the company's online sites and at its flagship stores in many cities, including New York, London, and Melbourne. Instead of being marketed as a Muslim collection, it was presented as merely one season's iteration of Uniqlo's popular LifeWear collection. The common narrative in coverage of the story by NBC News, the *Daily Mail,* and *Huffington Post* was that Uniqlo had become the first mainstream clothing retailer to offer pious fashion. In an interview with *Vogue,* Tajima discussed her own hope that the collection would appeal to a wide range of women: "I like this idea that someone from a completely different background or a completely different style could see a piece in the collection and think, 'I could really work that into what I want to wear.'"[3]

In 2016, Western journalists also reported on the increasing importance of pious fashion in high-profile fashion events, one in Istanbul and one in New York. The first Istanbul Modest Fashion Week (IMFW) took place in May at Haydarpaşa, a gorgeous Ottoman-era railway station in Kadıköy. The location was a geographic symbol of the fashion event's goals. "It was Mr. Türe's idea," Franka Soeria, one of the event's organizers, told the Turkish newspaper *Daily Sabah*. Kerim Türe is the cofounder of Modanisa.com, an online platform for modest fashion that sponsored IMFW. "He liked the idea that Haydarpaşa is [where] Asia ends and Europe starts. It has its own story, it own philosophy. This is what we want for the IMFW too; we want to connect different regions and be the bridge for the modest fashion sector."[4] The event showcased a dazzling range of modest clothing, such as watery floral gowns by United Arab Emirates designer Annah Hairi that were paired with solid-color headscarves; Bahraini designer Samar Murad's puffy-sleeved blouses coordinated with high-waisted, wide-legged pants made from a Kufic calligraphic print; and Turkish designer Lazaza Gülcan's gowns featuring a feathery appliqué effect in fiery red. Both *Newsweek* and the *Christian Science Monitor* published photo essays of the event.

In September, pious fashion had a different sort of runway coming-out party when Jakarta-based fashion designer Anniesa Hasibuan became the first designer to showcase an entire collection of Islamic pious fashion at one of New York Fashion Week's official venues. Some of her forty-eight items were ready-to-wear; others were elaborate evening wear, in satins, silk, and chiffons. The clothing was embellished with gold-thread embroidery, sequins, and crystals. Necklines were high, sleeves were long, and skirt hems swept the floor. Some looks included chunky necklaces with large polished stones or rhinestone-studded eyewear. Every model went down the runway wearing a headscarf. Hasibuan received a standing ovation, and the *New York*

Times, CNN, and BBC News all reported it as a historic event. Though Hasibuan had shown the same collection at Istanbul Modest Fashion Week, it went virtually unnoticed by the Western media then, as just one of many "Muslim" collections. It was the collection's inclusion in New York Fashion Week that signaled its acceptance by the fashion world.

The next mention of pious fashion in mainstream news that caught my eye was the *New York Post*'s coverage of the launch of the digital version of *Vogue Arabia* in October 2016. Just a decade earlier, *Vogue*'s publisher, Condé Nast International, had rejected the idea of an Arab edition. In an infamous 2007 leaked email, Jonathan Newhouse, head of the company, had acknowledged that there was a market for an Arab version of *Vogue* but feared that an Arabic-language magazine might "provoke a strongly negative, even violent reaction." In this same email he referred to the region as the home of "bin Laden and most of the September 11 terrorists" and referred to a militant and violent element in the region that "rejects freedom of expression, equality for women and expression of sexuality," values presumably important to *Vogue.*[5]

Vogue was not the first fashion magazine to publish an Arabian edition—*Harper's Bazaar, Marie Claire,* and *Elle* were already doing so. This particular Arabian edition seemed newsworthy because of *Vogue*'s undisputed status as the grande dame of women's fashion. *Vogue Arabia* was distinct in at least one way, compared with other regional editions: its intended reach went much beyond the Gulf. The magazine's first editor in chief, the glamorous Deena Aljuhani Abdulaziz, described her readers as women who see themselves as global citizens of the world. They have ties to Arabia that are cultural and familial, but they are just as likely to live in Los Angeles as in Dubai.[6] Abdulaziz herself fits this mold: she is of Saudi Arabian descent but was born in California and shuttles between Riyadh and New York City. This hybrid identity is reflected in her own sartorial practices. She wears modest clothing but without a headscarf covering her signature super-short hair. For Abdulaziz, pious fashion is just fashion, albeit fashion that emphasizes taste and aesthetics from a particular region.

One last piece of pious fashion news was enthusiastically reported by the mainstream news media in 2016: CoverGirl's November announcement that Nura Afia would become their first headscarf-wearing Muslim spokesperson. At the time, Afia was best known as a popular American video blogger who shared tips on makeup application, skin-care routines, and headscarf wrapping. In her partnership with CoverGirl, Afia joined the lineup of the brand's most diverse group of ambassadors to date, including singer Katy Perry, actor Sofia Vergara, and teenage Internet sensation James Charles, to promote a new brand of mascara. With the tagline #Lash Equality, the high-profile campaign ran a series of advertisements, including a billboard in Times Square, designed to present an inclusive vision of beauty.

Read together, this journalistic celebration of new collections, fashion shows, and a *hijabi* spokesperson seem to provide evidence that mainstream Western culture is beginning to notice pious fashion, even to admire and desire it. Yet not everyone was thrilled with the crossover of pious fashion into more secular fashion forums. Conservative Muslims staged a Twitter backlash against Istanbul Modest Fashion Week. The night before the event began, the Turkish writer Yusuf Kaplan tweeted, "We won the headscarf battle, but we lost the practice" with the hashtag #tesettureihanet, or "betrayal of *tesettür*." His comment was retweeted more than 2,600 times and liked by 3,400 users. Others quickly chimed in with tweets such as "Veiling is not fashion, it is God's order" and "Modest Fashion Week is making veil a tool of capitalism!"[7] These critics were concerned that pious fashion's new mainstream acceptability indicated that designers and market forces, instead of Islamic values, were dictating the aesthetics of Muslim women's dress. To put it bluntly, they thought fashion was polluting Islamic practice.

The opposite concern, that Islam was polluting fashion, has also been voiced, echoing Jonathan Newhouse's assertion a decade ago that the freedom required for fashion is somehow incompatible with Muslim values. In March 2016, Pierre Bergé, French fashion mogul and cofounder of Yves Saint Laurent, publicly accused designers who create pious fashion of encouraging the enslavement of women. "Designers are there to make women more beautiful, to give them their freedom," he said during a radio interview. "Not," he continued, "to collaborate with this dictatorship which imposes this abominable thing by which we hide women and make them live a hidden life."[8] Later that month, in response to the launch of a full-body swimsuit line by British brand Marks & Spencer, Laurence Rossignol, France's minister for families, children, and women's rights, attacked modest fashion during an interview on French radio station RMC. "What's at stake is social control over women's bodies," she told listeners. "When brands invest in this Islamic garment market, they are shirking their responsibilities and are promoting women's bodies being locked up."[9] The increasing inclusion of Muslims in the creation, marketing, and representation of fashion and beauty has been occurring simultaneously with a backlash against Muslims throughout the West, not just in France. While the designer Anniesa Hasibuan was receiving a standing ovation at New York Fashion Week, Donald Trump was winning the U.S. presidential election on a brazenly Islamophobic platform.

This coincidence of increasingly intense celebration and rejection of pious fashion and all it is assumed to stand for is evidence of both the transitional moment we are in and the underlying anxieties that it has evoked. A *hijab*-wearing CoverGirl ambassador and the extreme vetting of Muslim immigrants are both acknowledgements that Muslims are transforming Western culture and political life. Of course, they are two very different ways of dealing with this realization. On the one hand, there is a doubling down on efforts to exclude, through extreme vetting, burkini bans, racial profiling, and other actions that treat Muslim-minority communities as threats. But on the other hand, we are seeing a response that looks more like a move toward inclusion, by which visible expressions of Muslim identity and taste are highlighted and celebrated.

Consider one image recently adopted for political resistance in the United States: a woman wearing a headscarf with an American flag pattern, from Shepard Fairey's 2017 "We the People" series. Feminists waved posters featuring this image during the 2017 Women's March. Optimists might see this as a sign that opinions about pious fashion are on the cusp of changing from negative to positive in the West. In Fairey's image, the headscarf is a symbol of solidarity and a powerful critique of forces trying to marginalize and exclude believers in Islam. Yet Fairey's image is powerful because it relies upon what many Westerners still see as a jarring juxtaposition: an American flag and a covered Muslim woman. Only when the combination no longer surprises will there be genuine cause for optimism.

The women in this book are real people trying to express their religious beliefs and look good at the same time. They are not merely symbols of something else—whether a universal form of Islamic politics or patriarchy. And their decisions and everyday actions related to pious fashion occur in extremely different fast-paced urban locations. Homa is confident that she can identify *bad hijab* and make sartorial choices for herself that are both modern and tasteful despite Iran's compulsory dress code. Raissa uses modest clothing and a hidden fake bun as part of her character formation in contemporary Indonesia, where public displays of Islam are increasingly valued. Nur asserts her own style expertise as she critiques the cover of *Âlâ* magazine and pursues a publicly Muslim lifestyle in the secular Republic of Turkey. These women and the others I have discussed through prose and displayed through photographs are not merely symbols of some cohesive "Muslim femininity." More than just "veiled women," these are women who wear pious fashion head to toe, motivated by various reasons and propelled by various style choices, creating various forms of political and social critique. They don't need Dolce & Gabbana to tell them what is stylish. As one young Indonesian woman said to me, "We are fashionable enough to be our own style icons."

NOTES

Introduction

1. Joanne Entwistle, *The Fashioned Body: Fashion, Dress, and Modern Social Theory* (New York: Polity, 2000), 65.

2. Malcolm Barnard, *Fashion Theory: An Introduction* (New York: Routledge, 2014), 42.

3. According to the CIA World Fact Book, 99.8 percent of Turkey's population of just over 80 million identify as Muslim (2016 estimate). The Iranian population of 82.8 million (2016 estimate) is 99.4 percent Muslim, with roughly 90 percent of Muslims (2011 estimate) belonging to the Shia sect, the official state religion of the republic. In Indonesia, with a population of about 258 million (2016 estimate), 87.2 percent identify as Muslim, making it the country with the world's largest Muslim population. See https://www.cia.gov/library/publications/the-world-factbook/fields/2122.html.

4. Amelie Barras, *Refashioning Secularisms in France and Turkey: The Case of the Headscarf Ban* (New York: Routledge, 2014); Reina Lewis, *Muslim Fashion: Contemporary Style Cultures* (Durham, NC: Duke University Press, 2015).

5. Sahdi Sadr, "*Bad hijab dar qanun, fiqh, va raviyah'ha-yi,*" *Zanan* 107 (1382 / 2004): 44.

6. Jean Taylor, "Identity, Nation, and Islam," *IIAS Newsletter* no. 46 (2008): 12.

7. Amel Boubekeur and Olivier Roy, eds., "Introduction," in *Whatever Happened to the Islamists? Salafis, Heavy Metal Muslims, and the Lure of Consumerist Islam* (London: Hurst, 2012), 2.

8. *The Devil Wears Prada* (2006), directed by David Frankel, screenplay by Aline Brosh McKenna based on a novel by Lauren Weisberger. A clip of this

monologue can be found at https://www.youtube.com/watch?v=Yj8mHwv FxMc.

9. Karen Hansen, "The World in Dress: Anthropological Perspectives on Clothing, Fashion, and Culture," *Annual Review of Anthropology* 33 (2004): 372.

10. Erving Goffman, *Encounters: Two Studies in the Sociology of Interaction* (Indianapolis: Bobbs-Merrill, 1961), 145–146.

11. Faegheh Shirazi, "Islamic Religion and Women's Dress Code: The Islamic Republic of Iran," in *Undressing Religion: Commitment and Conversion from a Cross-Cultural Perspective,* ed. L. B. Arthur (Oxford: Berg, 2000), 116.

12. Erving Goffman, *The Presentation of Self in Everyday Life* (New York: Anchor, 1959), 13.

13. Pierre Bourdieu, *Distinction: A Social Critique of the Judgment of Taste,* trans. Richard Nice (1979; Cambridge, MA: Harvard University Press, 1984), 57.

14. Sean McCloud, "Putting Some Class into Religious Studies: Resurrecting an Important Concept," *Journal of the American Academy of Religion* 75.4 (2007): 842.

15. See Elizabeth Bucar, *The Islamic Veil: A Beginner's Guide* (Oxford: Oneworld Publications, 2012), 28–48.

16. Michael Lambek, *Ordinary Ethics: Anthropology, Language, and Action* (New York: Fordham University Press, 2010), 3.

17. Barbara Metcalf, "Remaking Ourselves: Islamic Self-Fashioning in a Global Movement of Spiritual Renewal," in *Accounting for Fundamentalisms: The Dynamic Character of Movements,* ed. Martin E. Marty and R. Scott Appleby (Chicago: University of Chicago Press, 1994), 710.

18. As the anthropologist Saba Mahmood concludes from her study of the Islamic piety movement in Egypt, pious acts "inhabit" norms. Mahmood, *Politics of Piety: The Islamic Revival and the Feminist Subject* (Princeton, NJ: Princeton University Press, 2005), 15.

19. Elizabeth Bucar, "Dianomy: Religious Women's Agency as Creative Conformity," *Journal of the American Academy of Religion* 78.3 (2010): 662–686.

20. Ann Marie Leshkowich and Carla Jones, "What Happens When Asian Chic Becomes Chic in Asia?" *Fashion Theory* 7.3–4 (2003): 286. I explore play as a metaphor for the interaction of women and clerical authority in Bucar, *Creative Conformity: The Feminist Politics of U.S. Catholic and Iranian Shi'i Women* (Washington, DC: Georgetown University Press, 2011), 171–173.

21. From the *Saḥīḥ Muslim* collection.

22. Al-Ghazali, *Ihya' 'ulum al-din* (The revival of religious sciences) (Beirut: Dar al-Kutub al-'Ilmiya, 2001), vol. 2, 318. All translations in this book are my own unless otherwise indicated.

23. Ebrahim Moosa, *Ghazali and the Poetics of Imagination* (Chapel Hill: University of North Carolina Press, 2005), 235.

24. This diversity is a reflection of Aristotle's claim that virtue is "the mean relative to us," or as Miskawayh formulates it, virtue "should be sought separately for each individual person." This means that one person's courage is another person's timidity. Virtue as a "mean" can also be thought of as a mean relative to a specific cultural or political context. Aristotle, *The Complete Works of Aristotle*, vol. 2., ed. Jonathan Barnes, trans. St. George Stock (Princeton, NJ: Princeton University Press, 1984), 1106a28; Ahmad ibn Muhammad Ibn Miskawayh, *The Refinement of Character (Tahdhib al-akhlaq)*, trans. Constantine Zurayk (Chicago: Kazi, 2002), 22.

25. Barnard, *Fashion Theory*, 52.

26. Muslim men are also required to dress modestly: to cover their bodies at least from the navel to below the knee and to avoid other forms of exposure, like extremely tight clothing. Some hadiths describe the Prophet Muhammad as covering his face as a sign of respect, for example when he appeared before his father-in-law. And among the Tuareg, a Berber Muslim tribe, men, not women, wear long, flowing robes and a head covering comprising a low turban and a face veil. For the Tuareg, the veil is not a sign of femininity but rather of masculinity and male fertility. See Fadwa El Guindi, *Veil: Modesty, Privacy, and Resistance* (New York: Bloomsbury Academic, 2003), 119.

27. Sukarno, *Sukarno: An Autobiography*, trans. Cindy Adams (Indianapolis: Bobbs Merrill, 1965).

1. *Hijab* in Tehran

1. As quoted in Thomas Erdbrink, "Olympics 2012: FIFA Bans Headscarves for Iranian Women's Soccer Team," *Washington Post*, June 6, 2011, https://www.washingtonpost.com/sports/united/olympics-2012-fifa-bans-headscarves-for-irans-women-soccer-team/2011/06/06/AGzT1JKH_story.html?utm_term=.a4cb713570bc. FIFA first banned the *hijab* during play in 2007 for safety reasons. Pieces such as neck warmers are also banned from play, as they are considered a choking hazard. After the new regulations were put in place, the Iranian team modified their headscarves to fit more tightly. The team believed the modifications were in line with the new rules, and according to Reuters they continued to play in matches without any objection from FIFA officials until the Olympic qualifier. FIFA says it "thoroughly informed" the Iranian team before the qualifier that wearing headscarves would prevent the

team from playing. In January 2012, FIFA agreed to a trial period, starting in July, of allowing headscarves to be worn. In 2014, the trial period was deemed a success by the International Football Association Board, and the ban on head covers was lifted.

2. See http://www.farsnews.com/newstext.php?nn=8809171089.

3. I collected data on Tehran from textual sources in both Persian and English, online sources, such as Tumblr and Instagram, and three ethnographic sources: (1) observations and interviews I conducted in Iran for four months in 2004; (2) a qualitative survey on dress rules and norms that I conducted via email in 2011 with twenty-seven women between the ages of eighteen and thirty-five who live in Tehran (referred to by pseudonyms); and (3) a photo essay I solicited in 2011. My first stint of research (2004) was conducted in person; because of logistical and political difficulties, I conducted the second round (2011) remotely. I completed the qualitative survey via email with the help of my invaluable research assistant, Heeva Khadivar. In Tehran I was fortunate to find an art student, Dorsa Javaherian, who photographed pious fashion trends that same year. In addition to my own fieldwork, this chapter draws on two important articles on *hijab* published in Persian in Iran: Fatemeh Sadeghi, "Why We Say 'No' to the Compulsory Hijab?" trans. Frieda Afary, http://iranianvoice sintranslation.blogspot.com/2009/07/fatemeh-sadghi-is-assistant-professor .html (original version at http://www.meydaan.com/Showarticle.aspx?arid =548), and Shadi Sadr, "Bad ḥijāb dar qānūn, fiqh, va ravīyah'hā-yi 'amalī" (*Bad hijab* in theology, *fiqh*, and practice), *Zanan* 107 (2004): 44. My analysis was also informed by Alexandru Balasescu's excellent ethnography of Tehrani fashion, *Paris Chic, Tehran Thrills: Aesthetic Bodies, Political Subjects* (Bucharest: Zeta Books, 2013).

4. Emma Tarlo, *Clothing Matters: Dress and Identity in India* (Chicago: University of Chicago Press, 1996), 324–325.

5. Peter Chelkowski and Hamid Dabashi, *Staging a Revolution: The Art of Persuasion in the Islamic Republic of Iran* (1999; London: Booth-Clibborn Editions, 2002), 302.

6. Niloofar Haeri, "Clothes Make the Mullah," *Salon,* January 5, 2005. Available at http://www.salon.com/2005/01/05/iran_clergy/.

7. Although *bad hijab* is most often used to refer to young women's dress, in 2006 and 2007 the morality police began to detain young boys with spiked hair and upscale punk clothing.

8. Kulai was one of eleven women (out of 290 MPs) elected that year. Despite their small number, these women were able to form an important block in

the Majles through their shared focus on women's issues; they were successful in part because the Reform Party had gained control of the Majles that same year. See "Results of the 6th Majles Elections," *Bad Jens: Iranian Feminist News-letter* (May 13, 2000), www.badjens.com/secondedition/election.htm.

9. Norma Claire Moruzzi, "Trying to Look Different: *Hijab* as the Self-Presentation of Social Distinctions," *Comparative Studies of South Asia, Africa and the Middle East,* 28.2 (2008): 231.

10. See, for example, Quran 24:30.

11. As quoted in Richard Foltz, *Iran in World History* (New York: Oxford University Press, 2016), 102.

12. As quoted in Moruzzi, "Trying to Look Different," 231.

13. Murtadha Mutahhari, *The Islamic Modest Dress,* 3rd ed., trans. L. Baktiar (Chicago: Kazi Publications, 1992), 23.

14. Interview with Khomeini, *Sahifa-yi Nur,* vol. 4 (December 28, 1978), 103.

15. Sadr, "Bad ḥijāb," 45.

16. Ibid., 46.

17. Ibid., 48.

18. Sadeghi, "Why We Say 'No' to the Compulsory Hijab?"

19. Alexandru Balasescu calls this a particularly modern form of control, legitimized through "participant citizenship" and enacted through many various forms of ordinary daily life. Balasescu, *Paris Chic, Tehran Thrills,* 153.

20. Since about 2010, an underground fashion movement has begun to emerge, with pop-up stores and an emphasis on "slow fashion" that is sustainable. For discussion of this group of designers and photographs of their clothing, see Hoda Katebi, *Tehran Streetstyle* (Hoda Katebi, 2016).

21. Catherine Taylor, "A Designer Tugs at Iran's Fashion Straitjacket," *Christian Science Monitor,* April 15, 2002.

22. Balasescu, *Paris Chic, Tehran Thrills,* 205.

23. Mahla was able to publish five issues from 2001 until President Ahmadinejad shut down the magazine in 2012.

24. Balasescu, *Paris Chic, Tehran Thrills,* 208–209.

25. Parinoosh Arami, "High Fashion Makes Inroads in Modern Iran," *Globe and Mail,* January 28, 2003.

26. The interview with the *Atlantic Post* is no longer available online but was previously accessible at http://www.theatlanticpost.com/gab_gallery/true-colors-tehrans-street-fashion.

27. Kristen Gresh, *She Who Tells a Story* (Boston: MFA Publications, 2013), 35.

28. http://thetehrantimes.tumblr.com/post/33841826087.

29. http://thetehrantimes.tumblr.com/post/68068756253.

30. http://thetehrantimes.tumblr.com/post/32352220702/bitchy-mouse.

31. http://thetehrantimes.tumblr.com/post/32456850639.

32. See, for example, http://thetehrantimes.tumblr.com/post/72346179553.

33. Balasescu argues that the recent adoption of traditional fabric is, ironically, a sign of modernity: "Easily and light-heartedly bringing the past into the present also affirms one's separation from it." Balasescu, *Paris Chic, Tehran Thrills*, 227. The ethnic cloth is not only linked to the past but also to nonurban lifestyles. In this view a person who wears ethnic clothing conveys a sartorial form of confidence and makes a claim to be cosmopolitan and urban, not confined or overly determined by history, and thus able to reinvent markers of traditional and rural life.

2. *Jilbab* in Yogyakarta

1. Like many Indonesians, General Wiranto has only one name.

2. Jean Gelman Taylor, "The Sewing-Machine in Colonial Era Photographs: A Record from Dutch Indonesia," *Modern Asian Studies* 46.1 (2012): 81, 90.

3. From Sukarno's autobiography, as quoted in Jean Taylor, "Identity, Nation, and Islam," *IIAS Newsletter* 46 (2008): 12–13.

4. Ibid., 12.

5. Saskia Wieringa, *Sexual Politics in Indonesia* (New York: Palgrave Macmillan, 2002), 82.

6. The word *fitna* appears in a number of places in the Quran, where it means discord, temptation, or worldly disorder. It is not, however, used in the sacred text as a reason for veiling, or even to refer to seduction. Nevertheless, the majority of medieval legal scholars utilized a doctrine of *fitna* to explain why the covering of women was required: the disorder of *fitna* at stake is the chaos that sexual desire outside of a marriage can cause (such as distraction from completing other duties). Invoking *fitna* remains a common powerful rhetorical strategy today in Muslim communities.

7. Wieringa, *Sexual Politics in Indonesia*, 71.

8. Jean Gelman Taylor, *Global Indonesia* (New York: Routledge, 2012), 170; and Rachel Rinaldo, *Mobilizing Piety: Islam and Feminism in Indonesia* (Oxford: Oxford University Press, 2013), 45. See also Carla Jones, "Women in the Middle: Femininity, Virtue, and Excess in Indonesian Discourses of Middle-Classness," in *The Middle Classes: Theorizing through Ethnography*, ed. Rachel Heiman, Carla

Freeman, and Mark Liechty (Santa Fe: School for Advanced Research Press, 2012), 156.

9. Karen Strassler, *Refracted Visions: Popular Photography and National Modernity in Java* (Durham, NC: Duke University Press, 2010).

10. Rinaldo, *Mobilizing Piety*, 13, 51.

11. James Hoesterey describes the pornography debate as "a theatrics of national morality played out on the public stage." Hoesterey, *Rebranding Islam: Piety, Prosperity, and a Self-Help Guru* (Stanford, CA: Stanford University Press, 2015), 149.

12. Taylor, "Identity, Nation, and Islam," 12; Jones, "Women in the Middle," 162 (quotation).

13. Nancy Smith-Hefner, "Javanese Women and the Veil in Post-Soeharto Indonesia," *Journal of Asian Studies* 66.2 (2007): 390.

14. In May 2011, I spent a month on the island of Java, mostly in Yogyakarta, where I (1) interviewed and conducted focus groups with college students, (2) performed ethnographic observations of sartorial practices in shopping malls, university campuses, and popular pedestrian shopping areas, (3) photographed campus and street fashions, and (4) visited boutiques, large apparel stores, and small fashion houses. With the help of a research assistant, I translated advice literature for Muslim women about how to dress in proper *jilbab*. I also traveled to Bandung and Jakarta, cities where clothing is designed, produced, and sold. This chapter is also indebted to the published ethnographies of Carla Jones, Suzanne Brenner, and Nancy Smith-Hefner, which analyze the role dress plays in Indonesian constructions of women's public and pious personas. It is also informed by the work of Doreen Lee on Javanese youth and James Hoesterey on Indonesian visual culture.

15. Taylor, "Identity, Nation, and Islam."

16. My understanding of the use of lace in Indonesian *jilbab* is informed by an insightful, unpublished paper delivered by Carla Jones at "Re-Orienting the Veil," a conference cosponsored by Duke University and the University of North Carolina at Chapel Hill, Durham, NC, in February 2013.

17. "Ina's Scarf at Jakarta Fashion and Food Festival 2011," May 22, 2011, http://inasscarf.blogspot.com/2011_05_01_archive.html.

18. "One Shawl, Different Styles!" Hijab Tutorial Store, March 19, 2011, http://hijabtutorialstore.blogspot.com/2011/03/one-shawl-different-styles.html.

19. Carla Jones, "Materializing Piety: Gendered Anxieties about Faithful Consumption in Contemporary Urban Indonesia," *American Ethnologist* 37.4 (2010): 619.

20. Most Indonesians believe that the term *cadar* is derived from Arabic, although it actually seems to be an adoption of the Persian word *chador*. This etymological belief is linked to the fact that the practice of full-body covering was seen as an importation from the Gulf when it was first used in Indonesia.

21. Because *cadari* women were still very rarely seen in public in 2011, this group was not part of my case study. The anthropologist Eva Nisa has pointed out that although face veiling is not considered mainstream, it has what she calls "subcultural capital," which has increased its popularity among university students. *Cadaris* have a large online presence, a "virtual public visibility," even if offline they are still stigmatized: "Many *cadari* who study in big cities in Indonesia admit that they are often asked by their parents to take their *cadar* off when they return to their hometowns, because many people in their neighborhoods feel insecure when they see women wearing it." Nisa, "The Internet Subculture of Indonesian Face-veiled Women," *International Journal of Cultural Studies*, 16.3 (2013): 245.

22. The Arabic term *'awrah* is a reference to Quran 24:31, a verse often interpreted as requiring Muslim women to dress modestly in front of men except close male relatives or male servants. A woman's *'awrah* is usually interpreted as her genitals and breasts.

23. This is not to say that there is no Arabic literacy. In fact, Islamic studies scholar Anne Gade has written about women-only Quran study groups based in Indonesia. See Gade, *Perfection Makes Practice: Learning, Emotion, and the Recited Quran in Indonesia* (Honolulu: University of Hawaii Press, 2004). As in all Muslim communities, the Quran is recited in Arabic for ritualized prayer, and status is given to those who can read it for themselves. But that aside, the majority of Indonesian women do not have reading knowledge of Arabic.

24. On instruction regarding gender roles, see Nancy Smith-Hefner, "The New Muslim Romance: Changing Patterns of Courtship and Marriage among Educated Javanese Youth," *Journal of Southeast Asian Studies* 36.3 (2005): 442.

25. For discussion of the role of popular preachers in creating authority for themselves, see Hoesetery, *Rebranding Islam*.

26. *Adab* is a genre of Islamic literature that is concerned with Islamic etiquette and how to acquire good manners and cultivate a good character. For discussion of a classic *adab* text written by Miskawayh (d. 1030) and how it helps explain the role of modest clothing in character formation, see Elizabeth Bucar, "Islam and the Cultivation of Character: Ibn Miskawayh's Synthesis and the Case of the Veil," in *Cultivating Virtue: Multiple Perspectives,* ed. N. Snow (Oxford: Oxford University Press, 2014), 197–226.

27. My understanding of this literature is informed by James Hoesterey's account, in *Rebranding Islam,* of the Indonesian celebrity preacher known as Aa Gym, who combines Sufi ethics with pop psychology.

28. Nining Suryadi, ed., *Pesona Gaya Kerudung* (The charm of the headscarf style) (Jakarta: Dian Rakyat 2009), 31; *Creations from a Single Scarf,* 3rd ed. (Jakarta: Penerbit Dian Rakyat, 2011), 8.

29. Giliarsi Wahyu Satijono, "Introduction," in Suryadi, ed., *Pesona Gaya Kerudung,* 7.

30. Dewi Priyatni, *Kerudung Instan: Modis and Praktis* (Jakarta: Penerbit Pt Gramedia Pustaka Utama, 2007), 2.

31. Kurniati Rahmadini and Tirza Arsminda, *Aneka Kreasi Kerudung Cantik: Gaya dasar memakai kerudung segi empat & selendang* (Jakarta, Demedia Pustaka, 2011), 2.

32. Rahmadini and Arsminda, *Aneka Kreasi Kerudung Cantik,* 2.

33. Ibid.

34. Suryadi, *Pesona Gaya Kerudung,* 9.

35. Ibid.

36. Ibid., 8.

37. Ibid., 9.

38. Ibid.

39. I. Fitri and K. Nurual, *60 Kesalahan Dalam Berjilbab* (60 Common veiling mistakes) (Jakarta: Basmallah, 2011), xl.

40. In the publication in question, aesthetic mistakes are differentiated from mistakes according to the sharia (for example, wearing *jilbab* that does not cover the chest) or mistakes related to perceptions of *jilbab* (for example, wearing *jilbab* in order to obtain praise from others).

41. Rahmadini and Arsminda, *Aneka Kreasi Kerudung Cantik,* 6.

42. Ibid.

43. Jones, "Women in the Middle," 152.

44. Ibid., 152, 159, 161. Jones described the concern with this type of veiling in Indonesia as being connected to *imej,* an Indonesian word that expresses anxiety over the possibility that appearances can be misleading. Regarding fashion veiling, *imej* is invoked to criticize a perceived pursuit of piety through surface rather than depth.

45. Claire-Marie Hefner's ethnography of large Islamic boarding schools in Yogyakarta provides insight into the training of modern Indonesian women. These programs not only require uniforms for girls that include a headscarf but learning how to correctly pin the headscarf is one of the disciplinary practices

that separates new students from upperclass students who have mastered the complicated tuck and pin. Hefner, "Models of Achievement: Muslim Girls and Religious Authority in a Modernist Islamic Boarding School in Indonesia," *Asian Studies Review* 40.4 (2016): 564–582. Similar training occurs in Indonesian finishing schools, which teach women not only how to be good wives but also how to become part of the modern and urban workforce; see Carla Jones, "Better Women: The Cultural Politics of Gendered Expertise," *American Anthropologist* 112.2 (May 2010): 270–282. Most often run by a member of the Priyayi or local aristocracy whose authority is based on their class position and perceived worldliness, these programs train women how to have good taste and to avoid aesthetic failures ranging from the underconsumption of rural backwardness to the overconsumption of the nouveau rich. *Jilbab* is not traditionally a central part of these trainings, insofar as it is neither encouraged nor discouraged, but these finishing programs are also based on specific conceptions of public femininity.

46. Eve Warburton, "Regulating Morality: Compulsory Veiling at an Indonesian University," presented at the 17th Biennial Conference of the Asian Studies Association of Australia, Melbourne, July 2008. Available online at http://artsonline.monash.edu.au/mai/files/2012/07/evewarburton.pdf.

47. Carla Jones, "Images of Desire: Creating Virtue and Value in an Indonesian Islamic Lifestyle Magazine," *Journal of Middle East Women's Studies* 6.3 (2010): 99.

48. Translation of statement from *NooR*'s website, www.noor-magazine.com/tentang-kami/.

49. Early on, *NooR* had a challenge to overcome. Because it was a woman's magazine, it had to publish images of women. But as an Islamic magazine, it had to be careful that the circulation of images of a modestly dressed woman did not contradict the goals of her covering. In other words, if the modestly dressed woman is supposed to draw less attention to herself, the commodification of her body for public consumption is a moral problem. Ultimately, *NooR* resolved this tension through the idea that pious fashion reflects the inner pious character of the woman. *NooR* even collaborated with a leading fashion designer, Itang Yunasz, to produce a volume of advice literature on the subject. See Jones, "Images of Desire," 105.

50. Jetti Hadi, editor in chief of *NooR*, as quoted in Anthony Deutsch, "Jakarta's Chance to Lead Fashion for Faithful," *Financial Times*, August 12, 2010.

51. As quoted in Sylviana Hamdani, "Indonesian Fashion Brand Keeping Muslim Women Up2date," *Jakarta Globe*, January 20, 2013.

52. As quoted in Hamdani, "Indonesian Fashion Brand Keeping Muslim Women Up2date."

53. As quoted in Sylviana Hamdani, "Indonesia Becoming a Mecca for Muslim Fashion Trends," *Jakarta Globe*, August 8, 2012.

54. Rania Iswarani, Style Whimsical (blog), http://stylewhimsical.blogspot.com/search/label/Outfits?updated-max=2017-01-03T12:47:00%2B07:00&max-results=20&start=4&by-date=false.

55. On March 16, 2016, Rania moved her blog to stylewhimsical.blogspot.com.

56. Rania Iswarani interview by author, May 17, 2011.

57. Ibid.

58. Ibid.

59. Rania Iswarani, "Fresh Fun for Friends," Style Whimsical, December 10, 2011, http://stylewhimsical.blogspot.com/2011/12/fresh-fun-for-friends.html.

60. Rania Iswarani, "'Hiking' Look," Style Whimsical, November 29, 2011, http://stylewhimsical.blogspot.co.id/2011/11/hiking-look.html.

61. Rania Iswarani, "'Leaders in Hijab' Look: A Mother," Style Whimsical, November 27, 2011, http://stylewhimsical.blogspot.co.id/2011/11/leaders-in-hijab-look-mother.html.

62. Rania Iswarani, "Reader Question: One-Sleeve Dress," Style Whimsical, May 24, 2011, http://stylewhimsical.blogspot.com/2011/05/reader-question-one-sleeve-dress.html.

63. Rania Iswarani, "Simple and Practical, Yet Edgy," Style Whimsical, February 19, 2011, http://stylewhimsical.blogspot.com/2011/02/simple-and-practical-yet-edgy.html.

64. Ibid.

65. Rania Iswarani, "New Scarves . . . Made in Indonesia," Style Whimsical, May 17, 2011, http://stylewhimsical.blogspot.com/2011/05/new-scarves-made-in-indonesia.html.

66. Iswarani interview, 2011.

67. This phenomenon seems similar to what Doreen Lee describes in her study of street art in Indonesia. Lee, "Images of Youth: On the Iconography of Protest in Indonesia," *History and Anthropology* 22.3 (2011): 307–336. Lee describes how Indonesian street art is an aesthetic critique of an immoral regime, which creates a precedent of gaining and leveraging moral authority through aesthetic practices that pious fashion can appear to be participating in.

68. As quoted in Jones, "Images of Desire," 105.

3. Tesettür in Istanbul

1. Banu Gökarıksel and Anna Secor, "Between Fashion and Tesettür: Marketing and Consuming Women's Islamic Dress," *Journal of Middle East Women's Studies* 6.3 (2010): 132.

2. As quoted in Tim Arango, "Turks Debate Modest Dress Set for Takeoff," *New York Times*, February 24, 2013.

3. Niyazi Berkes, *The Development of Secularism in Turkey* (Montreal: McGill University Press, 1964), 385–386.

4. Umat Azak, *Islam and Secularism in Turkey: Kemalism, Religion, and the Nation State* (London: I. B. Tauris, 2010), 11. See also Banu Gökarıksel and Katharyne Mitchell, "Veiling, Secularism, and the Neoliberal Subject: National Narratives and Supranational Desires in Turkey and France," *Global Networks* 5.2 (2005): 155.

5. The administrative provision read in part, "Staff and students at the higher educational institutions must be in plain attire that is compatible with Atatürk's reforms and principles . . . [the] head will be uncovered and it will not be covered inside the institutions." As quoted in Merve Kavakçı, *Headscarf Politics in Turkey: A Postcolonial Reading* (New York: Palgrave Macmillan, 2010), 51.

6. Jenny White, "Islamic Chic," in *Istanbul between the Global and the Local*, ed. Çağlar Keyder (Boulder: Rowman and Littlefield, 1999). See also Jenny White, *Islamist Mobilization in Turkey: A Study in Vernacular Politics* (Seattle: University of Washington Press, 2002), and Gökarıksel and Secor, "Between Fashion and Tesettür," 121.

7. Özlem Sandıkcı and Güliz Ger, "Veiling in Style: How Does a Stigmatized Practice Become Fashionable?" *Journal of Consumer Research* 37.1 (2010): 24.

8. There is a large body of scholarship on pious fashion in Turkey. Researchers have described the tremendous shifts in sartorial practices in the last thirty years, as well as the emerging *tesettür* apparel industry. Analytical frameworks in this research include consumption and marketing, geographies of space, class, and social power, and neoliberal subjectivity. Other works engage ethics and aesthetics directly and therefore inform the theoretical framework not only of this chapter but also of the entire book. Because of this vast literature on Turkey, the nature of my ethnographic research differed slightly from the other two locations. I completed three research trips to Turkey (September 2004, April 2012, and April 2013). In lieu of one-on-one interviews of the kind I conducted in Indonesia, or the online survey I conducted in Iran,

I traveled around Istanbul observing how modest styles differed from neighborhood to neighborhood. I focused on pedestrian shopping districts with a high concentration of *tesettür* shops. In the upscale Muslim neighborhood of Fatih, for example, I visited eighteen boutiques and noted what *tesettür* items were for sale, how they were displayed, what salesclerks wore, and what the overall shopping experience was like. As in the other locations, I conducted focus groups. I began with a couple of college students I met through my research assistant, and through snowballing I was able to recruit fourteen *tesettürlü* women (aged twenty to twenty-four) who described themselves as wearing fashionable modest dress. Where appropriate, I also draw on the ethnographies of other scholars who have studied *tesettür.*

9. Gökarıksel and Secor, "Between Fashion and *Tesettür,*" 126.

10. Banu Gökarıksel and Anna Secor, "Islam on the Catwalk: Marketing Veiling-Fashion in Turkey," in *The Changing World Religion Map,* ed. S. D. Brunn (New York: Springer, 2015), 2594. See also Banu Gökariksel and Anna Secor, "'Even I Was Tempted': The Moral Ambivalence and Ethical Practice of Veiling-Fashion in Turkey," *Annals of the Association of American Geographers* 102.4 (2012): 847–862.

11. Özlem Sandıkcı and Güliz Ger, "Aesthetics, Ethics, and Politics of the Turkish Headscarf," in *Clothing as Material Culture,* ed. Susanne Küchler and Daniel Miller (New York: Bloomsbury Academic, 2005), 73.

12. This is similar to the critique that one of Gökarıksel and Secor's informants makes, that is, that the display of brand names is a form of showing off and thus constitutes an aesthetic failure: "Sometimes I see it and I go 'Well, she's surely gone over the top, it's so obvious that she's displaying the brand name.' I find it odd . . . because there are people who can't afford that." Gökarıksel and Secor, "'Even I Was Tempted,'" 6.

13. Banu Gökarıksel and Anna Secor, "The Veil, Desire, and the Gaze: Turning the Inside Out," *Signs* 40.1 (2014): 184.

14. Ali Çarkoğlu and Binnaz Toprak, *Religion, Society, and Politics in a Changing Turkey,* trans. Çiğdem Aksoy Fromm (Istanbul: TESEV Publications, 2007), 64.

15. Banu Gökarıksel and Anna Secor, "'You Can't Know How They Are Inside': The Ambivalence of Veiling and Discourses of the Other in Turkey," in *Religion and Place: Landscape, Politics, and Piety,* ed. Peter Hopkins, Lily Kong, and Elizabeth Olson (Springer Netherlands, 2013): 104.

16. Gökarıksel and Secor, "'You Can't Know How They Are Inside,'" 103.

17. Kavakçı, *Headscarf Politics in Turkey*, 51.

18. Gülşen Demirkol Özer, *Psikolojik Bir İşkence Metodu Olarak İkna Odaları* (Istanbul: Beyan Yayinlari, 2005), 271.

19. Benajmin Bleiberg, "Unveiling the Real Issue: Evaluating the European Court of Human Rights' Decision to Enforce the Turkish Headscarf Ban in *Leyla Şahin v. Turkey*," *Cornell Law Review* 91.1 (2005): 163.

20. Nilüfer Göle, *The Forbidden Modern: Civilization and Veiling* (Ann Arbor: University of Michigan Press, 1997).

21. Grand Chamber decision in the case of *Leyla Şahin v. Turkey*, European Court of Human Rights, Application no. 44774/98, November 10, 2005, para. 15–16. Available at http://hudoc.echr.coe.int/eng (search by application number).

22. *Leyla Şahin v. Turkey*, para. 17, 21–24.

23. Ibid., para. 14.

24. Ibid., para. 39.

25. Ibid., para. 106.

26. Ibid., para. 105.

27. Kavakçı, *Headscarf Politics in Turkey*.

28. As cited in Murat Çemrek, "How Could the Rights of Education and Representation Challenge National Security? The Headscarf Conflict in Turkey Revisited," *Human Security Perspectives* 1.2 (2004): 56.

29. Kavakçı, *Headscarf Politics in Turkey*, 76–78.

30. https://www.youtube.com/watch?v=gpR84XF7N5s.

31. http://www.uludagsozluk.com/k/emine-erdo%C4%9Fan-%C4%Bın-giyim-zevksizli%C4%9Fi/.

32. Pinar Tremblay, "The Erdogans' Lavish Lifestyle," *Al-Monitor*, April 2, 2015, http://www.al-monitor.com/pulse/originals/2015/04/erdogan-familys-attempt-to-appear-modest-backfire.html#.

33. Kavakçı, *Headscarf Politics in Turkey*, 124.

34. Banu Gökarıksel and Anna Secor, "Islamic-ness in the Life of a Commodity: Veiling-Fashion in Turkey," *Transactions of the Institute of British Geographers* 35.3 (2010): 318.

35. Gökarıksel and Secor, "Islam on the Catwalk," 2587–2590.

36. Gökarıksel and Secor, "Islamic-ness in the Life of a Commodity," 317.

37. Gökarıksel and Secor found that neither corporate charity practices nor strict gender segregation in the workplace was common, leading them to conclude that "while 21 per cent of the [*tesettür* apparel] firms surveyed felt that the Islamic character of a company was an important or very important consider-

ation for establishing business relationships, there were no other significant characteristics that these firms shared." Gökarıksel and Secor, "Islamic-ness in the Life of a Commodity," 319.

38. See http://www.tekbirgiyim.com.tr/default.aspx (accessed January 26, 2016).

39. As translated by Gökarıksel and Secor, "Between Fashion and Tesettür," 119. Originally published in the Turkish Magazine *Yeni Bizim Aile,* July 1992, 9–11.

40. Banu Gökarıksel and Anna J. Secor, "New Transnational Geographies of Islamism, Capitalism, and Subjectivity: The Veiling-Fashion Industry in Turkey," *Area* 41.1 (2009): 12.

41. As quoted in Yael Navaro-Yashin, *Faces of the State: Secularism and Public Life in Turkey* (Princeton, NJ: Princeton University Press, 2002), 95, 235.

42. Gökarıksel and Secor, "New Transnational Geographies of Islamism, Capitalism, and Subjectivity," 13.

43. Dan Bilefsky, "A Fashion Magazine Unshy about Baring a Bit of Piety," *New York Times,* March 29, 2012 ("Sex and the City" quotation); Daniel Steinvorth, "Turkish Women's Magazine Targets the Chaste," trans. Christopher Sutlan, *Spiegel Online,* January 25, 2012 ("diktat of nudity" quotation), available at http://www.spiegel.de/international/world/the-vogue-of-the-veiled-turkish-women-s-magazine-targets-the-chaste-a-811161.html.

44. As quoted in Steinvorth, "Turkish Women's Magazine Targets the Chaste."

45. Author interview with Zeynep Hasoğlu, April 5, 2013.

46. A similar practice of displaying *tesettür* women alongside women with uncovered heads is used by the Turkish apparel industry in *tesettür* catalogues. Gökarıksel and Secor point out that these images are designed to make covered women feel "that they are able to participate in 'fashion' in a way that includes them within a broad consuming class." Gökarıksel and Secor, "Between Fashion and *Tesettür*," 129.

47. Nihat Hatipoğlu, "Televizyonlarin Ençok Izlenen Hocasi," *Âlâ* (April 2013): 48.

48. Zeynep Hasoğlu, "Editorial," *Âlâ* (April 2013): 16.

49. http://www.pantone.com/about-us?from=topNav (accessed January 31, 2016).

50. Banu Çaycı, "Is Your Waist Getting Thicker?" *Aysha* (April 2013): 184.

51. Ayşe Eryılmaz, "Vücut Tipinize göre stillinizi olusturun," *Âlâ* (April 2013): 106.

52. In virtue ethics, we would call this an improperly habituated desire.

53. Gökarıksel and Secor, "The Veil, Desire, and the Gaze," 193.

54. Ibid., 194.

4. Pious Fashion across Cultures

1. Emma Tarlo, *Clothing Matters: Dress and Identity in India* (Chicago: University of Chicago Press, 1996).

2. Erving Goffman, *The Presentation of Self in Everyday Life* (New York: Anchor, 1959), 35.

3. As Malcolm Barnard puts it, there is "no non-cultural way of performing modesty." Barnard, *Fashion Theory: An Introduction* (New York: Routledge, 2014), 52.

4. Gökarıksel and Secor, "The Veil, Desire, and the Gaze: Turning the Inside Out," *Signs* 40.1 (2014): 186–191.

5. According to Timothy Mitchell, expertise is "a politics of techno-science" that is used to bring our reality more in line with our ideal. Mitchell, *Rule of Experts: Egypt, Techno-Politics, Modernity* (Berkeley: University of California Press, 2002), 15.

6. Sean McCloud, "Putting Some Class into Religious Studies: Resurrecting an Important Concept," *Journal of the American Academy of Religion* 75.4 (2007): 845.

7. Carla Jones, "Better Women: The Cultural Politics of Gendered Expertise," *American Anthropologist* 112.2 (May 2010): 271.

8. Peter Awn, who describes this shift, explains that "instead of being the pawn of his or her human instincts, the Sufi is able to employ both interior strengths and the world of creation to foster continued progress. Asceticism, seen in this light, is transformed from the violent wrenching of spirit from matter enjoined by a dualistic perception of the universe into a force for moderation, temperance, and harmony. The good is to be found even in the world, for a healthy body, sharp mind, and integrated emotional life are assets, not deficits, to continued spiritual growth." Awn, "The Ethical Concerns of Classical Sufism," *Journal of Religious Ethics* 11.2 (1983): 245–246.

9. Amel Boubekeur and Olivier Roy describe this as a shift to an activist culture of consumption, in which various modes of production and consumption are used "to re-introduce an Islamic ethos into the various forms of leisure that they once shunned." Boubekeur and Roy, "Introduction," in Boubekeur and Roy, eds., *Whatever Happened to the Islamists? Salafis, Heavy Metal Muslims, and the Lure of Consumerist Islam* (London: Hurst, 2012), 9.

10. Carla Jones, "Images of Desire: Creating Virtue and Value in an Indonesian Islamic Lifestyle Magazine," *Journal of Middle East Women's Studies* 6.3 (2010): 103.

11. Jones, "Images of Desire," 111.

12. Karen Hansen, "The World in Dress: Anthropological Perspectives on Clothing, Fashion, and Culture," *Annual Review of Anthropology* 33 (2004): 383.

13. Ayala Fader, *Mitzvah Girls: Bringing Up the Next Generation of Hasidic Jews in Brooklyn* (Princeton, NJ: Princeton University Press, 2009), 147–148.

14. Max Weber, *"Class, Status, Party,"* in *Essays in Sociology (From Max Weber)*, trans. H. H. Gerth (Oxford: Oxford University Press, 2015), 180–195.

15. Mike Savage, *Class Analysis and Social Transformation* (Buckingham, UK: Open University Press, 2000), xii; McCloud, "Putting Some Class into Religious Studies," 844–845.

16. "O Prophet! Tell your wives and daughters, and the believing women, that they should cast their outer garments [*jalibab*] over their persons (when abroad): that is most convenient, that they should be known (as such) and not molested. And God is Oft-Forgiving, Most Merciful." *The Qur'an: Translation*, trans. A. Y. Ali, ed. S. Smith, 26th U.S. Edition (New York: Tahrike Tarsile Qur'an, Inc., 2010), 320.

17. Samantha Kwan and Mary Nell Trautner, "Beauty Work: Individual and Institutional Rewards, the Reproduction of Gender, and Questions of Agency," *Sociology Compass* 3.1 (2009): 50. See also Murray Webster and James Driskell, "Beauty as Status," *American Journal of Sociology* 89.1 (1983): 140–165.

18. Nining Suryadi, ed., *Pesona Gaya Kerudung* (The charm of the headscarf style) (Jakarta: Dian Rakyat 2009).

19. Kwan and Trautner, "Beauty Work," 59.

20. Marilyn Robinson Waldman, "Tradition as a Modality of Change: Islamic Examples," *History of Religions* 25.4 (1986): 326.

Epilogue

1. Thomson Reuters, *State of the Global Islamic Economy Report, 2016 / 17*. Available at https://ceif.iba.edu.pk/pdf/ThomsonReuters-stateoftheGlobalIslamicEconomyReport201617.pdf.

2. Dina Torkia, "Designer Abayas, What's New?" http://www.dinatorkia.co.uk/style/designer-abbayas-whats-new/.

3. As quoted in Steff Yotka, "Uniqlo's Collaboration of Hijabs and Ready-to-Wear with Muslim Designer Hana Tajima Is Coming to the U.S.," *Vogue*, February 15, 2016.

4. *Daily Sabah*, April 30, 2016.

5. Lukas Alpert, "Conde Nasty," *New York Post*, June 1, 2007.

6. Elizabeth Paton, "Asserting a Muslim Fashion Identity," *New York Times*, November 1, 2016.

7. Riada Asimovic Akyol, "Muslim Conservatives Unveil Anger at Turkey's Modest Fashion Week," *Al-Monitor*, May 19, 2016.

8. As quoted in Jessica Chasmar, "French Fashion Mogul Says Islamic Clothing Trend Promotes 'Enslavement of Women,'" *Washington Times*, March 31, 2016.

9. As quoted in Henry Samuel, "France Says Marks and Spencer Burkini 'Irresponsible.'" *The Telegraph*, March 30, 2016.

FURTHER READING

The following pages provide readers guidance as to where to find further information on the topics discussed in this book. Suggestions are arranged by chapter, approximately in the order in which the topics are covered.

Introduction

A good introduction to the theory of fashion is Malcolm Barnard's *Fashion Theory: An Introduction* (New York: Routledge, 2014). For scholarship in anthropology on dress as practice, see Karen Hansen's excellent review essay, "The World in Dress: Anthropological Perspectives on Clothing, Fashion, and Culture," *Annual Review of Anthropology* 33 (2004): 369–392. Hansen provides an overview of research on clothing, highlighting trends in scholarship on agency, practice, and consumption. The interdisciplinary journal *Fashion Theory* has published some of the most cutting-edge and solidly researched studies on clothing and culture. For book-length treatments of clothing, see Emma Tarlo's *Clothing Matters: Dress and Identity in India* (Chicago: University of Chicago Press, 1996) and *Visibly Muslim: Fashion, Politics, and Faith* (London: Bloomsbury Academic, 2010).

Reina Lewis treats pious fashion in Muslim-minority communities in *Muslim Fashion: Contemporary Style Cultures* (Durham, NC: Duke

University Press, 2015). For a scholarly study of everyday Islamic clothing in Muslim-minority immigrant communities, see Emma Tarlo and Annelies Moors's edited volume *Islamic Fashion and Anti-Fashion: New Perspectives from Europe and North America* (London: Bloomsbury Academic, 2013). A terrific book on issues of modest clothing in the Hasidic community in Brooklyn is Ayala Fader, *Mitzvah Girls: Bringing Up the Next Generation of Hasidic Jews in Brooklyn* (Princeton, NJ: Princeton University Press, 2009).

For understanding how Muslims have turned to Islam to cope with change, see Marilyn Robinson Waldman's "Tradition as a Modality of Change: Islamic Examples," *History of Religions* 25.4 (1986): 318–340. Not only does she give an overview of scholarly explorations of the relationship between modernity and tradition but she also provides her own definition of tradition as a process that works through renewal, reform, and maintenance. One place the debate between tradition and modernity plays out is in nation building, and there is excellent scholarship on how women become central to these debates in Muslim-majority countries. A good place to start is Nikki R. Keddie and Beth Baron, eds., *Women in Middle Eastern History: Shifting Boundaries in Sex and Gender* (New Haven, CT: Yale University Press, 1991). See also Lila Abu-Lughod, *Remaking: Feminism and Modernity in the Middle East* (Princeton, NJ: Princeton University Press, 1998); Leila Ahmed, *Women and Gender in Islam: Historical Roots of a Modern Debate* (New Haven, CT: Yale University Press, 1993); and Margot Badran, *Feminists, Islam, and Nation: Gender and the Making of Modern Egypt* (Princeton, NJ: Princeton University Press, 1996).

Lila Abu-Lughod's *Do Muslim Women Need Saving?* (Cambridge, MA: Harvard University Press, 2013) counters the idea that Muslim women's lives are completely dictated by religious doctrine. Abu-Lughod presents a nuanced critique of the claim that Islamic societies are radically "other" because they are inherently more patriarchal. Other insightful treatments of agency and freedom for religious women are Saba Mahmood, *Politics of Piety* (Princeton, NJ: Princeton University Press, 2005); R. Marie Griffith, *God's Daughters: Evangelical*

Women and the Power of Submission (Berkeley: University of California Press, 1997); and Azam Torab, "Piety as Gendered Agency: A Study of Jalaseh Ritual Discourse in an Urban Neighborhood in Iran," *Journal of the Royal Anthropological Institute* 2.2 (1996): 235–252.

Chapter 1: *Hijab* in Tehran

For a good history of the role of women in twentieth-century Iranian politics, see Parvin Paidar, *Women and the Political Process in Twentieth-Century Iran* (Cambridge: Cambridge University Press, 1997). Ziba Mir-Hosseini's *Islam and Gender: The Religious Debate in Contemporary Iran* (Princeton, NJ: Princeton University Press, 1999) provides great insight into religious debates about women in Iran through a series of interviews with clerics. For a concise summary of the Iranian dress code, see Faegheh Shirazi, "Islamic Religion and Women's Dress Code: The Islamic Republic of Iran," in *Undressing Religion: Commitment and Conversion from a Cross-Cultural Perspective*, ed. Linda B. Arthur (Oxford: Berg, 2000), 113–130.

For more on fashion in Tehran I suggest starting with Hoda Katebi's self-published book of street fashion photography, *Tehran Streetstyle* (Hoda Katebi, 2016) or Alexandru Balasescu's *Paris Chic, Tehran Thrills: Aesthetic Bodies, Political Subjects* (Bucharest: Zeta Books, 2013). To view more images of *hijab* in Tehran, see the following blogs and Instagram accounts: www.thetehrantimes.com; www.instagram.com /ir.streetstyle/?hl=en; and www.instagram.com/honarmandanplus/.

Chapter 2: *Jilbab* in Yogyakarta

For an overview of Indonesia's particular take on Muslim politics, a good place to start is Robert Hefner's *Civil Islam: Muslims and Democratization in Indonesia* (Princeton, NJ: Princeton University Press, 2000). For histories of Indonesia that emphasize the role of women, see Saskia Wieringa, *Sexual Politics in Indonesia* (New York: Palgrave Macmillan, 2002), and Rachel Rinaldo, *Mobilizing Piety: Islam and*

Feminism in Indonesia (Oxford: Oxford University Press, 2013). Suzanne Brenner's "Reconstructing Self and Society: Javanese Muslim Women and 'The Veil,'" *American Ethnologist* 23.4 (1996): 673–697 is groundbreaking early work on headscarves. For an excellent analysis of the post-Suharto changes in women's dress, see Nancy Smith-Hefner, "Javanese Women and the Veil in Post-Soeharto Indonesia," *Journal of Asian Studies* 66.2 (2007): 389–420.

On the topics of consumption and virtue related to pious fashion in Indonesia, Carla Jones's work is extremely illuminating. I recommend starting with the following three essays: "Fashion and Faith in Urban Indonesia," *Fashion Theory* 11.2–3 (2007): 211–232; "Images of Desire: Creating Virtue and Value in an Indonesian Islamic Lifestyle Magazine," *Journal of Middle East Women's Studies* 6.3 (2010): 91–117; and "Materializing Piety: Gendered Anxieties about Faithful Consumption in Contemporary Urban Indonesia," *American Ethnologist* 37.4 (2010): 617–637.

Rania Iswarani's fashion blog gives a good sense of everyday fashion in Yogyakarta: www.stylewhimsical.blogspot.com. Other popular fashion blogs in Indonesia include Indah Nada Puspita's www.sketchesofmind.com and Puput Utami's www.pupututami.com.

Chapter 3: *Tesettür* in Istanbul

An accessible introduction to Turkish politics is Stephen Kinzer's *Crescent and Star: Turkey between Two Worlds,* rev. ed. (New York: Farrar, Straus and Giroux, 2008). Jenny White's *Muslim Nationalism and the New Turks* (Princeton, NJ: Princeton University Press, 2012) shows how Muslim nationalism in Turkey blurs the line between secularism and Islam, often in ways that are detrimental to women.

Banu Gökarıksel and Anna Secor have produced a series of terrific essays about *tesettür* over the last ten years. On the marketing of pious fashion in Turkey, see their "Between Fashion and Tesettür: Marketing and Consuming Women's Islamic Dress," *Journal of Middle East Women's Studies* 6.3 (2010): 118–148. On the role of ethics and aesthetics in modest dress, see their "The Veil, Desire, and the Gaze: Turning the Inside Out," *Signs: Journal of Women in Culture and Society* 40.1 (2014): 177–200; and "'Even I Was Tempted': The Moral Ambivalence and Ethical Practice of Veiling-Fashion in Turkey," *Annals of the Association of American Geographers* 102.4 (2012): 847–862. For more about the change of pious fashion from stigma to icon, see Özlem Sandıkcı and Güliz Ger, "Veiling in Style: How Does a Stigmatized Practice Become Fashionable?" *Journal of Consumer Research* 37.1 (2010): 15–36.

Many of the most popular fashion blogs in Turkey post only occasionally on *tesettür*, but two good Instagram accounts that cover pious fashion on the street are: www.instagram.com/everyday.turkey/and www.instagram.com/street_style_istanbul/.

Chapter 4: Pious Fashion across Cultures

For more on "ethnic chic," see Emma Tarlo's early work on dress in India, "The Transformation of Hauz Khas Village," *India International Centre Quarterly* 23.2 (1996): 30–59. In this essay, Tarlo shows the power dynamics behind the promotion of "village clothing," a style defined by boutique owners, while villagers prefer a less "marketable" set of aesthetics. An excellent edited volume by Aliakbar Jafari and Özlem Sandikci provides a good overview of recent scholarship on Islam and consumption in a variety of fields: *Islam, Marketing and Consumption: Critical Perspectives on the Intersections* (New York: Routledge 2016).

ACKNOWLEDGMENTS

Pious Fashion has been enriched by my interlocutors, colleagues, and research assistants. The book would not have been possible without the women in all three locations who shared with me their opinions about Muslim women's clothing. I also learned a tremendous amount from existing scholarship on Muslim women's dress, especially from the work of Carla Jones, Emma Tarlo, Banu Gökarıksel, and Anna Secor. Many colleagues have read portions of the manuscript, but Victoria Cain and Lori Lefkovitz did me the favor of reading a draft in its entirety and then giving me comments that helped refine the argument. A group of peer mentors have helped me to fit in writing times among all the other responsibilities of work and life. At crucial moments Kirsten Wesselhoeft, Lea Schweitz, and Liza Weinstein held me accountable as a writer.

My research was deepened with the help of research assistants Dorsa Javaherian in Tehran, Yasim Özata in Istanbul, and Ashika Prajnya Pramita in Yogyakarta. My thanks also go to my research assistants at the University of North Carolina at Greensboro and at Northeastern University, especially Heeva Kadivar, Meghan Murphy, Charina Hanley, and Larissa Witte.

I am thankful for invitations to present portions of this book at several venues, including the Middle East Beyond Borders Workshop at Harvard University; the Women's Voices series at Wesleyan University;

the Institute on Culture, Religion, and World Affairs at Boston University; the Religion and Critical Thought Workshop at Brown University; the Religious Studies Department at Florida State University; and the Berkley Center for Religion, Peace and World Affairs at Georgetown University. One invitation deserves special recognition: the Luce Project on Religion and Its Publics at the University of Virginia hosted me for a full-day workshop devoted to my manuscript. Feedback from faculty and graduate students helped enormously with the final round of revisions.

Generous institutional grants supported my fieldwork and the writing of this book, including funding from the Humanities Center at Northeastern University, the Theology of Character Project at Wake Forest University, the Kohler International Travel Fund at the University of North Carolina at Greensboro, and the Human Rights Program at the University of Chicago.

It is not an exaggeration to say that Sharmila Sen understood what this book was about before I did. Working with her was not only a pleasure; she helped me produce a much better book than I could have on my own. Heather Hughes made sure we stuck to the production schedule by staying on top of logistics. Louise Robbins made the final manuscript a much more enjoyable read through her fabulous editing.

At home, my partner Alexis Zubrow and daughter Zoe Zucar put up with the travel required for this research and with my regime of "writing units." They also put up with my talking about pious fashion. A lot. When Zoe's second-grade teacher asked each student in the class to write a sentence using the word "scarf," her sentence was, "Some scarfs can be worn for religious reasons and to keep you warm and to look nice." Atta girl, Zoe!

INDEX

Attractiveness: cultivating, 186–189; enhancing, 186; of *jilbab*, 75. *See also* Aesthetics; Appearance; Beauty; Values, aesthetic

Authorities, aesthetic, 11, 12–13; as experts on pious fashion, 180–182; effects on women's clothing choices, 166; in Indonesia, 98–117; in Iran, 54–70; struggle for, 167; in Turkey, 146–166

Authority: government as, 180; tastemakers, 180–181

Avicenna, 189

'Awrah, 206n22

Aysha, 159, 163

Bad hijab. See *Hijab, bad*

Balasescu, Alexandru, 65

Bani-Sadr, Abolhassan, 28

Barras, Amelie, 4

Basij (morality police), 53, 58–61, 181, 202n7

Batik, 79, 83–84, 92

Beauty, 19; as accepted religious ideal, 188–189; and character, 82; cultivating, 186–189; in ethical theory, 188–189; inclusive vision of, 195; influenced by foreign ideals, 187; intelligible vs. sensible, 189; Javanese aesthetic of, 81; and pious fashion, 119; Western conceptions of, 117. *See also* Aesthetics; Appearance; Attractiveness; Values, aesthetic

Beauty work, 186–188

Behavior, and pious fashion, 95

Bergé, Pierre, 195

Bella, Laudya Chintya, 95

Birer, Ibrahim Burak, 158–159

Blogs / bloggers: Afia, 195; in Indonesia, 187; in Iran, 67–70; for *jilbab*, 114–117; as tastemakers, 67; Torkia, 192

Body, women's: concealing shape of, 175; emphasizing, 57; enhancing attractiveness of, 186; and ideals of beauty, 188; regulation of, in Indonesia, 80; revealing outline of, 164, 166; shape of, 163–164

Boroujerdi, Hossein, 58

Boubekeur, Amel, 7

Brand names, 130, 140–143, 166

Bun ciput, 75, 82, 89

Butler, Judith, 18

Cadar, 91, 206nn20,21

Çarşaf, 143, 145–146, 153, 167, 179

Chador, 25, 26, 30, 41, 70; among leaders of civil society, 49; Arab, 41–42, 44; ban of, 29–30; and class, 49–50; and political power, 48; symbolism of, 47–50

Chanel, Coco, 161

Character: appearance and, 19, 22, 51, 82; *bad hijab* and, 51, 178; beauty and, 82; and consumption, 105; cultivation of, 16, 17; failures related to, 169–170; *jilbab* and, 115; relation to clothing, 119; view of in Turkey, 169. *See also* Ethics; Morality

Charisma, 181

Charm of Headscarf Style, The (Pesona Gaya Kerudung), 101

Chastity, public, 56

Mohammad Reza Pahlavi, 27
Moral authority, women's claim
 to, 73
Morality, 16–20; aesthetics linked to,
 82, 169–170; appearance linked
 with, 64; and *bad hijab*, 50–54; and
 consumption, 104, 182–185; dress
 linked to, 56–57; vs. fashion, 108;
 and full-body coverage, 146; and
 modesty, 175; norms in Indonesia,
 118; and occasional *jilbab*, 178–179;
 piety connected to, 3; in Turkey,
 129; women linked with, 56, 118;
 women's clothing as marker of, 22.
 See also Character; Ethics
Morality, public, 56, 81
Morality police (Basij), 53, 58–61, 181,
 202n7
Moruzzi, Norma Claire, 49
Mousavi, Mir Hossein, 29
Mozafar, Shahrzad, 26
Murad, Samar, 193
Mutahhari, Murtadha, 55–56
Mutiara, Irna, 87, 111,
 112–114, 117

National Islamic University in
 Yogyakarta (UIN), 108
National Security Council and the
 Council of Higher Education
 (YÖK), 127, 147
Neckties, 22, 44
Nefis, 169
Neo-Ottomanism, 129
Newhouse, Jonathan, 194, 195
New York Times (newspaper), 12
NooR (magazine), 111, 112–113,
 208n49

Norms: and beauty work, 188;
 women as shapers of, 118
Norms, gender, 2

Orientalism, 153
Ottoman Empire, 129
Overconsumption, 152–153, 184

Pahlavi Dynasty, 26–27
Pancasila, 77
Peci, 92
Performance practices, 18
Persia, 65, 70
Photographs, 11–12
Piety: *çarşaf* as expression of, 145;
 ethics connected to, 39; fashion
 and, 91, 160–161, 189–190; in Islamic
 tradition, 189
Pious, use of term, 3
Pious fashion. *See* fashion, pious
Politics: and *chador*, 48; and
 headscarves in Turkey, 149; *hijab*'s
 impact on, 70, 72; in Indonesia,
 76–81; and meaning of *jilbab*, 119;
 and motivations for wearing *jilbab*,
 98, 103–105; and overconsumption,
 184; political Islam, 7, 20–21,
 128–129; women's dress and, 6–7,
 20–23
Pornography, 80
Practice, clothing as a, 18

Qom, Iran, 66
*Question of Hijab, The (Masaleyeh
 hijab)*, 55–56
Quran, 27, 203n23; and men's dress,
 55; and women's dress, 7, 15,
 98–100, 160, 185, 204n6, 206n22